LOST SAINTS
Silence, Gender, and
Victorian Literary Canonization

VICTORIAN LITERATURE AND CULTURE SERIES
Karen Chase, Jerome J. McGann, *and* Herbert Tucker, *General Editors*

LOST SAINTS

Silence, Gender, and

Victorian Literary

Canonization

———◆∞◆———

Tricia Lootens

UNIVERSITY PRESS OF VIRGINIA
Charlottesville and London

THE UNIVERSITY PRESS OF VIRGINIA
© 1996 by the Rector and Visitors
of the University of Virginia

First published 1996

Library of Congress Cataloging-in-Publication Data

Lootens, Tricia A.
 Lost saints : silence, gender, and Victorian literary canonization / Tricia Lootens.
  p. cm.—(Victorian literature and culture series)
 Includes bibliographical references and index.
 ISBN 0-8139-1652-6 (cloth : alk. paper)
  1. English literature—19th century—History and criticism—Theory, etc. 2. English literature—Women authors—History and criticism—Theory, etc. 3. Feminism and literature—
Great Britain—History—19th century. 4. Women and literature—Great Britain—History—
19th century. 5. Browning, Elizabeth Barrett, 1806–1861—Criticism and interpretation—
History. 6. Rossetti, Christina Georgina, 1830–1894—Criticism and interpretation—History.
7. Shakespeare, William, 1564–1616—Criticism and interpretation—History—19th century.
8. Shakespeare, William, 1564–1616—Characters—Women. 9. Criticism—Great Britain—History—19th century. 10. Femininity (Psychology) in literature. 11. Authorship—Sex differences. 12. Canon (Literature) I. Title. II. Series.
PR468.F46L67 1996
820.9'9287'0934—dc20
                                                                    95-48316
                                                                         CIP

⊗The paper used in this publication meets the minimum
requirements of the American National Standard for
Information Sciences—Permanence of Paper for Printed
Library Materials, ANSI Z39.48-1984.

Printed in the United States of America

TO
those who have taught me,
both inside the classroom and beyond it—
and to my students

Contents

Acknowledgments

I AM GRATEFUL to the staffs of the Library of Congress, the British Museum, the Rockefeller Library of Brown University, and the Indiana University Library for their assistance. Special thanks go to the University of Georgia Library staff, in particular the Interlibrary Loan department. A generous fellowship from the University of Georgia Humanities Center provided a course release and financial support; the University of Georgia Research Foundation also granted a summer's funding.

On a more personal level, my thanks go back for many years, to more people than I can name. I am grateful to Michael Berkvam for challenging me to write more frankly; to Wendy Kolmar for showing me my first photocopy of *Aurora Leigh;* to Susan Gubar for directing the dissertation that arose out of that discovery; and to my other committee members, Linda Dégh, Don Gray, and Christoph Lohmann, for offering me crucial support and advice, both during and beyond the writing of my dissertation.

C. Blue Calhoun, Christy Desmet, Margaret Dickie, Jean Friedman, Simon Gatrell, Susan Gubar, Linda K. Hughes, Paula M. Krebs, Frances Teague, Herbert S. Tucker, Anne Williams, and Katharina Wilson have all read parts of the manuscript and offered encouragement or useful suggestions; though Frances Teague and Anne Williams have critiqued certain chapters several times, their patience and attention have never failed. Coburn Freer and Hugh Ruppersburg were supportive department chairs. No other acquisitions editor could have matched the humor, efficiency, and patience of Cathie Brettschneider. Thanks, too, to Ellen Goldlust and Gerald Trett for their editing and to Suzanne Gilbert for indexing.

Miranda Pollard, who has read virtually every word of this manuscript, teased and badgered me over the rough spots: I owe her several years' worth of coffee at Espresso Royale. Carol

Anne Douglas devoted hours to hearing me talk chapters through, long distance and in person; Christy Desmet cheerfully led me through the mysteries of master documents. Kasee Clifton Laster, Phyllis Gussler, Barbara Schmitt, and especially Patrick McCord, willingly found and lugged dozens upon dozens of volumes from the University of Georgia Library; JoEllen Childers, Suzanne Gilbert, Lisa Kozlowski, Barbara Lootens, Patrick McCord, and Kate Montwieler helped proofread. Russ Greer regularly dropped tantalizing photocopies in my mailbox; other, anonymous graduate students (I think I know who you are) tacked them to my door.

On a more general level, Kathy Simpson, Leann Tigges, and Karen Maschke, my "Tenure Anonymous" group, helped me learn to work and rest more sanely; the University of Georgia Lilly Program, under Ron Simpson, Gina Dress, and Bill Jackson, taught me to celebrate as well as negotiate the necessity of balancing teaching and research. Generations of Interdisciplinary Dog Walk groups encouraged me to break for comic relief and forgave me when I had to work instead: thanks especially to Christy Desmet, David Schiller, and Dita; Merrill Morris and Rosie; Libby Tisdell, Ruth Largay, Rachel, Naomi, and Sheba; and, of course, JoEllen and Watson and Mackinac.

My parents, Barbara and Bernard Lootens, were there for me, as they always have been: I feel lucky to be their daughter. My grandfather, Carl W. Meyer, read part of this manuscript for fun, which gave me great joy: If my grandmother Rose had lived to see its completion, I'm sure she would have done hilarious dramatic readings. Thanks, too, to my brother and sister-in-law, Jim and Sara Lootens, my nieces, Katherine, Amy, and Anne, and my grandmother Madeleine Lootens Johnson, for all they have taught me through their stories and their love.

As always, Paula M. Krebs gave me her friendship, her clearsighted criticism, and her love. Without her, I would never have written this book or any other. In all these years, JoEllen Childers has never once asked me when I was going to "get that thing done": of all the ways in which she has shown her faith in me and her generosity of spirit, that is the one for which I am most grateful.

Finally, I would like to thank the women and men with whom I have done political work in the years since I first began wondering about the disappearance of women's texts: the members of Zurich's Frauenbefreiungsbewegung (especially Madeleine Buess and Susanne

Hess); Xanthippe Women's Collective and friends (especially Karen Klebofski); the Bloomington Organization for Abused Women (especially Lynette Carpenter, Wendy Kolmar, Sam Milkes, and Linda Peyton); and the past and current *off our backs* collective (especially Carol Anne Douglas, Alice Henry, Jennie Ruby, and Ruth Wallsgrove); as well as the board, volunteers, and staff of the Northeast Georgia Rape Crisis Center. I also owe a great deal to the women who worked at the Arlington Community Temporary Shelter and the women and men who stayed there. Sometimes without knowing it, all these people have supported me in my attempts to write. At certain points, my work on this project has seemed to speak directly to the life we have shared; at others, it has seemed thoroughly alien. Both perspectives have been invaluable; both have helped this work to reach completion.

The lines I quote from "Cartographies of Silence" are reprinted from *The Fact of a Doorframe: Poems Selected and New, 1950–1984,* by Adrienne Rich, by permission of the author and W. W. Norton & Company, Inc. Copyright © 1984 by Adrienne Rich. Copyright © 1975, 1978 by W. W. Norton & Company, Inc. Copyright © 1981 by Adrienne Rich.

"In an Artist's Studio," by Christina Rossetti, is reprinted by permission of Louisiana State University Press from *The Complete Poems of Christina Rossetti, Volume III,* edited by R. W. Crump. Copyright © 1990 by Louisiana State University Press.

LOST SAINTS
Silence, Gender, and
Victorian Literary Canonization

Introduction:
Statues, Saints, and Silence:
Canonical Forms and Authorities

LIKE SO MUCH FEMINIST CRITICISM, *Lost Saints* began with a woman standing in a library looking for a book that was not there. I was the woman, a beginning graduate student in English. The book was Elizabeth Barrett Browning's *Aurora Leigh*. I had heard rumors that it was delightful, exhilarating; I believed that Barrett Browning's name and face should be familiar to anyone who had studied high school English; I expected to find several copies of the book in my university's excellent library. Yet *Aurora Leigh* was absent. It had already been out of print, as a separate volume, for more than fifty years. Eventually, I did find the poem, of course, in a *Collected Works* from the beginning of the century. I also discovered, however, that other feminist students had read it in another form: in pirated photocopies. *Aurora Leigh* might have been a scurrilous tract or a recent underground newspaper instead of the most ambitious work of nineteenth-century England's most famous woman poet—a woman still considered highly respectable, if not a writer still highly respected.

Within a few years, that situation had changed.[1] Still, awareness of *Aurora Leigh*'s near disappearance and anxiety about such potential literary losses—both material and metaphoric—continued to haunt me. Through a reception study of Barrett Browning, I decided to use my dissertation to trace the growth and establishment of silence with respect to *Aurora Leigh*. This work, I imagined, would be analogous to a slow-motion study of magic tricks: progressing step by step, review by review, I would document the verbal and institutional sleight of hand whereby an influential work was made virtually to disappear from literary consideration. Gaps would begin to emerge—moments at which later critics silently transformed mid-Victorian censure into doubly effective, because unacknowledged, censorship. Such critics, I assumed, would be mostly male, and the sexual politics that informed their work would clearly, if at points subtly, transform hostility into neglect.[2] Along the way, I also hoped to find an opposing group of (mostly female) writers who had resisted or challenged attacks, who had broken critical silence to insist on the poem's existence, its right to be what Barbara Smith has called "real and remembered" (159).

Hundreds of reviews, essays, textbooks, biographical sketches, and encyclopedia entries later, I began to acknowledge that the process of decanonization was much more complex and ambiguous than I had thought. Where I had expected to find hostility, I often found profuse expressions of reverence; where I had sought relatively clear divisions along lines of gender or sexual politics, I discovered not only strange alliances but deeply conflicted responses, both among and within critics. Sexual politics and gender mattered—but not in ways I could have predicted. Most surprisingly, where I had looked for silence as absence, I found instead what Adrienne Rich has called

> *The technology of silence*
> *The rituals, etiquette*
>
> *the blurring of terms*
> *silence not absence*
>
> *of words or music or even*
> *raw sounds.*

(17)

Slowly, I came to understand that what is silenced within discourses—and what remains unprinted, untaught, and virtually unread within institutions—is inseparable from what is written and from what remains "real and remembered" within a canon.[3] Again, Rich's warning springs to mind:

> *Silence can be a plan*
> *rigorously executed*
>
> *the blueprint to a life*
>
> *It is a presence*
> *it has a history   a form*
>
> *Do not confuse it*
> *with any kind of absence.*

(17)

The silence around Barrett Browning—and around other poets—turned out not to be an absence. It had and has a history, a "form"; indeed, I have come to believe that it may represent one of the most powerful conventions within nineteenth-century literary history. For the ambitious, controversial author of *Aurora Leigh* and *Poems before Congress* did not merely fade out of literary historiography; rather, she entered it in the guise of a series of idealized—and standardized—heroines, as the center of a literary legend.

In so doing, Barrett Browning served as an exemplar of female authorship throughout her century and well into our own. Why else, for example, would Margaret Atwood number E. B. B.'s biography among the "most lurid cautionary tales provided by society" to discourage her, as a young woman, from writing (224–25)? When Janet Sternburg exhorted prospective female authors, in

1980, to exorcise visions of "the woman writer as we've stereotypically known her," why else would she describe that writer as a "recluse, sufferer, woman in mauve velvet on a chaise, woman who flees the stifling rooms of her father's house" (xvi)? Clearly, by the time I discovered *Aurora Leigh,* Barrett Browning had become a popular counterpart to Virginia Woolf's notorious "Angel in the House." For the author of *Aurora Leigh,* that impassioned defense of women's desire to write, no fate could have been more ironic.

Thus, what began as a reception study was transformed into a study of the formation of a literary legend. Now, that study has led further, into the investigation of nineteenth-century literary canonicity itself. *Lost Saints* still explores what disappears from the canon, but it does so by focusing on canonical presences rather than absences.[4] For I have come to believe that if we are to understand what canonicity has created and cost, we must address the power of legend—and must acknowledge, too, how significantly such power has been shaped by cultural traditions linked to the legends of saints.

To make this assertion is not to deny that nineteenth-century literary canonization was a secular process. As we shall see, what mattered in literary terms was less that ecclesiastical authorities should have conferred (and still be conferring) sanctity upon given religious figures than that in so doing they should have provided newer modes of reverence with invaluable precedents and rhetorical resources.[5] Nineteenth-century faith in religious sanctity took its own shapes, and sparked its own controversies; but these controversies bore no primary or inevitable relation to the development of reverence toward literary figures.[6] Indeed, given frequent assumptions that literary sanctity had superseded its religious model, the project of canonizing literary figures might be even easier for skeptics.

Religious sanctity is thus not the point of this study. In many ways, however, it remains a point of departure. For in seeking to turn traditions of sanctity to the greater glory of literature, nineteenth-century literary canonization not only mobilized and transformed complex discourses and practices of reverence but was inscribed by them in turn. As nineteenth-century writers appropriated saints' canonization, it appropriated them—a process that continues into our own day.

This latter claim runs counter to the current of much recent writing. As students of canon formation have first weathered accusations that their work was destructively radical and then dismissals of it as passé (DeJean and Miller vii), their work has remained primarily (and sometimes exclusively) cast in contemporary terms.[7] After all, who remembers ever hearing of literary canons until the "wars" broke out? What is more, most commentaries assume that the relationship between the literary canon and religious tradition is superficial at best.[8] Again, this has seemed to reflect common sense. Who could resist Wendell V. Harris's rejection of the "seductive apparent parallel between the creation and closing of the biblical canons and the formation of lists of literary works that . . . have been called 'canons,'" for example? After all, as Harris notes, "literary canons have always implicitly allowed for at least the possibility of adding new or revalued works," while "the very entelechy of the process of biblical canonizing was toward closure" (110–11).

Harris's formulation implicitly raises another possibility, however. Perhaps the seductiveness to which he refers lies less in the parallel between religious and literary canonization than in the reduction of *canon* to "lists of literary works." Indeed, it seems that rather than drawing parallels between religious and literary canonization too literally, most current discussions may be drawing them too rigidly—and as a result, too ahistorically. Consider, for example, the question posed by W. Macneile Dixon in an 1895 *Westminster Review* article entitled "Finality in Literary Judgment." "Dare we flatter ourselves," he asks, "by believing . . . that ours is the age whose critical representative has . . . won his way to the just canons of a final and unassailable criticism?" (402). Dixon's use of "just canons" here may seem to bear only the most tangential relation to the term employed in recent debates. Within a few pages, however, Dixon's "canon" emerges as bearing more than an accidental or marginal relationship to canonization as we understand it. Francis Turner Palgrave, Dixon writes, is "the high priest who performs the rites proper to the canonisation of a lyric poet" (406). Here is the canonization we recognize. Not incidentally, it is also a canonization that we misrecognize—for although Dixon's usage could not be more familiar, it refers to the sanctification not of "texts" but of "poets."

Simultaneously anthologist, high priest, and juridical representative of "a final and unassailable criticism," Palgrave plays a highly suggestive role within the world evoked by "Finality in Literary Judgment." As editor of the wildly successful *Golden Treasury,* he assumes the status of a kind of Chief Canonizer: he wields the merged powers of textual, personal, and historical glorification. By virtue of his wise choices—his application of "just canons"—he is claimed to have rendered the *Golden Treasury* so authoritative that mere inclusion in its pages is equivalent to sanctification for a lyric poet and so sacred that the anthology, in turn, has become a testament to his own sacred authority as a "high priest." Both processes have established Palgrave's "age" itself as a focus for reverence, a source of critical canons that are not only "just" but "final" and "unassailable."

Along with other, similar nineteenth-century texts, "Finality in Literary Judgment" suggests the extent to which recent debates have shifted and transformed rather than created the discourse (and practices) of canonization.[9] If we are to understand the power of this inheritance, we must turn back to the nineteenth century and beyond—indeed, back to classical Greece.

Few feminists could resist pointing out the implications of Jan Gorak's assertion that modern meanings of *canon* reside "embryonically" in the *kanōn* of classical Greek, "whose earliest meaning is glossed in Liddell and Scott's *Greek-English Lexicon* as 'any straight rod or bar'" (9). Apparently, canonicity and phallic authority have had strong metaphorical as well as historical links. At least equally suggestive for my purposes, however, is the extent to which Gorak's classical "canon" merges measurements, figures, and texts—much as does the Victorian example cited above.[10] Gorak notes that "two of the most influential ancient canons appeared as teaching manuals," for example (10). Their subjects are quite suggestive. One, Epicurus' *Of the Standard: A Work Entitled Canon,* opposed Plato's philosophical claims concerning standards of truth (13); the other, composed by the famous sculptor Polycletus, dealt with "the representation of the human body" (10). So great was the reputation of the *Doryphorus,* one of Polycletus' statues, that according to Pliny the Elder, Polycletus "alone of mankind is deemed by means of one work of art to have created the art itself" (Gorak 11). Polycletus, Pliny wrote, "made what artists call a canon, or model statue, from which they draw their artistic proportions, as from a sort of standard" (11). Bodies, books, statues, standards of truth: all intersect in—and depart from—the "straight rod" of the classical "canon."

As Ernst Robert Curtius's influential *European Literature and the Latin Middle Ages* makes clear, moreover, such multiplicity of meaning found analogues in medieval religious terminology. Curtius traces the Middle Ages' first use of *canon* to the fourth century, where it referred not to a list of texts or even of standards but to a "catalogue of authors" (256).[11] "The formation of a canon," Curtius notes, "serves to safeguard a tradition. There is the literary tradition of the school, the juristic tradition of the state, and the religious tradition of the Church: these are the three medieval world powers, *studium, imperium, sacerdotium*" (326).

Classical society sculpted and revered a pantheon whose forms were textual, personal, and architectural; the sacred texts, standards, and saints of the medieval church glorified not only each other but the educational, legal, and religious structures of the society that sanctified them. Thus, canonization has been a figurative as well as a textual process: if the canon's home is a library, it is a library with busts. This last metaphor suggests a central illustration of the importance of acknowledging the multiple historical modes of canonization. For the canon does indeed have a home, and one whose shape and functions we can only understand by considering earlier conceptions of canonization, be they Victorian, medieval, or classical.

Officially, current debates tend to limit the definition of *canon* to a list of texts. In practice, however, the language actually used by the debaters often tells another story. Not only does it slip between lists of texts and of figures, but it vividly and repeatedly invokes a mythic canon that has, or is, a place—an architectural canon filled with the solid, plastic figures of High Art. Like the personal subjects of canonicity, the imaginary architecture of canon-as-place emerges, as if naturally, throughout current discussions, including those whose focus might seem at first to be exclusively textual. Envisioned as a museum, church, courtroom, library, or pantheon, this canon is what Allan Bloom praises as a "spiritual edifice" (53): it is a creation whose metaphoric halls are fit to house the cultural "monuments" invoked by works such as T. S. Eliot's "Tradition and the Individual Talent" (5).[12]

This architectural canon did not build itself, of course. As Lawrence Levine points out, for example, nineteenth- and early-twentieth-century American public institutions, bent upon reverence for "the Eurocentric products of the symphonic hall, the opera house, the museum, and the library," deployed architecture as a means of "sacralizing" high culture (136). The resulting structures assisted in establishing not only "canons that identified the legitimate forms of drama, music, and art, and the valid modes of displaying them" but also the "disciplining and training" of properly genteel audiences (184). It is surely no accident that imaginary Halls of Literature so often resemble Victorian libraries, or that so many students and teachers of literature, in the United States and elsewhere, still reach our classrooms, offices, and card catalogues by passing under the names and faces of the Great.

Not all architectural canons take the same form. For Matthew Arnold and Charles Altieri, the canon may be a kind of legislative chamber or courtroom, a meeting place for that imagined "Amphictyonic Court of final appeal" capable of authenticating "definitive" literary "glory" (Arnold, "Wordsworth," 334), or the point at which one sits to imagine oneself at the center of a "circle" of "judges for the canon," "projections from within the canon as it develops over time" (Altieri 52). Here, textual canonization is an open process, and positively conceived—though selection procedures for judges remain somewhat obscure. To others, however, the architectural canon is a form of what Audre Lorde terms the "Master's House" (Lillian Robinson 34–35). Like "tradition" in Raymond Williams's description, it is a more fixed, negatively conceived entity, "an object, a projected reality, with which we have to come to terms on its terms, even though those terms are always and must be the valuations, the selections and omissions, of other men"—or men, period, a feminist might add (quoted from Chandler 197).

No matter what one's attitude toward canonization as a process, however, the architectural canon as metaphor exercises a power of its own that both opens up and forecloses conceptual possibilities. Conceived as an enclosed physical space, the canon is a place of containment: its contents are almost inevitably defined by exclusion and shaped through competition. When T. S. Eliot notes that the addition of a "really new" monument to an ideal order shifts those already present, for example, he simultaneously celebrates an ongoing process and implicitly raises the possibility of a selective domino effect (5). Given the "dynamics of endurance," older monuments may not be easily "'dislodged,' to use Dr. Leavis' celebrated word" (Barbara Herrnstein Smith, 47–53; Kermode 81); but dislodged they may be—and perhaps must be, if the walls of imaginary halls of culture are as rigid as those of their historical models. Once displaced, moreover, monuments seem to face uncertain futures. With luck, they may be "relegated to the canonical attic"; without it, they may even end in "the trash can" (Wendell V. Harris 113).

Moreover, though the canon's moral authority may be transcendent, its defenders and tour guides are merely mortal. Required to open the canon's doors to the reverent public as well as to those cultural construction workers who note (or undertake) shifts, they must also carefully monitor access. For the "hall of fame" may admit "gatecrashers" as well as "gatekeepers" (Lawrence 5). Surely Walter Benjamin is not alone in imagining a House of Literature forcibly occupied by soldiers—and literary historians—who are more interested in a suitable place from which to take aim than in the treasures surrounding them ("Literaturgeschichte," 287).

Nor is carelessness the only threat to the architectural canon's reified monuments. Witness, for example, Nigerian-born critic Chinweizu's responses to a *Times Literary Supplement* article that objected to what it termed the "painfully irrelevant" comparison of Langston Hughes's work to that of T. S. Eliot and Ezra Pound: "Who says that Shakespeare, Aristophanes, Dante, Milton, Dostoevsky, Joyce, Pound, Sartre, Eliot, etc., are the last word in literary achievement, unequalled anywhere? . . . The point of these comparisons is not to thrust a black face among these local idols of Europe which, to our grave injury, have been bloated into 'universality'; rather, it is to help heave them out of our way, clear them from our skies by making clear . . . that we have among our own the equals and betters of these chaps" (quoted in Barbara Herrnstein Smith 27). With a shift in perspective, icons become idols.

In the eyes of many early Christians, even the Polycletus statue whose perfection earned it the name of "Canon" might have seemed just so much pagan rubbish. Standing on "frozen and unalterable exhibit" in the "classical museum [or church or pantheon] of supreme and sacred compositions," the architectural canon's imaginary monuments are not only as "eternal" as Polycletus' statue but as fragile (Levine 240). And thus, as current writing more or less casually mobilizes the multiple meanings of *canon,* it assumes and elaborates upon a paradoxical juxtaposition of "universal" value and irretrievable vulnerability. Building upon an architectural image of canonical order that derives from and evokes a violent siege mentality, such writing remains captive to metaphors that not only associate openness and change with disruption and desecration, but radically limit human interactions with "great" art. As Alastair Fowler puts it, "A literary museum that could only be extended might well call for the destructive attentions of a terrorist-critic" (2). "She's done a Samson thing on the whole damn church," the *Chronicle of Higher Education* reports novelist David Bradley as having said in reference to scholar Shelley Fisher Fishkin's effect on the canon of American literature. Her action? The composition of a book that considers how African-American individuals, rhetoric, and culture may have inspired Mark Twain's *Huckleberry Finn* (Winkler A6).

One may admire the architectural canon's existing monuments; one may attempt to calibrate, list, or even rearrange them, perhaps by "thrusting" new monuments into their ranks; one may even try to heave them out of the way. Yet one can never negotiate, expostulate, or play with them. For in a sense, they are dead: visions of the architectural canon evoke, among other sites, the "cemeteries of tradition" (Fowler 2; Caroline Newman).

As Ben Jonson's famous poem to Shakespeare suggests, both visions of the architectural canon and anxieties over the connections between its monuments and funerary statuary surfaced well before the nineteenth century:

(42)

My Shakespeare, rise; I will not lodge thee by
Chaucer, or Spenser, or bid Beaumont lie
A little further to make thee a room:
Thou art a monument, without a tomb,
And art alive still, while thy book doth live.

There is something sinister as well as glorious about canonical monuments, as Jonson implies: their rigidity is that not only of ideals but of effigies. To join them is, in T. S. Eliot's terms, to be set among "the dead" (5). They are not only as solid but as brittle as marble: they inhabit and require an imagined physical space that is always, in some sense, under siege and always held by force.

One central point of *Lost Saints,* then, is to consider how we still use discourses drawn from religious canonization and how they use us—a process that becomes possible only through the acknowledgment that in our usage as in that of earlier cultures the term *canon* evokes far more than a list of texts. Another central point is best expressed by a far less scholarly, if no less serious, definition of the subject at hand: "Saint: a dead sinner, revised and edited." The definition is the devil's own, according to Ambrose Bierce, and it is fiendishly suggestive. For Bierce's account of the canonization of a "dead sinner" does more than succinctly represent religious sainthood as a form of artifice. It implicates scholarly textual practices in canonization's workings. Revision and editing are creative endeavors here: they make saints. Yet they do so, it seems, by transforming sinners. Silence thus stands at the heart of the canonization of religious saints, Bierce implies; and saints' canonization, this book insists, stands at the heart of literary canonization. Always a process of creation, canonization is also inevitably a process of loss. This has no doubt been especially true in the cases of "sinners" who are already subject to (and subjected by) the status of the Other—including women.

Chapter 1, "Saint Shakespeare and the 'Body' of the Text: Legends and 'Emendatory Criticism,'" is most directly—and perhaps most abstractly—concerned with canonization's interplays of creation and omission. Paradoxically, it demonstrates, critical consideration of the canon's figurative aspects reveals how thoroughly textual the canonization process actually is. For the conception of saints' canonization as a model for literary reverence does not substitute figures for texts. Rather, as Bierce's definition suggests, it builds upon the recognition that saints are in some sense texts. Like those "dead sinners" who become religious saints, canonical writers achieve (secular) sanctity only through being "revised and edited"; they "live," if at all, through the power of legends. Part of the chapter is thus devoted to the precedents for and functions of such legends. In the remainder of the chapter, I explore nineteenth-century critics' self-presentation as the shapers of legendary figures. The nineteenth century inherited a tradition of associating bodies of literature with physical bodies, and even though early references to editorial "castrating" or "purging" of texts gave way to more reverent hopes of reuniting Carlylean "*disjecta membra*," many critics still proclaimed themselves authorized to reshape the "bodies" of texts. Some modestly cast themselves as archaeologists reconstructing monuments to genius; others assumed the grandiose guise of angels at a literary resurrection, capable of restoring the "relics" of genius not only to their proper forms but to "eternal" literary life. Such faith in a literary version of what medievalist Caroline Walker Bynum calls the "fragmentation and redemption" of sacred bodies might seem to demand painstaking attention to textual relics; and of course the nineteenth century marks an explosion of bibliographic, scholarly, and curatorial activity, all aimed at establishing or preserving textual accuracy. As a brief consideration of the fates of Carlyle's Saint Shakespeare and his works suggests, however, such achievements could be counterbalanced by an equally active emendatory criticism. For when writers and editors sought to reconstruct or resurrect the essential, unified genius of canonized literary figures, they were often capable of considering their subjects' actual lives and works as merely the expendable textual fragments from which a more sacred monument was to be constructed.

While any writer's transformation into a saint might entail literary loss, that of women writers was particularly dangerous. Chapter 2, "Poet Worship Meets 'Woman' Worship: Victorian Femininity and Fictionality," draws upon recent research into the history of medieval sainthood and Mariology as well as upon the works of conduct-book writers such as Sarah Stickney Ellis; intellectuals such as John Ruskin, Anna Jameson, and Frederic Harrison; novelists such as George Eliot, Charles Dickens, and William Makepeace Thackeray; and poets such as Coventry Patmore and Elizabeth Barrett Browning to demonstrate how Victorian literary canonization of women echoed, exacerbated, and partially transcended the problems it inherited from medieval models of female sanctity. In transforming the heritage of female medieval sanctity, Victorians tended to create a feminine canonicity whose most glorious monuments were doomed to collapse under their own weight.

At their most inventive, as in the works of Ellis, conservative constructions of feminine glory may have succeeded in domesticating feminine sanctity as never before. Partly as a result, nineteenth-century feminine literary canonization became a virtual recipe for critical disappearance. For while the glory of the Romantic poet-hero was believed to arise from purely individual genius, the "genius of woman" was often seen as both generic and radically ahistorical. Trapped between the demands of poet worship and "woman" worship, historical women writers became mythic impossibilities. Efforts to accord them canonicity thus tended to split between casting them as honorary Great Men and lauding them as vessels of the unitary, eternal, and ultimately silent sanctity of womanhood. More like pâpier-maché than marble, the metaphoric figures of such canonized nineteenth-century women poets were shaped around vacancy: if their literary "relics" were revered, it was not as embodiments but as representations of a transcendent and definitively absent feminine glory.

Chapter 3, "Developing Character(s): Shakespeare's Heroines and Nineteenth-Century Literary Study," offers the first of a series of case studies. Based not only on formal criticism but on pedagogical texts, popular magazines, minutes of Shakespeare study groups, and conduct manuals, it traces two interconnected tendencies within the shifting, conflicted canonization of the nineteenth century's only popular feminine equivalent to Saint Shakespeare, the female characters of Shakespearean plays. The first, beginning with Thomas De Quincey and Samuel Taylor Coleridge and continuing through Sarah Stickney Ellis, John Ruskin, and A. C. Bradley, reads Shakespearean heroines as "van-

ishing monuments": it elevates them as basically interchangeable, "characterless" revelations of the timeless and essentially incorporeal glory of "the sex."
The second tendency, represented most powerfully by writers such as Mary
Lamb, Anna Jameson, and Ellen Terry (and ultimately Virginia Woolf), also
elevates the "heroines" as models to womanhood. It does so, however, precisely
by insisting upon their historicity, their irreducible individuality, and their
moral complexity.

It is scarcely accidental that actresses and their friends should have played
such a strong role in this latter criticism. To "Shakespearian Gallery" illustrators
such as Daniel Maclise, the beauty of Shakespearean heroines might be as interchangeable as it was ideal and incorporeal: like certain visual treatments of medieval saints, such reverent portraiture might distinguish one ideal figure from
another only through stock attributes. To admirers of "Ellen Terry's Ophelia"
or "Fanny Kemble's Juliet," however, Shakespeare's heroines could appear as
concrete, powerfully individual presences—and as presences, moreover, whose
performative "lives" literally depended upon the bodies and imaginations of
specific historical women. Thus, critical glorifications of fictional heroines challenged as well as shaped nineteenth-century tendencies to identify feminine
virtue with transcendent absence.

In chapter 4, "Canonization through Dispossession: Elizabeth Barrett
Browning and the 'Pythian Shriek,'" I investigate nineteenth-century attempts
to canonize Victorian England's most influential woman poet. Author of a literary autobiography while still in her teens, Elizabeth Barrett made a name
for herself, early on, as a woman poet whose commitment to ascetic suffering
conflated the virtues of the dutiful daughter, the Christian, the invalid, and
the genius. Not surprisingly, her marriage precipitated a crisis both of self-
representation and of reception. By midcentury, however, those admirers who
had mourned the loss of a "saint—sister—comforter" might nevertheless rejoice in E. B. B.'s accession to a more public honor: the (barely) unofficial title
of England's Queen of Song.

No sooner had Barrett Browning attained such status, however, than her
vehement and often witty political verse initiated a second canonic crisis. Particularly in response to the controversial *Poems before Congress,* a number of reviews
mobilized metaphors aimed at exonerating the Queen of Song from blame for
the complete works of Elizabeth Barrett Browning. (Like the Pythia, Barrett
Browning had prophesied while "not herself": she had been figuratively, [or,
one writer claimed, literally] "possessed.") Such determination to protect the
poet's canonicity, even at the cost of symbolically dispossessing her of some of
her own writing, foreshadowed the long process whereby the range of Barrett
Browning's "characteristic" verse was rendered increasingly restrictive, increas-

ingly subordinate to readings of her "womanly" (or later, "Victorian") character. Always unstable, the shape of this character underwent numerous complex
and suggestive transformations. By the first decades of the twentieth century,
however, the overall tendency of Barrett Browning's canonization had become
clear. Revered and (sometimes tenderly) mocked as some form of Andromeda
in Wimpole Street, E. B. B. had attained canonicity, in great part, at the cost of
being reduced to a romantic heroine of literary history. Even the *Sonnets from
the Portuguese,* which often seemed to exhaust her claim to literary fame, had
devolved from the status of serious poetry to that of a mere relic or valentine,
a verse counterpart to the Browning love letters. What had begun as a process
of limited exorcism ended in something perilously close to erasure.

The final chapter, "Competing Sainthoods, Competing Saints: The Canonization of Christina Rossetti," traces the fate of a major "vanishing monument" to nineteenth-century feminine canonicity. By the time Rossetti began
publishing verse, Barrett Browning's right to the exclusionary role of "supreme"
Victorian woman poet was already well established. Thus, Rossetti's canonization was marked from the beginning by competition with the earlier poet. As
detailed reception study of the years from 1861 to 1910 reveals, fin-de-siècle
critical assumptions and cultural anxieties were instrumental in shaping the
lengthy (and still ongoing) process whereby Rossetti's canonization was linked
to the decanonization of her predecessor. Each poet appeared both as a transparent medium of generic womanly love and as deplorably artificial; each served
both as an emblem of and a threat to vanishing feminine virtue; and each served
both as a symbol of and a stay against sexual anarchy. In one strain of reception,
Rossetti emerges as a representative of "artless art," a quintessentially modest
and spontaneous songbird-poet whose feminine purity renders her a useful
symbol in struggles against the professionalization and politicization of women's
writing. Here, Barrett Browning may be denigrated as unnaturally ambitious
and self-aware, while her verse may reap condemnation as stylistically "un-
chaste." In another strain, as E. B. B.'s once-controversial *Sonnets from the Portuguese* are retroactively packaged as the ultimate Victorian valentines, the Brownings come to stand as patron saints of old-fashioned romance and marriage.
Here, Rossetti is made to look suspiciously like a "marriage resister"; and her
own ambitious sonnet sequence, "Monna Innominata," is accordingly dismissed
as inauthentic.

In the end, Barrett Browning's triumph may be as inevitable as it is hollow.
For while insistence upon Rossetti's definitive literary modesty could do much
to win her praise as a spontaneous, natural poet, it scarcely encouraged close
critical reading of works such as "Monna Innominata," an artistically ambitious
"sonnet of sonnets" whose preface overtly marks it as a deliberate intervention

in a tradition tracing back not only to (the immodest) Barrett Browning but also to Dante and Petrarch. For the moment, Rossetti might have achieved highest status as an exemplary woman; but to do so—to become so fully identified with the shifting but always secondary literary virtues of her sex—was to lose out as a writer. Ironically, of course, mere literary sainthood had never been Rossetti's great goal: indeed, her expressions of the religious "call to be saints" represented a spiritual ambition for which the vast majority of her canonizers were unprepared.

At many points, especially early on, the arguments of *Lost Saints* slide over boundaries of class, nation, ethnicity, religion, period, and even gender. Such ranging does not aim at reinscribing some static, monolithic version of the nineteenth century or of "English literature" (see Crawford). Rather, by demonstrating that earlier conceptions and practices of canonization permeate our thinking about literature, even across crucial ideological and historical divisions, I seek to create a useful prerequisite for exploring such divisions' power and implications. The book's closing case studies, which analyze how canonization practices have been deployed in specific cultural locations, begin such exploration. Speaking more directly to conflicts and discontinuities within literary legends and to historical shifts within legend formation, these analyses complicate the book's earlier arguments—and in the process, I hope, suggest how attention to canonization, widely conceived, can open up new understandings of specific conflicts over literary and cultural value.

Lost Saints is a far cry from my original starting point: to the student facing the bookshelf where *Aurora Leigh* should have been, it might have seemed fairly tame. From years of feminist activism as well as work in the academy, though, I have learned to accept and honor the deep, everyday bases of certain kinds of political power as well as the extent to which effective political action can remain rooted in the messiness and intransigent materiality of day-to-day existence. I began in a stance of clear-cut political anger, fueled by dramatic fantasies of censorious (and dead) patriarchs burying a brilliant feminist text. I now find myself describing a process that is far more complex and ambiguous—and one in which my peers and I are implicated. As I celebrate the recovery of so many neglected nineteenth-century women poets, I find myself constantly aware of how my own readings and classroom practice can not only resist but inadvertently perpetuate the canonical processes whereby such poets came to be lost.

What is important now, it seems to me, is to educate ourselves and—if we have them, our students, and our colleagues—about the extent to which legend formation may have shaped and may still shape the "accessible canon" (Fowler

215–16). In addition to directing our critical attention beyond as well as within that canon, for example, we can be very clear about the impossibility of teaching the "essential" works of even the most canonical writers. We can also address the power of literary legends explicitly and critically, even when we have come to love them. Above all, perhaps, we can support the use (and, where possible, the production) of carefully edited, reasonably priced editions of poets' complete works—a privilege of canonization that has yet to be accorded even to the likes of Christina Rossetti and Elizabeth Barrett Browning. Limited and straightforward as such projects might sound, they would demand massive, consistent, and thoughtful effort—effort that would be both wide-ranging and deeply political, in the best sense of the term.

I have a working copy of *Aurora Leigh* now—a cheap paperback. When I take it in my hands, I hold a poem, a teaching text, and a materialized victory, both for Victorian studies and for the feminist movement. I hold, too, a living means of connection—however remote, fragmented, or mediated—to nineteenth-century women who were no saints—and who helped to make so many of my own joys and freedoms possible. It seems suitable that the words of one of them should close this chapter. When Susan B. Anthony traveled across the United States to lecture on behalf of women's suffrage, she carried a copy of *Aurora Leigh* with her. On Christmas Day 1901, she inscribed that copy with the following words: "This book was carried in my satchel for years and read and reread— . . . I have always cherished it above all other books—I now present it to the Congressional Library, Washington, D.C., with the hope that women may more and more be like 'Aurora Leigh.'"

I

——⫷⪥⫸——

Saint Shakespeare and the "Body" of the Text: *Legends and "Emendatory Criticism"*

WITHIN AT LEAST ONE nineteenth-century system of thought, authors could already achieve literal, though secular, sanctity. This was, of course, Auguste Comte's Religion of Humanity, whose precise, elaborate, and "scientific" appropriations and transformations of Catholicism extended to include an official "Positivist Calendar."[1] Creative writers figured strongly among the 558 historical worthies honored by inclusion in this secular answer to saints' calendars (Frederic Harrison, *New Calendar,* v). Indeed, so powerful were authors' positions that Homer, Dante, and Shakespeare belonged to a sort of immortals of the month club, joining the likes of Moses, Aristotle, Archimedes, Caesar, St. Paul, Charlemagne, Gutenberg, Descartes, Frederic II, and Bichat in presiding over lunar cycles (T. R. Wright 30–39; see fig. 1).

To be sure, outside positivist circles, canonization of literary secular saints was nearly always slightly tinged with irony or nostalgia, and positivist circles were never large. (As historian T. R. Wright notes, "The joke about their schism was that they had come to Church in one cab and left in two" [4].)[2] Yet these believers' "impact was out of all proportion to their numbers": from 1860 through 1880, according to Wright, English intellectuals felt compelled to assume and defend positions with respect to positivism, and "general interest" in the Religion of Humanity remained active until the end of the century (5). Moreover, though many Victorians rejected the positivists' ambitious extremism, even official monuments, such as the 1872 Albert Memorial, with its "169 portrait sculptors of benefactors of mankind," offer "an authentic, however inadvertent, witness to the power of positivist thinking . . . in the sixties and seventies" (Altick, *Lives,* 84; Piper 156–61). This was the age of (embattled, disputed) hero-worship, after all—the age "of the peopling of the capitals of Europe with statues, sometimes over life-size, of national heroes," including "heroic monumental" figures of poets (Piper 160, 156).

Although the literalism of the positivist calendar may have been unique, its analogues were legion. When the Pre-Raphaelites indited their secular "list

First Month — MOSES — THEOCRATIC CIVILISATION | Second Month — HOMER — ANCIENT POETRY | Third Month — ARISTOTLE — ANCIENT PHILOSOPHY | A

#	MOSES (Theocratic Civilisation)	HOMER (Ancient Poetry)	ARISTOTLE (Ancient Philosophy)	A
1	Prometheus. ....*Cadmus*	Hesiod.	Anaximander.	Theoph...
2	Hercules. ....*Theseus*	Tyrtæus.......... ....*Sappho*	Anaximenes.	Heropl...
3	Orpheus. ....*Tiresias*	Anacreon.	Heraclitus.	Erasist...
4	Ulysses.	Pindar.	Anaxagoras.	Celsus.
5	Lycurgus.	Sophocles. ....*Euripides*	Democritus. ....*Leucippus*	Galen.
6	Romulus.	Theocritus. ....*Longus*	Herodotus.	Avicen...
7	NUMA.	ÆSCHYLUS.	THALES.	HIPPO...
8	Belus ....*Semiramis*	Scopas.	Solon.	Euclid.
9	Sesostris.	Zeuxis.	Xenophanes.	Aristæ...
10	Menu.	Ictinus.	Empedocles.	Theodo...
11	Cyrus.	Praxiteles.	Thucydides.	Hero.
12	Zoroaster.	Lysippus.	Archytas. ....*Philolaus*	Pappus
13	The Druids. ....*Ossian*	Apelles.	Apollonius of Tyana.	Diopha...
14	BUDDHA.	PHIDIAS.	PYTHAGORAS.	APOLL...
15	Fo-Hi.	Æsop. ....*Pilpay*	Aristippus.	Eudoxu...
16	Lao-Tse.	Plautus.	Antisthenes.	Pytheas...
17	Mencius.	Terence. ....*Menander*	Zeno.	Aristar...
18	The Theocrats of Thibet.	Phædrus.	Cicero. ....*Pliny the Younger*	Eratost...
19	The Theocrats of Japan.	Juvenal.	Epictetus. ....*Arrian*	Ptolem...
20	Manco-Capac. ....*Tamehameha*	Lucian.	Tacitus.	Albateg...
21	CONFUCIUS.	ARISTOPHANES.	SOCRATES.	HIPPA...
22	Abraham. ....*Joseph*	Ennius.	Xenocrates.	Varro.
23	Samuel.	Lucretius.	Philo of Alexandria.	Colume...
24	Solomon. ....*David*	Horace.	St. John the Evangelist.	Vitruvi...
25	Isaiah.	Tibullus.	St. Justin. ....*St. Irenæus*	Strabo.
26	St. John the Baptist.	Ovid.	St. Clement of Alexandria.	Frontin...
27	Haroun-al-Raschid. *Abderrahman*	Lucan.	Origen.... ....*Tertullian*	Plutarc...
28	MAHOMET. [*III.*	VIRGIL.	PLATO.	PLINY

Eighth Month — DANTE — MODERN EPIC POETRY | Ninth Month — GUTENBERG — MODERN INDUSTRY | Tenth Month — SHAKESPEARE — THE MODERN DRAMA | ...

#	DANTE (Modern Epic Poetry)	GUTENBERG (Modern Industry)	SHAKESPEARE (The Modern Drama)	...
1	The Troubadours.	Marco Polo. ....*Chardin*	Lope de Vega. ....*Montalvan*	Alberti...
2	Boccaccio. ....*Chaucer*	Jacques Cœur...........*Gresham*	Moreto...........*Guillem de Castro*	Roger B...
3	Rabelais. ....*Swift*	Vasco da Gama.........*Magellan*	Rojas.....................*Guevara*	St. Bon...
4	Cervantes.	Napier. ....*Briggs*	Otway.	Ramus.
5	La Fontaine. ....*Burns*	Lacaille.....................*Delambre*	Lessing.	Montai...
6	De Foe.....................*Goldsmith*	Cook. ....*Tasman*	Göthe.	Campan...
7	ARIOSTO.	COLUMBUS.	CALDERON.	ST. TH...
8	Leonardo da Vinci..........*Titian*	Benvenuto Cellini.	Tirso.	Hobbes
9	Michael Angelo. .....*Paul Veronese*	Amontons. ....*Wheatstone*	Vondel.	Pascal.
10	Holbein.................*Rembrandt*	Harrison.............*Pierre Leroy*	Racine.	Locke.
11	Poussin. ....*Lesueur*	Dolland.....................*Graham*	Voltaire.	Vauven...
12	Velazquez.................*Murillo*	Arkwright.................*Jacquard*	Metastasio....................*Alfieri*	Diderot
13	Teniers....................*Rubens*	Conté.	Schiller.	Cabanis...
14	RAPHAEL.	VAUCANSON.	CORNEILLE.	LORD...
15	Froissart....................*Joinville*	Stevin. ....*Torricelli*	Alarcon.	Grotius
16	Camoens.....................*Spenser*	Mariotte. ....*Boyle*	Mme. de Motteville. *Mme. Roland*	Fontene...
17	The Spanish Romancers.	Papin. ....*Worcester*	Mme. de Sévigné. *Lady M. Montagu*	Vico...
18	Châteaubriand.	Black.	Lesage. ....*Sterne*	Fréret.
19	Walter Scott. ....*Cooper*	Jouffroy. ....*Fulton*	Mme. de Staal. .....*Miss Edgeworth*	Montes...
20	Manzoni.	Dalton. ....*Thilorier*	Fielding.................*Richardson*	Buffon.
21	TASSO.	WATT.	MOLIERE.	LEIBN...
22	Petrarch. [*and Bunyan*	Bernard de Palissy.	Pergolesi. ....*Palestrina*	Robert...
23	Thomas à Kempis. *Louis of Granada*	Guglielmini..................*Riquet*	Sacchini. ....*Grétry*	Adam S...
24	Mme. de Lafayette...*Mme. de Staël*	Duhamel (du Monceau). *Bourgelat*	Gluck. ....*Lully*	Kant...
25	Fénelon........*St. Francis of Sales*	Saussure. ....*Bouguer*	Beethoven. ....*Handel*	Condorc...
26	Klopstock....................*Gessner*	Coulomb. ....*Borda*	Rossini. ....*Weber*	Joseph...
27	Byron. ..*Elisa Mercœur and Shelley*	Carnot. ....*Vauban*	Bellini. ....*Donizetti*	Hegel.
28	MILTON	MONTGOLFIER.	MOZART.	HUME.

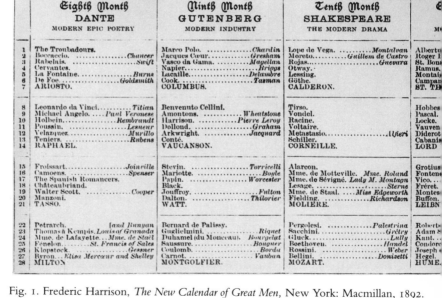

Fig. 1. Frederic Harrison, *The New Calendar of Great Men,* New York: Macmillan, 1892.

Top section

(partial)	Fifth Month — CÆSAR — MILITARY CIVILISATION	Sixth Month — ST. PAUL — CATHOLICISM	Seventh Month — CHARLEMAGNE — FEUDAL CIVILISATION
nth / ES / NCE			
..Averrhoes	Miltiades. / Leonidas. / Aristides. / Cimon. / Xenophon. / Phocion. ....Epaminondas / THEMISTOCLES.	St. Luke. ....St. James / St. Cyprian. / St. Athanasius. / St. Jerome. / St. Ambrose. / St. Monica. / ST. AUGUSTIN.	Theodoric the Great. / Pelayo. / Otho the Great. ..Henry the Fowler / St. Henry. / Villiers. ....La Valette / Don John of Austria. John Sobieski / ALFRED.
..Ctesibius	Pericles. / Philip. / Demosthenes. / Ptolemy I. / Philopœmen. / Polybius. / ALEXANDER.	Constantine. / Theodosius. / St. Chrysostom. ....St. Basil / St. Pulcheria. ....Marcian / St. Geneviève of Paris. / St. Gregory the Great. / HILDEBRAND.	Charles Martel. / The Cid. ....Tancred / Richard I. ....Saladin / Jeanne Darc. ....Marina / Albuquerque. ....W. Raleigh / Bayard. / GODFREY.
....Aratus / ...Nearchus / ..Berosus / ..Sosigenes / 'asir-Eddin	Junius Brutus. / Camillus. ....Cincinnatus / Fabricius................Regulus / Hannibal. / Æmilius Paullus. / Marius...............The Gracchi / SCIPIO.	St. Benedict.............St. Antony / St. Boniface.............St. Austin / St. Isidore of Seville. .....St. Bruno / Lanfranc. ....St. Anselm / Heloise. ....Beatrice / Architects of Mid. Ages. St. Bennet / ST. BERNARD. [the Less	St. Leo the Great. ....Leo IV. / Gerbert. ....Peter Damiani / Peter the Hermit. / Alexander III. ....St. Eligius / Suger. ....St. T. Becket / St. Francis of Assisi. ..St. Dominic / INNOCENT III.
	Augustus. ....Mæcenas / Vespasian....................Titus / Hadrian. ....Nerva / Antoninus. ....Marcus Aurelius / Papinian. ....Ulpian / Alexander Severus. ....Aëtius / TRAJAN.	St. Francis Xavier. Ignatius Loyola / St. Ch. Borromeo. Fredk. Borromeo / St. Theresa...St. Catharine of Siena / St. Vincent de Paul. L'Abbé de l'Epée / Bourdaloue. ....Claude Fleury / W. Penn.....................G. Fox / BOSSUET.	St. Clotilde. / St. Bathilda..St. Mathilda of Tuscany / St.Stephenof Hungary. Mathias Cor- / St. Elizabeth of Hungary. [vinus / Blanche of Castile. / St. Ferdinand III.......Alfonso X. / ST. LOUIS.

Bottom section

(partial)	Twelfth Month — FREDERICK II. — MODERN STATESMANSHIP	Thirteenth Month — BICHAT — MODERN SCIENCE	Day of ALL THE DEAD / Extra Day	Day of GOOD WOMEN / Additional Day in Leap-years
nth / ES / OPHY				
of Salisbury / monul Lully / ...Joachim / nal of Cusa / ..Erasmus / omas More / AS.	Maria de Molina. / Cosmo de' Medici the Elder. / Philippe de Comines. Guicciardini / Isabella of Castile. / Charles V..................Sixtus V. / Henri IV. / LOUIS XI.	Copernicus. ....Tycho Brahé / Kepler.......................Halley / Huyghens. ....Varignon / James Bernoulli. ...John Bernoulli / Bradley. ....Römer / Volta.....................Sauveur / GALILEO.		
...Spinoza / lano Bruno / alebranche / de Lambert / .....Duclos / orges Leroy	Coligny. ....L'Hôpital / Barneveldt. / Gustavus Adolphus. / De Witt. / Ruyter. / William III. / WILLIAM THE SILENT.	Vieta. ....Harriott / Wallis. ....Fermat / Clairaut. ....Poinsot / Euler. ....Monge / D'Alembert....Daniel Bernoulli / Lagrange........Joseph Fourier / NEWTON.		
......Cujas / Maupertuis / ....Herder / inckelmann / d'Aguesseau / ....Oken	Ximenes. / Sully. ....Oxenstiern / Colbert. ....Louis XIV. / Walpole. ....Mazarin / D'Aranda. ....Pombal / Turgot. ....Campomanes / RICHELIEU.	Bergmann. ....Scheele / Priestley. ....Davy / Cavendish. / Guyton Morveau..........Geoffroy / Berthollet. / Berzelius. ....Ritter / LAVOISIER.		
....Gibbon / ...Dunoyer / ...Fichte / ..Ferguson / ....Bonald / ie Germain	Algernon Sidney. ....Lambert / Franklin. ....Hampden / Washington. ....Kosciusko / Jefferson. ....Madison / Bolivar. ....Toussaint L'Ouverture / Francia. / CROMWELL.	Harvey. ....Charles Bell / Boerhaave. ....Stahl, Barthez / Linnæus. .....Bernard de Jussieu / Haller. ....Vicq-d'Azyr / Lamarck. ....Blainville / Broussais.................Morgagni / GALL.		

of Immortals" in 1848 (Altick, *Lives,* 84; 112–45); when Emily Dickinson hung one portrait of Elizabeth Barrett Browning on her bedroom wall and offered one to her cherished friend Thomas Wentworth Higginson ("Persons sent me three—") (Capps 86); when Leigh Hunt amassed his treasured collection of authors' hair; or when scores of holiday-makers undertook "pilgrimages" to Abbotsford, Casa Guidi, or Stratford and bought "relics," often of dubious provenance (Altick, *Lives,* 116–21), their actions and rhetoric clearly announced debts to earlier traditions of canonization. Thus, Victorian reverence for literary figures both undercuts and underscores Virgil Nemoianu's assertion that "it is virtually impossible to find even one example of . . . actual [literary] sacralization or sanctification. . . . Literary canons remained always *as if.* They were either frankly metaphorical, or relativized by implied linguistic markers of distance, approximation, and diminishment" (217).

Though the sway of *as if* was not always fully operative in nineteenth-century transformations of religious sanctity, it remains true that distancing, playfulness, and even overt parody played unmistakable roles within most such transformations. Like other versions of "sage discourse," texts aimed at literary canonization existed in a state of self-contradiction. Shaped by shifting and "competing affectional voices and ideological interests," canonizing texts attempted to mediate between positions that were both highly charged and, at points, fundamentally incompatible (Thaïs Morgan 3). Indeed, it is no wonder that impulses toward self-protection seem to have played instrumental roles in shaping Thomas Carlyle's literary "Universal Church" as, among other things, a church of self-parody (111). For outside "Catholicism without Christianity," as Thomas Huxley called positivism (Baldick 51), secular sainthood remained a contradiction in terms. On the one hand, its proponents faced challenges from continued faith in exclusively religious sainthood; on the other, they encountered thoroughgoing skepticism with respect to literature's allegedly divine powers. As has long been noted, nineteenth-century glorifications of high literature, with their concomitant sacralization of the language of literary criticism, arose just as the value of such literature was being radically called into question (Williams, "Romantic Artist").

As Linda Hutcheon notes, however, "Even in the nineteenth century, when the ridiculing definition of parody was most current . . . reverence was often perceived as underlying the intention of parody" (57). Parody's "appropriating of the past, of history, its questioning of the contemporary by 'referencing' it to a different set of codes, is a way of establishing continuity" (110). By choosing to build upon the conventions of religious sanctity, parodic secular sainthood not only subverts but simultaneously reinscribes their power. When Carlyle evokes a canonization without the benefit of clergy, for example, he dramatizes delight not only in the transformation but in the trivialization of earlier notions of sainthood. "Here in these ages, such as they are, have we not two mere Poets, if not yet deified, yet we may say beatified? Shakspeare and Dante are Saints of Poetry; really, if we will think of it, *canonised,* so that it is impiety to meddle with them. The unguided instinct of the world . . . [invests them with] a certain transcendentalism, a glory as of complete perfection. . . . They *are* canonised, though no Pope or Cardinals took hand in doing it!" (85). In such passages, the tone of irreverence seems clear. At other points, however, Carlyle seems to second Percy Bysshe Shelley's assertion that "no nation or religion can supersede any other without incorporating into itself a portion of that which it supersedes" (Shelley 289). When Carlyle writes that religion is "the soul of Practice" (102); when he insists that "the writers of Newspapers, Pamphlets, Poems, Books, these *are* the real working effective Church of a modern country" (162); or when he casts Shakespeare as the "noblest product" of "Middle-Age Catholicism" (102), the "Priest of a *true* Catholicism, the 'Universal Church' of the Future and of all times" (111), his appropriation of sanctity's cultural authority seems to be attempted in all earnestness. Secular sanctity is the genuine, if playful, heir to religious tradition. "If we do not now reckon a Great Man literally divine," Carlyle asserts, "it is that our notions of God . . . are ever rising higher" (84). "Perhaps there is no worship more authentic" than that of literary figures, he suggests (163). In so doing, he captures both the ambition and the ambiguity of secular sainthood's approaches to its religious models.

As celebrations of literary glory explicitly played with indebtedness to older traditions of reverence, they often incurred unacknowledged debts to such traditions: Carlyle's "working effective Church" may have been more like an older church than he acknowledges. This chapter, which turns upon treatments of Shakespeare, nineteenth-century England's greatest saint of poetry, draws from a wide range of writers—from Alexander Pope, Samuel Johnson, and Lewis Theobald to Carlyle, Ralph Waldo Emerson, and Matthew Arnold to Edward Dowden and Walter Raleigh, to virtually unknown compilers of pedagogical material such as Frank V. Irish. I will not pretend to represent such writers' thinking, much less to represent Shakespeare's reception or nineteenth-century literary study as a whole.[3] Rather, I will tease out certain strains within a literary reception—strains that may stand in uneasy, even explosive, juxtaposition to other approaches not only within the same author's thought but within the same text. Two access points will open up connections between literary and religious canonizations. The first, which is metaphoric, hearkens back to the architectural canon by locating sites at which nineteenth-century literary criticism and historiography explicitly undertake to construct and erect writers as idealized, monumental figures. Like Polycletus' "Canon," such glorified literary figures may become standards by being standardized: indeed, critics, editors, and pedagogues may even assert that devotion to a writer's "essential" glory authorizes or downright requires the "purging" or "pruning" of imperfections from the "body" of that author's works. Such figures are history's transcendent representatives. At the same time, however, their very glory elevates them beyond historic specificity. The second access point, the development of literary legends, links practices rather than metaphors. Addressing both the logical challenges and the institutional activities involved in according authors' biographies the values ascribed to sacred lives, it considers the potential force of such lives in establishing and policing texts' claims to be "characteristic" of their authors. In both cases, I argue, canonical creations and losses are inextricable. At points, they may even be indistinguishable.

In figurative glorifications of Shakespeare, as elsewhere, the nineteenth century offers a convenient starting point for analysis but no clear point of origin. The "cult of Shakespeare" was inherited, as was a long history of Shakespearean reception in which reverence and revision seemed inextricably, if variously, linked. Indeed, in Michael Dobson's words, by the eighteenth century, "adaptation and canonization, so far from being contradictory processes, were often mutually reinforcing ones. . . . The claiming of Shakespeare as an Enlightenment culture hero both profited from, and occasionally demanded, the substantial rewriting of his plays" (5; see Halliday and Babcock). Heirs to an already complex history of controversies over adaptations and editions, nineteenth-century writers heightened and elaborated upon, as well as transformed, already extant metaphors for critical and editorial practices when they attempted to define the "body" of the Bard's works or insisted upon the sacredness of his "character."

Even when Pope literally marginalized those "low and vicious parts and passages" that he presumed to have been corrupted or "unworthily charged upon" Shakespeare, for example, he became only one of the most famous of a lengthy series of editors whose omissions and emendations sought to present Shakespeare's "character in a light very different from that disadvantageous one in which it now appears to us" (46–47). Such editors, whether scholarly or not (and Pope was apparently less so than Theobald, the rival he pilloried in the *Dunciad*), often explicitly justified their textual emendations by the need to vindicate either the wonder of the Bard's poetry or its (and his) pretensions to true virtue—that is, the need to assert or maintain Shakespeare's legendary "character." (As folklorist Hermann Bausinger notes, wonder and virtue are the prerequisites for a figure's inclusion in the legends of saints [186].) What was at stake, these editors implied, was not merely the glory of the poet but the health and integrity of the body of his works (Dobson 10). Theobald, for example, wrote that Pope had "attacked" Shakespeare "like an unhandy slaughterman": he had "not lopped off the errors, but the poet" (69). The editor is thus charged with violence against the body of the text, and by extension, against the symbolic body of the Bard himself. Johnson echoes both Theobald's point and his metaphor when he charges that Pope "rejected whatever he disliked, and thought more of amputation than of cure" (148).

Theobald's and Johnson's evocations of the body of the text were relatively reserved, given earlier terms for expurgation—as Johnson's own biographer reveals. "Talking of Rochester's Poems," Boswell records, Johnson "said he had given them to Mr. Steevens to castrate for the edition of the Poets" (quoted in Perrin 44).[4] To a modern reader, the usage seems both shocking and paradoxical: how can writers so casually link the "straight rod" of canonical rule to textual "castration?" Yet link them they did, if Noel Perrin is correct: "'Castrate,' 'geld,' and 'mutilate' were the customary English verbs for expurgation until around 1800, when the euphemisms 'purge,' 'prune,' and 'chasten' begin to crop up alongside them" (44).[5]

As Theobald's reference to the "unhandy slaughterman" suggests, perhaps the key to such usage is its metaphoric link to husbandry: the "bodies" of eighteenth-century texts, already subject to being "disciplined and punished" by the kind of culture Michel Foucault discusses, are still conceived as objects, much as domestic animals may be. Medicinal and punitive, the metaphors for expurgation are also agricultural: one "gelds" or "prunes" to satisfy, not to limit, human appetites.[6]

By the time of Johnson, such attitudes were shifting: indeed, "shortly before his death [in 1795], James Boswell knelt before the 'miraculously discovered' manuscripts of two Shakespearean plays (actually forged by William Ireland) and kissed them" (Altick, *Lives,* 116). Playful though it is, a letter by Sir Walter Scott suggests the extent to which earlier metaphors for revising the body of the text had begun to prove both disturbing and painful: "I will not castrate John Dryden," Scott wrote of his projected edition of that writer's works. "I would as soon castrate my own father" (quoted in Perrin 56).[7] Like the body of the father, that of the text might be sacrosanct.

How much more sacred, then, must be the earthly remains of a "Saint of Poetry"? Surely these remains might be expected to be left untouched? Perhaps, Carlyle's discussion of Shakespeare implies—if only the body of the Bard's works had been intact at the start. As it is, however, what the "Saint of Poetry" leaves the world is not a full, monumental body of literature. Indeed, "all his works seem, comparatively speaking, cursory, imperfect," written under the "cramping circumstances" of history; they give "only here and there a note of the full utterance of the man." True, "passages there are that come upon you like a splendour out of Heaven, bursts of radiance." "Such bursts," however, "make us feel that the surrounding matter is not radiant; that it is, in part, temporary, conventional." For "Alas, Shakspeare had to write for the Globe Playhouse: his great soul had to crush itself, as it could, into that and no other mould. It was with him, then, as it is with us all. No man works save under conditions" (Carlyle 110). Thus, the body of Shakespeare's works comes to us already crushed, fragmented from its passage through history: its "bursts of radiance" are already obscured by "surrounding matter." For "the sculptor cannot set his own free Thought before us; but his Thought as he could translate it into the stone that was given, with the tools that were given. *Disjecta membra* are all that we find of any Poet, or of any man" (250).

Here, as elsewhere in a certain strain of critical writing that stretches from the Romantics to early in this century, Shakespearean texts become flesh or at the very least marble in the form of flesh, while critics become the masters who must reassemble the poet-hero's disjointed textual members, revealing (or reviving) the true, transcendent body that gave them life. What the canon creates and celebrates, in these terms, is less texts or even historical writers than "Thought," or, as David Masson calls it, a "ground-melody." "We cannot rest satisfied with a mere picture" of Shakespeare's "exterior in its aspect of repose, or in a few of its common attitudes," Masson writes. "We seek, as the phrase is, to penetrate into his heart—to detect and fix in everlasting portraiture that mood of his soul which was ultimate and characteristic; in which, so to speak, he came ready-fashioned from the Creator's hands; towards which he always sank when alone; and on the ground-melody of which all his thoughts and actions were but voluntary variations" (8).

The historical writer's "thoughts and actions" matter insofar as they are "voluntary variations" on the God-given grace from which they spring. In Edward Dowden's terms, if "no relic" of Shakespeare is "wholly without interest," it is because each text or fact may enrich a reader's "feeling for the man Shakespeare, who for ever lurks beyond the dramatist" (*New Studies,* 438). "All my writings are fragments of a great confession," Dowden quotes Goethe as saying, and adds, "And so it is and so it will be with every great writer who writes not merely out of head . . . but out of his head and heart, with intellect, imagination, passions, senses, conscience, will, all conspiring to one common result" (438–39). The critic's role, then, is not merely to read and interpret texts; it is to integrate these fragmentary remains into a "great confession" capable of flushing out the unified, essential "man" who "lurks" behind them.

The process of establishing transcendent canonical characters from such historically fragmented remains is a delicate one. Succeed, and one may not only restore a monument to the Hall of Literature but even attain a kind of reflected divinity as an interpreter of genius, a Great Narrator. Like an angel at the Resurrection, one may enact the "gathering together of bones, the reclothing of skeletons, the restoring of exactly those bits of matter scattered at death to the four winds," redeeming fragmentation by reviving the unified, sacred life that gave rise to literary "relics" (Bynum, *Fragmentation,* 284; 270–97). Fail, and one risks ending up as an incarnation of Victor Frankenstein.

Lest this discussion seem overly gothic or apocalyptic, let me allow two influential critics in this tradition to speak for themselves. In an essay first published in 1847, Thomas De Quincey writes, "Woman, sister, there are some things which you do not execute as well as your brother, man; no, nor ever will. Pardon me if I doubt whether you will ever produce a great poet from your choirs, . . . or a great philosopher, or a great scholar. By which last is meant—not one who depends simply on an infinite memory, but also on an infinite and electrical power of combination; bringing together from the four winds, like the angel of the resurrection, what else were dust from dead men's bones, into the unity of breathing life. If you *can* create yourselves into any of these great creators, why have you not?" ("Joan of Arc," 406). Walter Raleigh, whose reading list was used in the first English literature course taught in British universities (Kaplan and Rose 10), asserts, "The main business of Criticism, after all is not to legislate, not to classify, but to raise the dead. Graves, at its command, have waked their sleepers, oped, and let them forth. It is by the creative power of this art that the living man is reconstructed from the litter of blurred and fragmentary paper documents that he has left to posterity" (quoted in Baldick 78).[8]

At stake in constructing such canonical monuments was literature's relation to eternity. For like saints (or the undead), great authors do not decompose. "Emily Dickinson Is Dead," proclaims the title of a recent mystery novel centered on a literary cult, and the claim's effect is suitable (Langton). Of course she is, one thinks, smiling, after a suitable pause for shock. "Addison and Steele Are Dead," asserts the title of an academic book. The shock here seems intended to be far from comic. The *Spectator's* authors should be "alive," author Brian McCrea makes clear—if only in the way that Dickinson is—as living monuments whose *disjecta membra* have been reassembled and revived in the eternal life of the canon.[9]

Great authors must "live" on, and within the terms set by Carlyle's *disjecta membra,* they rely upon the unifying power of criticism to do so. They live, that is, through compositions (or composites) meticulously crafted from their texts—or at least from some of their texts. To be fair, critics and biographers need not lay claim to the right of "picking and choosing certain fragments" of an author's life and works "and constructing from these a charming vision to gratify" their "own peculiar sentiment[s]"; as Dowden puts it, "A man compassed about with infirmity, yet a heroic man, is after all better worth knowing than either a phantom or a fragment of a man." Nevertheless, "unless we know the whole man we shall comprehend no fragment aright" (*New Studies,* 443). And given enough faith in one's own capacity to "know the whole [literary] man" and, through such knowledge, to "comprehend" that whole subject's "fragment[s] aright," certain critics might lay claim to a fair bit of leeway in reconstructive efforts. Indeed, as Chris Baldick asserts in quoting Raleigh, some such criticism "can be seen to have elevated the personal greatness of the author to such a point that any interest in the litter of paper documents seems sacrilegious" (78).

As an 1896 *Athenaeum* review notes, for example, certain literary "remains" might be better left untouched: "There is much reason in the wrath of Tennyson and other great poets against the 'literary resurrection man,' who, though incapable of understanding the beauties of a beautiful work, can take a very great interest in poring over the various stages through which that work has passed on its way to perfection"—not to mention, presumably, juvenilia or compositions suppressed during the author's lifetime (Watts-Dunton, "*New Poems,*" 207). Such *disjecta membra,* it seems, may not be sacred relics; rather, like the grave robber's wares, they may be corrupt, fit only for dissection. To attempt to graft them to the living body of a writer's authorized publications would be desecration.

Even worse, perhaps, would be the attempt to canonize certain writers' remains in the first place. Another *Athenaeum* piece speaks directly to that point: "Beneath a slab of grey stone, marked by an almost illegible inscription, in the Cloisters of Westminster Abbey, lie the remains of the woman known as Aphra Behn. If it had entered the mind of any one of the present day to tear open the grave, and carry about, for the inspection of the public, the rottenness of that infamous person, he would have conceived an act only second in revolting loathsomeness to that of digging up this unwomanly creature's literary remains" (quoted in Perrin 247). Behn's corruption seems dual here: she was not only a writer who failed to be great but also a female who failed to be womanly.

Skepticism as to critics' ability to flush out, reassemble, or compile the essential writer remained lively throughout the nineteenth century. As late as 1910, however, even that sometime-skeptic Edward Dowden was still returning to Carlyle's image of Shakespeare's works as "so many windows, through which we see a glimpse of the world that was in him" (Carlyle 110), still asserting that "though what Browning calls the 'spirit-sense,' an educated tact, is the surest instrument for the discovery of a dramatist . . . in his work, some few canons of discovery can be formulated" (Dowden, *Essays,* 274).

Dowden's attempt to formulate "canons of discovery" is explicitly peda-gogical. Toward the century's end, teaching materials emerge as particularly rich sources for the glorification both of writers' and nations' "souls." Alfred H. Welsh's 1883 *Development of English Literature and Language,* for example, asserts that "personal genius remakes the society which evolves it. In so far as it rises above the table-land of national character, it not only expresses but intensifies the national type" (ix). Moreover, "since the desire of unity, and the necessity of referring effects to their causes, are the mainsprings of energy," what matters is less "the knowledge that . . . a certain author wrote certain books" than how that author is related "to some dominant idea or moral state . . . how beneath literary remains we can unearth the beatings of living hearts centuries ago, as the lifeless wreck of a shell is a clue to the entire and living existence. The one is a knowledge of objects as isolated; the other, of objects as connected. The first gives facts; the second gives *power*" (x–xi).

Though Welsh's rhetoric may be scientific, his echoes of De Quincey are unmistakable. The "laboratory method" of J. Scott Clark's 1900 *A Study of English and American Poets* offers similarly mixed claims: indeed, in defending his method's claim to being "inductive and scientific," Clark explicitly cites "the old scholastic dictum, 'First learn what is to be believed'" (viii).[10] In Clark's words, "The central idea of this volume is found in the quotation from Leslie Stephen given on the title-page: 'The whole art of criticism consists in learning to know the human being who is partially revealed to us in his written and spoken words'" (ix).

The metaphors of relics, monuments, and dismembered flesh that perme-ate the extremes of nineteenth-century attempts to assert the integrity of Shake-spearean texts may help to explain the apparently paradoxical coexistence of open emendation or expurgation with the development of ambitious scholarly editions. As canonized authors' bodies of work become sacred, and as "lopping off" comes to sound like sacrilege, developments in scholarly textual editing prefigure the caution with which later academics approach questions of textual integrity. Conversely, as the body of the text becomes merely the external and necessarily imperfect manifestation of an author's "spirit" (Altick, *Lives,* 94–99), an editor might well promise to alter or expurgate a writer's works, in Thomas Bowdler's words, "not only without injury, but with manifest advantage . . . to the sense of the passage and to the spirit of the author" (quoted in Perrin xv). As Frank V. Irish puts it in his unusually explicit 1896 "Hints to Teachers," "All facts *about* an author and his works are of minor importance, and should only be used to lead to an appreciation of his choicest writings and his noblest traits of character. . . . Literature should bring our pupils noble ideals. Avoid speaking of the personal deformities or failings of authors. . . . A beautiful poem or a piece of noble prose is a work of art. You have no more right to mar it than to mar a beautiful statue" (5).

"Formerly we used to canonize our heroes," Oscar Wilde wrote. "The modern method is to vulgarize them. Cheap editions of great books may be delightful, but cheap editions of great men are absolutely detestable" ("Epigrams," 494). In practice, the two sorts of cheap edition may often have been difficult to separate. Some readers, after all, might be seen to require simpler manifestations of the author's Thought than others; some literary monuments might hence encompass fewer textual relics. Editorial "disciplining" of scholarly texts might become more discreet (and more discrete), but the bodies of "popular" Shakespearean texts remained "chastened." F. T. Palgrave, that representative of "unassailable canons," did his part for such a process, for example: when he issued an edition of Shakespeare's *Sonnets,* he omitted four or five poems as having "a warmth of coloring unsuited for the larger audience" (quoted in Perrin xiii).[11] As students, middle-class women, and working-class readers of both sexes gained increasing access to relatively cheap literary texts, the shapes of popular and scholarly monuments diverged; and the latter were often covered by editorial fig leaves.[12] "What would you say to any man who would castrate Shakspere? . . ." Scott himself wrote. "I don't say but that it may be very proper to select correct passages for the use of boarding schools and colleges" (quoted in Perrin 56). It is scarcely accidental that one tends to think of popular classics as those that have been abridged or otherwise watered down. Unexpurgated texts were—and to some extent still are—reserved for those privileged enough to find and pay for them.

Thus, for creators of canonical monuments, a given writer's works may be both holy relics and expendable fragments; their significance is determined by their relation to the "soul," the "Thought," the glorious and essential (if somewhat malleable) character of their author. When a gap opens up between this sanctified soul and given *disjecta membra*—whether literary or biographical—the texts may have to go. As was already clear by the eighteenth century, for example, admirers of an ideal Shakespeare could be prepared to "redeem the 'essential' Shakespeare" from the "archaic or immoral lapses" of the historical writer's "uncorrected texts" (Dobson 187). By the time the Baconian Society developed, even the historical author was in danger of being tossed out. "Poet worship overreached itself," Richard D. Altick notes, "by making manifest the painful discrepancy between the idol (as constructed from a reading of the plays) and the real man (so far as he could be seen in the historical records). The trouble could be corrected simply by deciding that they were two different persons" (*Lives*, 139). At its most extreme, then, as in the formation of the Baconian society, canonization of the body of a writer's work might not merely smooth out or lop off textual rough edges: it might even create an ideal figure whose form overshadowed or blocked out that of the historical writer altogether.[13]

As the opening of an 1891 *Academy* review by Richard Le Gallienne suggests, certain nineteenth-century critics themselves perceived that secular sanctification involved transformation and perhaps even loss: "One by one, the *dii majores* of modern song are passing into the classic one-volume. . . . Till a fame has attained to that it is more or less nebulous . . . Till 'Endymion, a Poetic Romance' and 'Lamia, Isabella, &c.,' have merged into 'Keats'; till 'In Memoriam' and 'Maud,' and how much else of the fairest art, have merged their identity in 'Tennyson'—the poet has not yet undergone disembodiment, but still walks, so to say, in the dress of the period. With the one volume the poet enters into mythology" (130).

Le Gallienne's account of figurative canonization captures not only the sense in which separate texts may blend into a unified, perhaps homogenized canonical whole—*In Memoriam* and "Maud" into "Tennyson," for example—but the complexities of the relationship of such transformations to history. "Modern song" has created literary gods, it seems. Such transfiguration requires, however, that one become disembodied, divesting oneself of the dress of the period.

The power of the "classic one-volume" is thus indissolubly bound to that of the classical gods, or of the secularized saints with whom nineteenth-century literary reverence often interchanged them. In an almost literal sense, Le Gallienne's standard edition is the gateway to myth. As Great Men, Keats and Tennyson seem to have been gods even before they passed the portals of the one-volume edition. Yet however divine their power, before the appearance of the one-volume edition it could only be realized within the limitations of history and the flesh. Once the bodies of their work are transformed into a "classic" single volume, however, the writers become transfigured, disembodied. Into these figures, specific volumes and verses merge. "Lamia" and *In Memoriam* shuck off their "identity"; textual specificity, as well as historicity and physicality, vanishes into the "Keats," the "Tennyson," of myth. Paradoxically, all that remains tangible is the volume itself, as symbol of the fame, no longer "nebulous," that it both rewards and institutionalizes.

It was one thing to invoke a secularized pantheon or cathedral of art; it was another, as we have seen, to harmonize the desire for ideal literary figures with the practice of reading their texts, and yet another to combine the claims of sanctity with those of Romantic "genius."

Once more, Carlyle most vividly dramatizes the issues raised by literary secular sanctity. "Call it worship, call it what you will, is it not a right glorious thing, and set of things, this that Shakspeare has brought us?" he asks. "For myself, I feel that there is actually a kind of sacredness in the fact of such a man being sent into this Earth. Is he not an eye to us all; a blessed heaven-sent Bringer of Light? . . . He is the grandest thing we have yet done. For our honour among foreign nations, as an ornament to our English Household, what item is there that we would not surrender rather than him?" (111–13).

For Carlyle, Shakespeare is household ornament, saint, and poet-hero. Beyond doubt, the cultural icon forged by such conflations is a powerful one. At the same time, however, the yoking of sanctity to heroism—the project of locating sacred (literary) transcendence within the realm of mortal, national histories—presents serious, perhaps irresolvable problems. Such problems, in turn, elicit new constructions of cultural power.

Religious "saints share collectively in the luminous life of the incarnate Christ": their "sanctity is derived from the sacred, which is radically singular" (Heffernan 7; 20, 63, 87, 115). Granted, saints may be distinctive individuals whose actual or recounted lives serve powerful national and economic interests; they may even be heroes, whose glory derives from individual courage and achievement. What (officially) matters, however, is not their specific historical existence but their glory, which is a free, radically generic gift of God.

What of the glory of the sacred "poet-hero," then? If it is not literally supernatural, is it natural? Historical? Is the source of literary genius distinctive or collective? Does it derive from or transcend historical circumstance? Is it a matter of grace, courage and grace, or merely courage? Such questions shape much Victorian literary writing. Theoretically, for example, one can force one's way into the ranks of the heroic, given the proper circumstances. As influential Victorian poems remind us, however, it is not clear whether one can (or should be able to) buy, badger, or even suffer one's way into glory. Robert Browning's bishop may order his tomb at St. Praxed's under the popular belief that saints remain present in their burial places (Wilson 11), for example; but even he comes to doubt whether he himself will "lie through centuries, / and hear the blessed mutter of the mass / And see God made and eaten all day long" ("Bishop," lines 80–83). And while the futility of Tennyson's St. Simeon Stylites may seem less clear (he did become a saint, after all), St. Simeon's project of whining and bullying his way into heaven seems dubious at best. If a Simeon achieves sainthood, what, if anything, does that suggest about grace?

Genius—like religious grace—may be a gift. Can one can prove unworthy of it? Can one gain it by proving one's worth? In the context of such questions, it seems scarcely surprising that Browning's Renaissance bishop should remind readers that the passionate assembling of grotesque, rich beauties is no guarantee of eternal glory, or that the future author of *In Memoriam* should play with similar doubts about the efficacy of public displays of suffering. Embattled from without and conflicted from within, nineteenth-century canonizing texts often engage in delicate balancing acts between the generic sanctity of religious divinity and the distinctive glory of Romantic "genius." Such balancing acts become especially difficult where women writers are concerned.

De Quincey offers one possibility: one might accord the Bard an inborn grace explicitly akin to the generic sanctity of religion. "We feel," he writes, "that the little accidents of birth and social condition are so unspeakably below the grandeur of the theme, . . . that a biographer of Shakspeare at once denounces himself as below his subject if he can entertain such a question as seriously affecting the glory of the poet. In some legends of saints, we find that they were born with a lambent circle or golden aureola about their heads. This angelic coronet shed light alike upon the chambers of a cottage or a palace; . . . but the cottage, the palace . . . were . . . equally incapable of adding one ray of color or one pencil of light to the supernatural halo" ("Shakspeare," 37).

At their most ambitious, however, as with Emerson and Carlyle, nineteenth-century canonizing texts do not pit halos against history. Instead, they seek to adopt De Quincey's rhetoric of sanctity without thoroughly dismissing the "little accidents of birth and social condition." Attempting a new relationship between sacred glory and history, they suggest that the poet-hero's representative sanctity rescues the distinctiveness of historical existence from the realm of the accidental.[14] Genius in the abstract may transcend history, these texts assert; but history alone allows genius embodiment. Shakespeare, whose notoriously transparent, objective, Protean status as a "World-Poet" or "Universal Poet" (Carlyle 82) accords with his work's status as a "world-book" (Emerson 115), is a central model of such paradoxical glory.

What enters is election by history—or, in Carlyle, by Nature working through history (103)—rather than by divine grace. In Emerson, history is the source of great poets' sacred force: although "the essence of poetry [is] to abolish the past, and refuse all history" (118), "what is best written or done by genius in the world was no man's work, but came by wide social labour, when a thousand wrought like one, sharing the same impulse" (115). For "the genius of our life is jealous of individuals, and will not have any individual great, except through the general. There is no choice to genius. A great man . . . finds himself in the river of thoughts and events, forced onward by the ideas and necessities of his contemporaries" (109).

Filled with the spirit of his age, Emerson's "genius" cannot help but create: "What an economy of power! And what a compensation for the shortness of life! . . . Men, nations, poets, artisans, women, all have worked for him, and he enters into their labours. Choose any other thing, out of the line of tendency, out of the national feeling and history, and he would have all to do for himself: his powers would be expended in the first preparations. Great genial power, one would almost say, consists in not being original at all; in being altogether receptive; in letting the world do all, and suffering the spirit of the hour to pass unobstructed through the mind" (110). History floods this "great man" to achievement; "the rude warm blood of the living England" circulates in the drama of Shakespeare's time, giving "body . . . to his airy and majestic fancy" (111).

Carlyle's poet-hero is very differently placed. Such a Hero may live "in the inward sphere of things, in the True, Divine and Eternal, which exists always, unseen to most, under the Temporary, Trivial"; his life may be "a piece of the everlasting heart of Nature herself" (155); and yet he must shape himself "according to the kind of world he finds himself born into" (78). He must "cramp himself into strange shapes" (155). Here, too, though, as with Emerson, what matters about history, be it personal or cultural, is that it gives rise to an embodiment of eternal genius. "Given your Hero," Carlyle writes, "is he to become Conqueror, King, Philosopher, Poet? It is an inexplicably complex controversial-calculation between the world and him! He will read the world and its laws; the world and its laws will be there to be read. What the world, on *this* matter, shall permit and bid is . . . the most important fact about the world" (80). Not only is the Great Man the great reader of the world, but his character, as constituted by an "inexplicably complex controversial-calculation between the world and him," represents the most "important fact" of that world.

When the grace of literary genius has become the most important fact about a point in history—and a place on the globe—literary canonization attains powerful national significance. In this context, the implicit sanctification of a historical time and place never disappears, even from the most adamant assertions of transcendence. Thus, even the likes of Ben Jonson's famous assertion that Shakespeare "was not of an age, but for all time!" may resound as "a historically charged articulation of British imperialist pride" (Howard and O'Connor 281; see Longhurst).

Once more, Carlyle is the most eloquent and influential proponent of such an approach to canonization. Significantly, his Saint Shakespeare is both heaven's and England's doing. As a "Bringer of Light" and an ornamental household object, this Shakespeare simultaneously offers spiritual blessings and practical benefits: "If [foreign nations] asked us, Will you give-up your Indian Empire or your Shakspeare, you English; never have had any Indian Empire or never have had any Shakspeare? . . . Should not we be forced to answer: Indian Empire, or no Indian Empire; we cannot do without Shakspeare! Indian Empire will go, at any rate, some day; but this Shakspeare does not go, he lasts for ever with us; we cannot give-up our Shakspeare!" (113). "Nay," he continues, "apart from spiritualities; and considering him merely as a real, marketable, tangibly-useful possession," Shakespeare remains indispensable: "before long," England "will hold but a small fraction of the English: in America, in New Holland, east and west to the very Antipodes, there will be a Saxondom covering great spaces of the Globe." "What is it," Carlyle asks, "that can keep all these together into one Nation?" Not political rulers: for "Acts of Parliament, administrative prime-ministers" have failed to unify the "Nations of Englishmen." "America is parted from us, so far as Parliament could part it." What political rulers cannot do, however, poet-heroes can: "Here, I say, is an English King, whom no time or chance, Parliament or combination of Parliaments, can dethrone! This King Shakspeare, does not he shine, in crowned sovereignty, over us all, as the noblest, gentlest, yet strongest of rallying-signs; *in*destructible; really more valuable in that point of view than any other means or appliance whatsoever?" (114).

Only cultural empires last. Transcendence and utility, sanctification and reification, thus merge in the single figure of the saint, king, and poet-hero. As "rallying-sign" (or standard, in all senses of the word), means, and appliance, the fully canonical Shakespeare could "shine over" an indestructible, peaceful empire bound in fealty to (the) English.[15]

Most often, when nineteenth-century writing on Shakespeare invokes a sacred, timeless "monarch Bard," a "king of England's kings," the monarch in question lends his authority to a political, not merely a cultural or spiritual empire (Sprague 120; Aldrich 233). Carlyle may preface his vision of eternal empire by asserting that "not the noblest Shakspeare or Homer of them can be remembered *for ever*," for example (82); he may insist that unlike "Middle-Age Catholicism," Shakespeare's "Revelation" entails no "narrow superstition, harsh asceticism, intolerance, fanatical fierceness or perversion" (111). Nonetheless, he scarcely expresses eagerness to cede any national "treasures," whether textual or geographic. It might be most important, in Algernon Swinburne's words, that "time" itself "bows down to [England] as Shakespeare's land" ("Sonnet," line 14), but for many writers, that was no reason to refrain from desiring others to bow down as well.[16]

Such characterizations were cornerstones of a larger reading of English literature. Here, for example, is the opening of the first chapter of Henry Morley's famous *A First Sketch of English Literature,* a work that reached seventeen editions between its first publication in May 1873 and the century's end: "The Literature of a People tells its Life. . . . Let us bring our hearts, then, to the study which we here begin, and seek through it accord with [the] true soul of our country. . . . [English literature] represents a people striving through successive generations to find out the right and do it, to . . . labour ever onward for the love of God. If this be really the strong spirit of her people, to show that it is so is to tell how England won, and how alone she can expect to keep, her foremost place among the nations" (1–2).

By helping to constitute England as a secular Holy Land, Saint Shakespeare not only unifies an imagined (and partly imaginary) empire but symbolizes the sanctified grounds for imperial expansion.[17] As Patrick Brantlinger points out in *Rule of Darkness,* the "reform optimism" of early Victorians such as Thomas Babington Macaulay seems to foreshadow Kurtz's essay for the "Society for the Suppression of Savage Customs" in Conrad's *Heart of Darkness* (30). It is probably no accident that Kurtz and his "gang of virtue" first appear like self-proclaimed secular saints or that Kurtz's faith in the "cause intrusted to us by Europe" should be so emphatically linked to high culture (Conrad 28). Millenarianism met nostalgia: new crusaders who could imagine an "imperishable empire" might follow the lead of the original Crusaders in asserting that reliance on forced conversions did not give their undertaking any less "title to glory."

In practice, as Gauri Viswanathan has noted in the case of India, colonial literary studies proved the effects of Saint Shakespeare's teachings to be far from predictable (159–65).[18] Moreover, no doubt in part due to the religious backgrounds for such glory, even the abstract realm of King Shakespeare sometimes seems to challenge or confute the claims of more earthly realms. Gerald Massey's untitled 1888 poem from *The Secret Drama of Shakespeare's Sonnets* may imply as much, for example:

> *Our Prince of Peace in glory hath gone,*
> *With no Spear shaken, no Sword drawn,*
> *No Cannon fired, no flag unfurled,*
> *To make his conquest of the World.*
>
> *For him no Martyr-fires have blazed,*
> *No limbs been racked, no scaffolds raised;*
> *For him no life was ever shed,*
> *To make the Victor's pathway red.*

And for all time he wears the Crown
Of lasting, limitless renown:
He reigns, whatever Monarchs fall;
His Throne is in the heart of all.

The true Prince of Peace, it seems, is Prince Shakespeare. Visions of secular heavens are not the only complicating factors in King Shakespeare's association with mortal empires. On more practical grounds, for example, many of the positivists who insisted on certain indissoluble bonds between earthly and "imperishable" empires were nevertheless strongly anti-imperialist (T. R. Wright 113, 119, 251).

Self-divided though they might be, evocations of secular sainthood promised tremendous cultural power, not only to canonized texts and authors but to both the critics who constituted them and the culture whose definitive spirit they were supposed to embody. Inevitably, however, they entailed losses as well. For though the specificity of secular saints is the prerequisite for their embodiment of genius within history, such figures are only manifestations of a higher order. Their significance derives only from integration into an eternal plot whose workings transcend both them and history itself. Thus, faith in election by history did not necessarily guarantee commitment to historical accuracy. Indeed, as De Quincey's essay on Shakespeare suggests, canonized figures could lose in historicity what they gained in glory. The costs of such canonicity could be both personal and textual.

However suspect "essentialist biography" may now appear (Young-Bruehl 414), much Victorian writing assumes that rendition of the "essence of a life" is biography's (as well as criticism's) highest aim. Serious consideration of attempts to create secular sainthood adds new significance to the "steady drift of nineteenth-century critical attention . . . away from the work and toward the writer": it allows for more explicit focus on the powerful religious and national incentives for critical attempts to capture "what was regularly called the 'soul' of the poet" (Altick, *Lives,* 95–96).

As has long been recognized, a key source of the notorious tensions between the drives of nineteenth-century literary biographies toward historical specificity and mythic significance lies in literary historiography's grapplings with its hagiographic heritage.[19] Indeed, as A. O. J. Cockshut puts it, the difference between most twentieth-century and nineteenth-century biographies "is a religious one, though it does not always correspond to the religious profession of the writer" (20). Within the dominant conventions of much nineteenth-century biography, "each life is felt to have a meaning, an objective meaning to which all interpretation is only a weak approximation. . . . It is possible to read a good biography as if it were a novel, paying attention to the author's mastery of form. But in the nineteenth century, another process was more common. The biographer himself reads the *evidence* of the life as if it were a novel, and God were the novelist. In that case, the finished biography is more accurately compared to literary criticism; it is a report upon an obscure but momentous work of art" (21). What matters in such a form of literary biography is what John Henry Newman calls "poetical" character: a "central and consistent character" that achieves its distinctive quality only when "unnatural peculiarities [are] laid aside, and harsh contrasts reconciled" ("Poetry," 203, 212, 203).[20] If such renditions require suppression of what we might call the "differences within" an individual subject—or that subject's works—so be it.

What has been less often recognized is that where literary biography draws upon the traditions of hagiography, it also draws, perforce, upon the folk origins of hagiography—which is to say, upon the legend. Like other casually used terms already addressed, the phrase *literary legend* demands literal, serious attention: its common deployment both marks and masks recognition of the power of religious and folk traditions within literary study.

Much of this book focuses on the development of specific nineteenth-century literary legends. Here, however, that century is merely my starting point; for if later, detailed analyses of legend formation are to resonate as they should, one must conceive of the saint's legend as a folk genre, and of legend formation as a folk practice that began long before the Romantics and continues to flourish in our own time.[21]

Legend has meant, among other things, an assigned reading: the word, which derives from the Latin *legere* (to read), once referred to those accounts of saints and martyrs that were read in monasteries during services and meals on saints' days (Rosenfeld 1). As a ritual of reverence and an educational process, the reading of fixed, official saints' lives helped to create and maintain a distinct and in some senses elite community. At the same time, however, it also bound that community to a larger culture whose understanding of oral saints' legends remained both fluid and influential. One might say that in the formal reading of legends, the saints' calendar and the syllabus meet: time is apportioned to and marked by figures whose glory is at once taught and celebrated. Analogies between the uses of saints' lives or legends and those of the texts that create literary legends must remain rough, of course: they can only suggest, not prove, correspondences.[22] By so doing, however, they help to clarify the debate over whether canonic authority inheres in elite institutions or popular culture. They suggest connections between canonization's textual and material practices, and they assist in identifying some of the specific processes whereby the communal, if always unstable and contested, authority of canonicity is established and exercised.

The legend's popular authority stands as the origin and undergirding of the formal process of making saints. In early Christianity, saints' cults sprang "spontaneously from the life of the Church," whose local communities "venerated their own heroes and other great" individuals "of whom they had heard," free from "ecclesiastical control" or "formal authorization" (Kemp 21). In time, centralization of Church power rendered the constitution of sainthood a hierarchical process ultimately dependent upon papal decree. Still, legends remained both prerequisites for canonization and potential competitors of fixed, authorized saints' lives (Heffernan 34). As such, legends speak to the interconnectedness of and tensions between institutional and popular power in the canonization process.

Literary legends serve no such official functions, of course. As Altick acknowledges, however, "In practice, biography has profoundly and continuously affected everyone's attitudes toward the literature he reads; toward, indeed, his very concept of the *institution* of literature. . . . To most people, [literary history] is a melange of more or less vaguely remembered biographical headnotes in anthologies, history-of-literature textbooks that ticked off authors in chronological sequence, fly-specked portraits (the subjects usually bearded and standing on their dignity) on classroom walls, biographical anecdotes inserted in teachers' lectures to restore the drooping spirit, and romantic legends of the sort propagated by *The Barretts of Wimpole Street*" (*Lives,* 403).

To be sure, legends and disciplinary secular saints are intrinsic to the hidden curriculum of any discipline, including the hard sciences (Becher 23, 25). For disciplinary cultures are, among other things, folk cultures whose "legendary aspects . . . serve not only as part of the machinery of socialization, but also as weapons to be deployed in the course of internal disputes and controversies" (25). Within such cultures, however, the legend's force is surely more powerful in certain disciplines. Sitting under the fly-specked icons to which Altick refers, students whose spirits have been restored by "romantic legends" might well come to love Victorian literature, say, as represented by *The Barretts of Wimpole Street*. Once initiated into (or repelled from) literary cults, they might well find, as Altick himself did, that such early impressions are difficult to efface ("Victorians," 327).

Indeed, to read about the function of legends is in some sense to learn about the paradigms of literary pedagogy, and thus to learn about literary study as a practice. As Tony Davies argues, "It is in the humdrum, everyday and generally quite 'untheoretical' activity of English teaching that the real effecti-

vity of 'Literature' as a practice is to be found" (34). Certainly the communal
authority of canonizing legends has clearest play in the introductory classroom.
Pedagogy has its own oral traditions, which extend beyond the apocryphal
(or actual) classrooms in which generations of old notes are refurbished and re-
cycled for new audiences. If truth be told, even teachers who express the most
severe skepticism toward the conventions of authorship may often find that Altick's "biographical anecdotes" and "romantic legends" are inseparable from
their own day-to-day pedagogical practice.[23]

If the classroom is the literary legend's most powerful institutional site in
terms of oral tradition, textbooks and reference books are its most powerful
institutional site in terms of written tradition. To understand this phenomenon,
it helps to consider the analogous functions of authority within medieval "sacred biographies," as analyzed by Thomas Heffernan, and within pedagogical
texts devoted to outlining literary canons.

Heffernan's research, which focuses on a clearly delimited range of medieval texts, offers analyses that speak to a much wider range of practices within
religious canonization as a whole. The successful account of a saint's life, he
argues, bears an intimate and circular relationship to a community of faith: it
both restates shared knowledge and extends the community's interpretations of
sanctity (16). The author of such a sacred (or, in my terms, canonizing) biography is not an expert, in the modern sense; "rather, the community is a collection of experts, and the narrative reflects this state of collective authority" (20).
Such popular collective authority contains subversive aspects—often in both
senses of the word *contains*. For the function of medieval sacred lives is hegemonic (14): their narratives perform a harmonizing function and represent a
dominant, if often temporary, compromise between divergent and shifting interests.

The disjunctions between such saints' lives and modern texts such as
teaching anthologies are clear. Nonetheless, the results of Glen M. Johnson's
research into current textbooks' constructions of the canon present suggestive
analogies. Like a successful sacred life, for example, the teaching anthology "rat-
ifies whatever consensus exists about the canon; it perpetuates that consensus
in the act of presenting it and preserves the consensus through assuring that the
works are accessible; and it is a forum for changing the consensus through addi-
tions, deletions, or changes in format" (113). Moreover, although texts such as
the Norton editions are ultimately authorized by influential representatives of
institutional authority, they rely directly upon market research aimed at literally
hundreds of academics. Such attempts at achieving "consensus," Johnson notes,
render the creation of major anthologies "inherently more democratic than the

pronouncements of prestigious editors," though such anthologies are not "necessarily more pluralistic" (114).[24]

Thus, like earlier canonizing texts, teaching anthologies exercise a hegemonic, conservative collective authority.[25] Like a medieval sacred life, a standard anthology is "designedly not a reflection of individual ability, of virtuoso excellence but is part of a tradition. . . . The major anticipation which unites author and audience is how the text reflects the received tradition, a tradition whose locus is in the community. Such tradition is neither monolithic nor frozen but changes as the community selects and reinterprets anew from within itself" (Heffernan 19). Such texts do not stand merely as "the artifacts of the dialogue between a high and low culture"; rather, they present a "model of intimate reciprocity" whereby canonical authority circulates between institutional and popular sites (20–21).

The concept of communal authority, which applies both to folk legends and to the more formal biographies that Heffernan analyzes, suggests a great deal about the forms as well as the authority claims of standard popular and pedagogical texts. Like the oral saints' legends to which they are intimately related, for example, written saints' lives exercise a power that springs in great part from convention. They are deeply intertextual: indeed, they may be more or less openly and deliberately constructed as dense pastiches of quotations from and references to other such works (Heffernan 18–20, 113–22). The same is true, of course, for any number of textual guides to literary study. There are anecdotes, quoted passages, and even phrases (or, as John Rodden would call them, "watchwords") without which introductions to certain authors would not be complete.[26] These words are, of course, the stuff of legend.

For example, according to F. W. H. Myers, George Eliot took a walk with him one evening, and as she walked, she took "as her text the three words which have been used so often as the inspiring trumpet-calls of men,—*God, Immortality, Duty,*—." Eliot pronounced, Myers reported, "with terrible earnestness, how inconceivable was the *first,* how unbelievable the *second,* and yet how peremptory and absolute the *third*" (269). As Dorothea Barrett's *Vocation and Desire* persuasively argues, Myers's narrative is a relatively unrevealing bit of "purple prose." "Most book-length treatments" of Eliot nevertheless manage to invoke Myers's sibyl, who stands in the darkness of Trinity Fellows Garden, surrounded by a "columnar circuit of forest trees." Why? Interestingly, Barrett's explanation partly echoes Curtius's enumeration of the three medieval world powers: "The passage suggests associations with every major establishment institution: 'text,' 'pronounced,' and 'scrolls,' suggest the ecclesiastical; 'trumpet-calls' the military; 'sovereignty' the governmental; and 'Law' the judicial" (7).

Specifically protesting against any intent to proclaim Eliot an "ideal type" or embodiment of "saintly holiness," Myers nonetheless locates her figure firmly within the realm of the canon (266). Cast as a sibyl, Eliot rules Myers's hellenized garden, which appears as kind of outdoor hall of literature. (Never mind, Barrett points out, that any actual, historical "female . . . of lower middle-class origins," however famous, remained an alien on ground governed by the Trinity Fellows [10].) How many readers of Eliot can repeat this anecdote? How many of them can name its author? As Barrett stresses, Myers's prose has attained a power that is "most insidious when its language seeps into the prose of other writers, and in doing so . . . takes on the appearance of a universally acknowledged truth" (8).

To appropriate a term of Heffernan's, Myers's anecdote has achieved "iconicity" (35–36). That is, the account has established itself as "a document worthy of reverence": in the context of saints' lives, it has "become a part of the community's worship," attaining the status of assigned reading during holy services (35, 37). Somewhat like the successful saint's biography, then, the successful literary canonizing text "becomes itself part of the sacred tradition it serves to document" (Heffernan 16). Consider Terence Hawkes's description of A. C. Bradley's *Shakespearean Tragedy,* a work to which he attributes "the authority—not unquestioned of course—of the divine scriptures." Bradley's work "almost functions, through a system of universal education which has established the study of Shakespeare as its linchpin, as part of the air we breathe" (31). Like Barrett's analysis of an iconized text, Hawkes's account of the nature of Bradley's influence alludes both to gender politics and to the sway of Curtius's medieval world powers. In attributing to Bradley's work "the kind of invisible or subliminal influence on our view of the world that proves deeply and lastingly persuasive," Hawkes aligns *Shakespearean Tragedy* not only with educational texts but with "works such as *Scouting for Boys* and *Hymns Ancient and Modern*" (31).

To be fair, this description of Bradley's text suggests the ways in which modern "definitive biographies" break from older traditions of sacred lives: the authority claimed by Bradley, as what Joan DeJean might call a "canonic critic," is far from primarily communal ("Fictions," 787).[27] Among those casual reviews, plodding literary histories, potted biographies, and bland "authoritative" textbook introductions that comprise the bulk of many students' literary readings, however—not to mention the posters, film biographies, tourist paraphernalia, and postage stamps that shape poets' everyday reputations—the operations of communal canonizing authority may nonetheless remain very much in evidence.

In Heffernan's terms, the authority behind a text that achieves iconicity is even less personal than communal authority: it transcends human authorship altogether. Iconicity arises through a process of "spiritualization": it requires either the "steady disassociation of the text from the unique historical author" or the simple declaration that the "document is the product of a divinely inspired minister of God" (36).

To the extent that works such as Bradley's have become anonymous sources of influence, "part of the air we breathe," they may well justify claims to having been spiritualized. One need only thumb through a stack of reference or pedagogical texts to realize how consistently descriptive phrases and even passages are detached from their original context and integrated into the pastiches of standard canonizing accounts. Such language may well have its origins in identifiable individual experts. When it appears as unattributed truth, however, it partakes of the iconicity of sacred lives.

Not all passages that attain iconicity in my terms have been spiritualized, of course; indeed, one key aspect of literary legends is the use of "selected passages" from literary poet-heroes' and heroines' own work—often detached from their original context within that work. In what might serve as a defense of such iconized quotations, Emerson explains that Shakespeare's "dramatic merit" is "secondary": "what he has to say is of that weight, as to withdraw some attention from the vehicle; and he is like some saint whose history is to be rendered into all languages, into verse and prose, into songs and pictures, and cut up into proverbs, so that the occasion which gave the saint's meaning the form of a conversation or of a prayer or of a code of laws is immaterial, compared with the universality of its application" (120). And thus, in an ironic sense, iconic literary historiography's sanctification of authorship may carry with it a specific fragmentation of its own.[28]

Much as saints' lives may become part of holy services, iconized watchwords or even entire critical and biographical texts may assume (semiofficial) sacred status, so that one can scarcely join the "cult" of a given author without reading and revering them.[29] Such canonizing texts may offer brilliant insights. At the same time, however, they may also contain material that has been shaped by generations of revision and editing. They may even relay "characteristic" anecdotes that have long since been demonstrated to be apocryphal. After all, whole cloth, too, forms part of the texture of canonization: as religious history reminds us, canonization and falsification have a long and intimate shared history.[30] When Martin Luther linked *Legende* with *Luegen* or *Luegenden* (lies or liars), more than an accidental similarity of sound was at stake (Rosenfeld 27).

Standing as they do next to literary works—both literally and metaphorically—critical and biographical passages that have attained iconicity shape readings of those works. Literally, iconized criticism often "introduces" poets and their poetry, thus shaping crucial first impressions. If beginning courses fail to raise the issue of literary legends, students often do so. They may not yet know what the term *modernist* means, but they are often fully conversant with early-twentieth-century characterizations of Victorian writers. They may "know," for example, that Tennyson was the stupidest poet in the English language; that Robert Browning was a smug, bouncing diner-out; that George Eliot was horse-faced, humorless, and doggedly moral; or that Elizabeth Barrett Browning's best poem was her elopement. They may have read *Wuthering Heights,* say, in an "enriched classics" edition that not only illustrates *basilisk* and quotes Swinburne on the novel's "passionate," "ardent," and "unconscious" "chastity" but prints an otherwise unidentified photo of Laurence Olivier over the caption, "Heathcliff at Forced Labor" ("Reader's Supplement," 31, 36, 14). Such students have already been "introduced" to Victorian literature; teaching can only build upon (or undermine) paradigms that may have been long established.

More subtly, but no less powerfully, canonizing texts may help to determine which literary works reach the general public at all. Though twentieth-century criticism has not spared acknowledgment of Victorian tendencies toward idealization of literary figures or expurgation of their works, it may have been less quick to consider the specific connections between such suppressions and the establishment of a textual canon, especially in popular or pedagogical contexts. Given how frequently poems are elevated, printed, and taught as "characteristic," for example, one might well wonder about the origins and outlines of the "character" that they purport to represent.[31] Does the pedagogical status of certain selections rest upon the sanction of often unarticulated primary readings, which are devoted not only to the "body" of an author's work but to a project of reconstructing that same author's transcendent and unitary character?

Granted: textbooks and teaching anthologies no longer refer to writers' "souls." Still, this development need not mean that they refrain from presenting selections or excerpts as *disjecta membra,* as compatible fragments of clear, monumental literary hero or heroine. How many students still believe that volumes of selected poems can offer the "essential Tennyson," say? How many instructors examine students on the most "characteristic" passages of "characteristic" works without addressing precisely what such character might mean?[32] For if certain texts are characteristic, in some transcendent sense, surely others must be uncharacteristic; if certain readings are essential, others must be inessential. Indeed, once the character of a canonized author has been established, insistence upon interpreting or republishing an uncharacteristic work may come to seem as shocking or even sacrilegious as the airing of intimate biographical secrets. So may the decision to "cover" a given poet in a class by looking at a little-known or unpopular work.[33]

When publication or classroom practices seem to define the essential author, or when they promise to identify a writer's transcendently characteristic texts, as well as when they offer up literary works as illustrative of biographical legends, they continue powerful traditions of sanctification and of suppression. One could argue, of course, that since the practices of legend formation may be strongest in introductory contexts, be they popular or pedagogic, they need not be taken too seriously. After all, interested parties are always free to read more, to go beyond the comfortable charms of poet-heroes and heroines. In thus arguing, though, one would be echoing Thomas Bowdler's reassuring introduction to the expurgated *Family Shakespeare in Eight Volumes:* "The critic need not be afraid of employing his pen" in editing Shakespeare, "for the original will continue unimpaired" (quoted in Stavisky 63). With us as with Bowdler, although the original may remain unimpaired, there may still be reason to fear that for many readers—including, perhaps, some of those who would have responded most passionately to literary challenges and complexities—it will remain unread or even undreamed of as well. The problem, of course, lies in great part in the promise of "covering" a writer at all—short of dealing with that author's complete works. The process of coming to terms with such expectations, as with the rest of the heritage of nineteenth-century literary legends, must be a slow one. Once an influential account of the essential nature of a poet has been spiritualized, it cannot be easily banished. As the Victorians themselves insisted, literary character has a life of its own; and sanctified, essential literary character is no exception (Auerbach, *Woman,* 198; 189–217). In Rodden's words, "'Facts' . . . just bounce off" established literary legends (132). Where facts bounce off, however, analysis need not. We can conceive of bodies of texts as rich in their roughness and irreducible fragmentation; we can work to reverse the process of spiritualization and to reinscribe literary legends within literary history; and we can not only accept but more effectively analyze and influence literary study's deep and powerful relations to folk and religious traditions.

Surely no single paragraph on the seriousness of certain nineteenth-century's arguments for positioning literary study as a direct heir to earlier traditions of reverence has been so often cited as the opening of Matthew Arnold's "The Study of Poetry." Arnold's celebrated, caricatured, and much-anthologized assertion of the religious implications of literary study reads as follows: "The future of poetry is immense, because in poetry, where it is worthy of its high destinies, our race, as time goes on, will find an ever surer and surer stay. There is not a creed which is not shaken, not an accredited dogma which is not shown to be questionable, not a received tradition which does not threaten to dissolve.

Our religion has materialised itself in the fact, in the supposed fact; it has attached its emotion to the fact, and now the fact is failing it. But for poetry the idea is everything; the rest is a world of illusion, of divine illusion. Poetry attaches its emotion to the idea; the idea *is* the fact. The strongest part of our religion to-day is its unconscious poetry" (161).

There is no doubt that both this paragraph's present curricular status and its characterization of relations between literature and religion underscore some of my central premises. Paradoxically, however, what is actually most striking about "The Study of Poetry" in the context of this book is the place Arnold gives to criticism of literary reverence. Central to Arnold's essay is Charles d'Héricault's assertion that the "cloud of glory playing round a classic is a mist as dangerous to the future of a literature as it is intolerable for the purposes of history" (164). As Arnold conveys them, d'Héricault's points anticipate many of those raised here. Reverence obscures rather than illuminates critical vision, d'Héricault argues: the classic's "cloud of glory," Arnold translates, "hinders us from seeing more than one single point, the culminating and exceptional point; the summary, fictitious and arbitrary, of a thought and of a work. It substitutes a halo for a physiognomy, it puts a statue where there was once a man, and hiding from us all trace of the labour, the attempts, the weaknesses, the failures, it claims not study but veneration" (164).

Arnold disagrees, of course, and it is significant that he does so by raising issues of accessibility. Too great an emphasis on the "labour, the attempts, the weaknesses, the failures" of a poet, he implies, may create its own form of cloud: it may obscure the pleasures of poetry from beginning readers in particular (164–66). Arnold's point is a reminder of the difficulties involved in balancing the claims of historicism, accessibility, and glory. It suggests an interplay of values whose complexity and significance are heightened by the realization that "The Study of Poetry" originally served to introduce a major popular anthology.

In this context, however, even "The Study of Poetry" pales beside Arnold's "Wordsworth," which had been published a year earlier. Arnold's preface to his own edition of Wordsworth's works, the 1879 Golden Treasury volume, explicitly attempts to sketch out what canonical glory might mean, to accord such glory to Wordsworth, and to open Wordsworth's works to a general audience. "What I had to think of, both in the preface and in the selection," Arnold wrote privately, "was the great public; it is this great public which I want to make buy Wordsworth's poems" (Super 338). Arnold succeeded. "In the sixty-eight years following the second edition" of the collection, R. H. Super notes, "there were thirty-seven reprintings; the book is still in print at its original publisher's, one of the very few volumes of the Golden Treasury series of which this is true" (339).

Like the *Legenda Aurea,* the Golden Treasury series promises by its very title to offer priceless texts. Wordsworth's appearance in Arnold's volume fulfills that promise. Invoking the key term *glory,* with its ties not only to heroism or divine splendor but also, in a significant, literal sense, to halos, "Wordsworth" proceeds to sketch out a vision of a spiritually unified Western world whose representatives serve, among other things, as an international board of canonizers: "Let us conceive of the whole group of civilised nations as being, for intellectual and spiritual purposes, one great confederation, bound to a joint action and working towards a common result; a confederation whose members have a due knowledge both of the past, out of which they all proceed, and of one another. . . . Then to be recognised by the verdict of such a confederation as a master, or even as a seriously eminent and worthy workman, . . . is indeed glory; a glory which it would be difficult to rate too highly" (38). Conceived in such terms, "real glory is a most serious thing, glory authenticated by the Amphictyonic Court of final appeal, definitive glory" (40).

Given its classical origins and democratic elements (democratic, at least for members of those "civilized" countries who are represented), Arnold's version of election by the "Amphictyonic Court" may seem a far cry from canonization by papal bull. Yet just as the religious canonization of saints seeks to provide individual worshipers and nations with an authorized, mediated means of focusing on the divine, so Arnold's glorification of poets provides readers and nations with a means of "having [their] attention fixed on the best things" by "putting a stamp" on them and "recommending them for general honour and acceptance" (38). "Every establishment of such a real glory is good and wholesome for mankind at large, good and wholesome for the nation which produced the poet crowned with it" (40).

In Arnold, then, as in other writers, reverence and cultural redemption are thus explicitly bound. In practice, however, as Arnold makes clear, there must be limits to reverence. It may be fine for "Wordsworthians," among whom Arnold numbers himself, to read the poet's complete works, for example. Even they would do well to distinguish between levels of poetic achievement, however. To do so would not merely deepen the critical understanding of Wordsworth within their own circles; it would also open the way to his recognition as "more than the pure and sage master of a small band of devoted followers." And this work must be done; for Wordsworth is "one of the very chief glories of English Poetry; and by nothing is England so glorious as by her poetry" (55).

Thus, Wordsworth becomes both a sacred and a national glory; and his anthologist's duty becomes that of attempting "to bring to pass, as widely as possible and as truly as possible," Wordsworth's "own word concerning his poems: 'They will co-operate with the benign tendencies in human nature and society, and will, in their degree, be efficacious in making men wiser, better, and happier'" (55). As such a saint is made, however, a sinner may be lost. To be sure, Arnold does not engage in wholesale revision and editing. In significant ways, however, he does replicate the metaphorical patterns already addressed. In so doing, he demonstrates how the most reverent of editors could support canonization's dual levels of speech and silencing.

Arnold states his duty clearly: as Wordsworth's proponent, his role is not only to print the poet's greatest verse but to clear away "a mass of inferior work . . . done before and after" Wordsworth's "golden prime" between 1798 and 1808. Such work is guilty of "imbedding the first-rate work and clogging it," of "obstructing our approach to it, chilling, not unfrequently, the high-wrought mood with which we leave it." Wordsworth needs to "be recognised far and wide as a great poet, to be possible and receivable as a classic"; to achieve this goal, he "needs to be relieved of a great deal of the poetical baggage which now encumbers him. To administer this relief is indispensable, unless he is to continue to be a poet for the few only" (42).

Thus, the anthologist implicitly presents himself as a literary archaeologist, painstakingly extracting "first-rate work" from the clogging dross in which it is imbedded—and perhaps as either a restorer, chipping away excrescences from a monument, or a strong young assistant, rushing to catch valises and packages as they slide from his predecessor's hands. What happens, one might wonder, to the dross? Where does the baggage go? Certainly not into the 1879 Golden Treasury edition, which explicitly omits *The Excursion* and the *Prelude,* both because they are too long and because they are "by no means Wordsworth's best work" (42). Arnold and other Wordsworthians may wish to read such texts; the "great public" need not (55).

Thus, even for Arnold, "To exhibit [the] body of Wordsworth's best work, *to clear away obstructions from around it,* and to let it speak for itself," was "what every lover of Wordsworth should desire" (44; emphasis added). To be fair, Arnold explicitly disclaimed any pretense that his volume contained "all which ·in Wordworth's poems is interesting" (54). Nonetheless, as "Wordsworth" suggests, even the most serious and sophisticated nineteenth-century critical writings on canonization may evoke metaphoric connections between celebrating and shaping the bodies of poets' works, between opening and controlling public access to writers' texts. Such connections play powerful roles in the heritage of nineteenth-century literary study as a whole.

II

Poet Worship Meets "Woman" Worship: *Victorian Femininity and Fictionality*

WHILE FAITH IN Romantic "genius" alone could fuel canonization of male writers, the drive to canonize nineteenth-century women writers confronted an associated but very different form of reverence—the worship, "not of women individually, but of the essential characteristics of woman as a genius" (Ellis, "Poetry," 112). Along with the "Angel in the House," the "cult of true womanhood," the "cult of domesticity," and the "doctrine of feminine influence," "woman worship" forms part of a constellation of phrases whereby students of Victorian womanhood may both signal and trivialize Victorian debts to earlier forms of reverence.[1]

As we have seen, poet worship idealizes and thus standardizes its subjects: the poet-hero expresses himself, and in so doing, his time and the universe. The canonical poet-heroine, however, most often represents not so much irreducibly individual Romantic genius as the "essential characteristics of woman as a genius." In so doing, she speaks not for the universe but for "the sex," and, moreover, the sex as understood in highly specific terms. For in practice, abstract, allegedly generic Woman has a class, a race, an ethnicity; and in Victorian practice, the genius of Woman is that of "respectable women"—preferably, if not always exclusively, white "Anglo-Saxon" ladies. Any other historical female—whether colonial subject, foreign, or outside the (somewhat variable) bounds of respectability—may be implicitly relegated to the category of what Elizabeth V. Spelman calls "inessential Woman" (ix–x, 1–17). Moreover, even those historical females who are demographically qualified to be aligned with essential Woman remain in danger of failing to do so; for conceptions of the generic genius of Woman tend to be both rigid and unstable.

Any position between the legend's poles of wonder and virtue is certain to be difficult to assume and maintain (Bausinger 186). Canonical positioning between the wonder of poetic creation and the virtue of true womanhood may be impossible, however, even in theory. And thus, any discussion of the shifting, sometimes explosive relations between Victorian poet worship and woman worship must extend beyond literary historiography: for powerful and deeply problematic associations between feminine virtue and literary character permeate Victorian culture as a whole. "In terms of the production of culture," Susan Gubar writes, woman has been an "art object" ("Blank Page," 244). In terms of nineteenth-century literary writing, woman has been a character. In one sense, this has been true from the beginning of English literature: if there was an Anglo-Saxon woman poet, her fame was lost, while that of Grendel's monstrous mother lived on. Yet as Nina Auerbach's *Woman and the Demon* brilliantly demonstrates, the Victorians brought a new, "essentially religious" element into conceptions of female literary characters (198). What emerged was nothing less than a "mythic alliance between woman and that potent, intensely Victorian abstraction, [literary] character itself" (9). Canonization study reveals this mythic alliance in a specific form, suggesting how its deeply divided powers draw upon much older concepts and practices of sanctity.

Such concepts and practices are not simple, either in themselves or in their relations to Victorian culture. Religious canonization's intimate connections to divergent interests, be they national, regional, political, personal, or theological, have created dramatically divergent forms of sanctity, and although certain Victorians—agnostics and Evangelicals among them—did know their saints (Schork 292–99), canonization of female figures, like that of religious figures in general, was appropriated less as a specific, ongoing ecclesiastical process than as a more or less abstract concept. Nonetheless, the project of canonizing female literary figures drew upon a long-standing, ambivalent, complex, and potentially explosive history of mediations between sanctity, femininity, and female bodies. Larger conflicts over the Woman Question often echoed and exacerbated contradictions within religious canonization itself. Indeed, a central source of the mythic alliance between womanhood and literary character may lie in constructions of female sanctity.

Canonization through Degradation: "Virile" Female Saints, Honorary Great Men, and the (Dis)Graces of Exceptional Gendering

For female saints, the call to grace has tended to be in some sense a call to rebellion. Divine authority supersedes earthly authority, after all: where the wishes of God the Father or of the spiritual Bridegroom conflict with those of mortals, higher authority must take precedence. The call to sainthood has released women not only from Pauline injunctions to silence, but from obedience to fathers, husbands, or even the state. For a woman called by God must answer, even if it means rejecting her family's choice of husbands—or, in the case of a married woman, her sexual "indebtedness" to her husband (Heffernan 185).[2] Indeed, so common are accounts of female saints' challenges to authority that they have even been seen as paradigmatic of certain forms of female sacred biography (292–93).

Partly for this reason, religious sainthood offered a promising, if deeply disturbing, model for feminine literary canonicity. Consider, for example, that Comtean answer to saints' calendars, the positivist calendar, or, as its English popularizer Frederic Harrison called it, the "New Calendar of Great Men." In neat, horizontal columns, the New Calendar offers sacred lists of "Great Men," some of whom are women. Queens, female saints, national heroines, and even a woman mathematician appear among the official rolls of the "choir invisible."[3] Metaphorically as well as typographically, female models such as St. Elizabeth of Hungary, Mme. de Staël, Sophie Germain, and Isabella of Castille serve as honorary great men: they are what Harrison himself was later to term "honest exceptions and real exemptions" to the limitations of their sex (*Realities,* 104).

Exemptions—not exempla. As Harrison stresses, the true Comtean "woman of genius" can "make herself felt without our turning society upside down on the chance of producing her" (123). She remains unmoved by the "specious agitation" that underlies "our" daughters' "desire to see their names in newspapers, to display the cheap glories of academic or professional honours, to contemplate their bankers' pass-books in private, and to advertise in public their athletic record" (82). She may require that the Calendar of Great Men admit her, but she does not demand that it be renamed or restructured in the process.

Through Comtean honorary great men, then, one model for canonization emerges. Women may be masculinized by grace, released by sanctity from the limitations ascribed to their gender. Such exemption had its religious precedents. "As long as a woman is for birth and children," wrote Jerome, for example, "she is different from man as body is from soul. But when she wishes to serve Christ more than the world, then she will cease to be a woman, and will be called man" (quoted in Marina Warner 73). In Caroline Walker Bynum's words, "Medieval thinkers used gender imagery fluidly, not literally" (*Fragmentation,* 218).[4] The gendering of holy figures might be more flexible than the gendering of holiness itself; it might be easier to masculinize a female saint than to challenge the direct correspondence between virtue and virility.

As problematic as it is powerful, masculinizing grace celebrates a canonic glory that is radically discontinuous from feminine virtue in its everyday sense. To the common female believer, whom it consigns to a lesser, earthly virtue, such canonization provides models that are as inimitable as they are glorious. In such contexts, as Elizabeth Petroff stresses, "the good woman is not the saint" (3).[5] Indeed, as Thomas Heffernan conjectures with respect to late medieval English accounts, narratives of such figures' divinely inspired female rebellion may even offer "a safe opportunity for female audiences to celebrate independence"—safe because saints and only saints are assumed to have the right to resist (294).[6]

Sanctity's ambiguous relationships to gender could do more than allow women to transcend the limitations of femininity, however. They could also open up the even more radical possibility of reformulating virtue itself. Catherine of Siena's biographer, Raymond of Capua, for example, doubted her visions until he himself received a vision in which "Catherine's face fused into or became a bearded male face, which Raymond understood to be Christ" (Bynum, *Fragmentation,* 39). Catherine herself, however, reported having been told by God that he, who had "created both sexes and all sorts of men" and could "create an angel as easily as an ant," saw no need for her to disguise herself as a man: she could preach perfectly well as a woman (39). Bynum sees a pattern here: "In the later Middle Ages, it is male biographers who describe women as 'virile' when they make religious progress" (38). Female saints tend to refer to themselves in nongendered or feminine terms (39–41).[7]

The implications of such sanctity could not be more dramatic. For if earthly women need not masculinize themselves to become saints, then the utmost glory need not be virile. At their most subversive, then, female saints who were accepted as exceptionally gendered might embody virtues that not only transcended their cultures' understandings of femininity but defied exclusionary equations of masculinity with spiritual glory. In Victorian terms, the potential power of such sanctified gender subversion was explosive, as both female artists and activists were quick to realize. If this book focused on literary production instead of reputation, it could easily be called *Made Saints:* it is surely no accident that writers from Charlotte Brontë to George Eliot to Florence Nightingale consistently evoked feminine sanctity or that suffragettes later took up (the as-yet uncanonized) Joan of Arc as one of their central figureheads. Indeed, as chapter 4 indicates, even within the framework of reputation study, certain women critics' employment of sacred metaphors suggests how powerful evocations of an exceptionally gendered female speaking sainthood might be.

Given the discontinuity between feminine virtue and the virtues of sanctity, women's aspirations toward religious sanctity have carried grave dangers, whether spiritual, social, or physical. On a spiritual level, success in recognizing and responding to the call to sainthood cannot be unambiguous during a person's lifetime. What if one mistakes the call to grace and ceases to be a good woman without becoming anything else in the process? The lines between female saints and witches have often been difficult to draw, even for saints themselves.[8] On a pragmatic level, prospective female saints who have disobeyed injunctions to silence or rejected an earthly heterosexual contract have symbolically joined the ranks of what feminist philosopher Janice Raymond calls "loose" women: they have refused primary allegiance to (mortal) men (62, 73–79). As a result, they have often been subjected to surveillance and even punitive attacks. Accounts of tortures inflicted on female saints by demonic forces and by unbelievers offer ample evidence of what we would call sadism, of course, and church authorities themselves often rendered religious women's lives anything but easy. In their study of saints from 1000 to 1700, Donald Weinstein and Rudolph Bell note that "a woman claiming divine inspiration was immediately subject to special supervision, a male confessor assigned to review her every manifestation; and a woman whose religious impulses led her into the streets became fair game for every form of ridicule and even violence" (232; see also Bynum, *Holy Feast,* 84–86).

Indeed, there is suggestive evidence that if women have experienced specific relations to sanctity, these relations have emphasized bodily suffering and deprivation. "Humility, expiation of guilt, ritual prayer, and self-mortification, admitted of degrees," Weinstein and Bell write, and "to a degree, these activities were more dominant in the lives of women than of men" (233). Among the saints studied, women not only "stand out as penitents and ascetics" but comprise an "absolute majority" in terms of "punishing illness" (235–36; see also Bynum, *Holy Feast,* 26). To be sure, sexual politics may shape such statistics: Bynum finds that "male biographies of women between 1200 and 1400 stressed sensationalist and masochistic performance," whereas "women writing about themselves or about other women stressed service and the details of ordinary life" (*Fragmentation,* 75). This fact serves as its own testimony to the force of cultural associations between female sanctity and somatic suffering, however. As Bynum writes, "Both men and women saw female saints as models of suffering and inner spirituality, male saints as models of action" (25).

Such associations of danger with canonicity provide suggestive counterparts to the monitory or punitive accounts of female literary genius that pervade nineteenth-century literary historiography. As a number of recent literary historians have noted, the sufferings popularly ascribed to female aspirants to literary genius tend both to exceed those generally associated with genius per se and to be cast in particularly humiliating sexual or somatic terms. For a notorious instance of such associations, one need only consider the career of one of nineteenth-century England's most famous women poets, L. E. L. During her lifetime, Letitia E. Landon openly suffered from a (probably unearned) reputation for engaging in sexual liaisons; when she died by poison, "the shady and much publicised nature of her end only intensified the punishing moral" at the heart of punitive literary canonization: "'The fruits of a successful literary career for a woman,' are, ultimately, death" (Leighton, *Victorian Women Poets*, 57).[9]

Benjamin Disraeli referred to Landon as the "snub-nosed Brompton Sappho" (quoted in Leighton, *Victorian Women Poets*, 46); and indeed, Victorian literary critics often invoked Sappho, the Pythia, and female saints as parallel figures. In so doing, they united the perils of religious canonization with those of an even older tradition. As Joan DeJean has demonstrated, "The complicity between female humiliation and canonical positioning . . . between physical abandonment and critical appropriation" goes back all the way to Ovid's appropriations of Sappho ("Fictions," 789–90).[10] "Through the centuries, the process whereby male writers simultaneously appropriate the voice of female passion and flaunt the physical humiliation of the desiring woman whose passion they recount has been a cornerstone of canon formation" (788).

Explicit fear of such a process haunts the writing of many nineteenth-century women poets, whether stated in the abstract or embodied in the persons of doomed poet-heroines such as Properzia Rossi, Mme. de Staël's Corinne, or Sappho herself. In Angela Leighton's words, Sappho's leap "connects female creativity with death, in a pact which the Victorian imagination finds endlessly seductively appealing." The "objectification of the woman's body as a compulsively impassioned art form, as a self-improvising poetry as well as a sexual spectacle, finds its originating myth in the figure of that first female poet and lover in one" (*Victorian Women Poets*, 35).[11]

Like Sappho, and like many female saints, Victorian women poets are popularly agreed to embody virtues presumed to be beyond everyday women. They do so, however, at their own peril. Celebration and degradation are never far apart.

Festival of the Holy Women:
The Angel and Her Marian Model

Honorary great man is not the only position available to women in the positivists' New Calendar year, or at least in the positivist cycle of four years. "Complementary Day . . . Festival of all THE DEAD" reads a vertical line on the calendar's side. "Additional Day in Leap Years . . . Festival of the Holy Women."

Though it may come only on Sadie Hawkins's Day, the Festival of the Holy Women confirms what Harrison insisted: positivism is "saturated" with ideal visions of womanhood (*Realities*, 103). As verticals to the horizontal order of positivist time, the holy women—like the dead—are everywhere as well as nowhere. In Christina Crosby's terms, such women are the constitutive "unhistorical Other" of nineteenth-century history (1). And in this context, as in so many other aspects of secular sanctity, the positivists articulate in extreme terms what many of their most influential contemporaries assume or imply.

"Prayer would be of little value unless the mind could clearly define its object," Auguste Comte wrote in the *Système*. "The worship of Woman satisfies this condition, and may thus be of greater efficacy than the worship of God" (quoted in T. R. Wright 35). Comte's substitution of "Woman" for God is striking enough. Equally significant, however, are its antimatriarchal implications, in both metaphoric and material terms. For positivist Woman is no pagan Goddess, with her aspects of maiden, mother, and crone. Rather, she exists as "three beautiful womanly types," represented by Comte's own "daughter of . . . choice," his beloved, and his mother (Comte, *Auguste Comte,* 315; Alexander Welsh 179). Any divinity this Woman embodies is thus fully defined by familial relations. She is what certain Victorians might have called a thoroughly "relative" creature. Moreover, in Comte's own words, she must be prepared to renounce "both power and wealth" in order to remain so (*Auguste Comte,* 383). "*Man ought to maintain woman,* in order that she may be able to discharge properly her holy function" (*Catechism,* 24).[12]

No longer a question of personal desire or even of the need to ensure individual social and economic stability, Comtean Woman's capacity to inspire love and reverence thus becomes a spiritual duty. This reformulation is crucial: it locates the source of Woman's spiritual value not within individuals themselves but within their effects on the emotions of others.

Significantly, as the stakes rise, so does the competition. If actual daughters, wives, mothers, or female acquaintances fail sufficiently to embody the glories of Woman, positivism fully authorizes its adherents to turn to dead, historical, and even imaginary women as sources of divine feminine inspiration (T. R. Wright 35). Such reverence undertakes feminine literary canonization with a vengeance. It suggests, moreover, that what we have learned to call woman worship may be heroine worship instead.

It is no accident that when the Comteans sought a visual symbol of sacred humanity, they chose Raphael's *Madonna di San Sisto* (T. R. Wright, frontispiece). In Comte's own words, "the moral providence" of "our Goddess" springs especially from that "personal influence that every true woman is unceasingly putting out in the bosom of her own family. The domestic sanctuary is the continual source of this holy impulse which can alone preserve us from the moral corruption to which we are ever exposed by active or speculative life." True Comtean women are nothing less than "real *guardian angels,* at once ministers and representatives of the Great Being" (*Catechism,* 84). In short, such women are intimately related to the notorious Angel in the House, whose great model is the Virgin Mary herself.

At once "a metaphor for femininity and for cliché," the Angel in the House has become such a "feminist cliché for the 'killing' of clichés" that she might well tempt frustrated Victorianists into metaphorically throttling her all over again (Michie 89–90). Like Virginia Woolf before them, however, such writers would find that the Angel dies hard ("Professions," 60). She thrives upon a religious tradition whose implications have been only partially acknowledged, and though her "fictitious nature" is now that of a cliché rather than an ideal, it still remains "of great assistance to her" (60).

The "Queen" of Ruskin's dream garden has long been recognized as heir to the Queen of Heaven: clearly, behind and before the Angel in the House stands the Virgin Mary in a number of guises (Gilbert and Gubar 20). For the purposes of nineteenth-century literary canonization, however, one of the most suggestive visions of Mary traces back to the thirteenth and early fourteenth centuries, when a Franciscan-led "revolution in Christian thinking on the Incarnation" helped lead to the identification of Virgin Mary with "women in their subject aspect" (Marina Warner 179). Along with increased emphasis on the humanity of Jesus and Mary, this period marked a crucial metaphoric shift in Mary's class status (179–91).[13] Long revered as the Queen of All Saints and thus as a representative of holy monarchy, the Mother of God now emerged in alignment with a different social group: "The convergence of a social code of behaviour with a [Marian] spiritual ideal becomes more pronounced during the course of the later middle ages and the growth of the prosperous urban class, which permitted an exclusively domestic life to the wives of merchants and tradesmen" (185). If Marina Warner is correct, this Mary marks the early "stirrings" of celebration of "the ideal bourgeois wife" (187).[14] Metaphorically, a middle-class Mary may stand most directly behind the domestic angel.[15]

In explicitly religious contexts, the Virgin Mother was a highly controversial figure, and with reason. In terms of Roman Catholic theology, Pope Pius IX's 1854 papal bull resolving the Church's "prolonged and epic struggle" over the Immaculate Conception merely ratified what had already become a generally accepted article of faith (Marina Warner 249, 238).[16] In an England shaped by anxieties over the Oxford movement, the Maynooth controversy, and Irish immigration, however—only three years after a whole range of religious controversies exploded in the widespread "Papal aggression" agitation of 1850–51—reception of the formalized doctrine of Immaculate Conception was inevitably charged in highly specific ways.[17] "Roman Catholic leaders placed the cult of the Virgin at the centre" of their "campaign to evangelize Britain after 1840" (Singleton 16). The Marian revival in Britain brought a dramatic and in some cases carefully orchestrated upswing in public expressions of reverence for the Mother of God, not only among Catholics but among High Anglicans. It also acted as a powerful catalyst for no less carefully orchestrated anti-Catholic sentiments, however. By midcentury, the Virgin's status served as an explosive focal point for religious and ethnic tensions within Victorian England (Singleton 21–34).[18] Indeed, Mary "personified all that was thought to be alien and idolatrous about Romanism" (23; see also Trudgill 261–62). There was thus nothing simple about nineteenth-century English fascination with and resistance to veneration for the Mother of God.

Mary as a literal religious figure was one thing, however; Mary as a glorious model was another. As Eric Trudgill's *Madonnas and Magdalens* amply demonstrates, once Marian virtue was embodied in the semisecularized forms of sentimental heroines, it won widespread reverence (257–76).[19] No mere holy mascot for sacred Comtean humanity, the Madonna served as a central reference point for widely ranging attempts to define feminine virtue. It is no accident, for example, that Anna Jameson's 1852 *Legends of the Madonna* was so central to her ambitious work on the literary and pictorial iconography of womanhood. "In the perpetual iteration of that beautiful image of THE WOMAN highly blessed," Jameson writes, "*there,* where others saw only pictures or statues, I have seen," standing like "a spirit beside a visible form," the "great hope" of the "coming moral regeneration, and complete and harmonious development of the whole human race, by the establishment, on a higher basis, of what has been called the 'feminine element' in society" (22).[20] Raphael's *Madonna di San Sisto* alone, Jameson writes, has attained her "own ideal" (51).

Like those of honorary great men, then, the household angel's particular, problematic virtues drew upon and transformed a long religious history. Among the wide range of Mary's powerful and sometimes contradictory aspects, two emerge as most crucial for Victorian appropriations and transformations: the unearthly purity of the Virgin's body, which not only transcends vulnerability to sexual "corruption" but defies the ravages of history, both personal and general; and the Virgin's spiritual freedom from any need for internal moral struggle. Queenly and submissive, a symbol of chastity and of maternity, Mary is definitively feminine. Her connection to mortal female flesh remains in many ways unclear, however. Capable of giving birth in a virgin state, she also seems invulnerable to the ravages of time (Marina Warner 89–95). As Coventry Patmore suggests in the poem that gave the Angel in the House her name, Victorian counterparts of Mary may partake of such immunities, at least with respect to aging. Witness, for example, the mother of the poem's central "angel," Honoria:

(29–30)

> *in all she said,*
> *I heard a peaceful seraph talk.*
> *She seem'd expressly sent below*
> *To teach our erring minds to see*
> *The rhythmic change of time's swift flow*
> *As part of calm eternity. . . .*
>
> *The years, so far from doing her wrong,*
> *Anointed her with gracious balm,*
> *And made her brows more and more young*
> *With wreath of amaranth and palm.*

Patmore's household angel seems actually to grow younger:

(80)

> *she grows*
> *More infantine, auroral, mild;*
> *And still the more she lives and knows*
> *The lovelier she's express'd a child.*

Though such a figure may attain what John Ruskin calls "that majestic peace, which is founded in the memory of happy and useful years," her queenly maturity—like that of Mary—betrays no susceptibility to age. Its "perfect loveliness" springs from "majestic childishness" (95). "While it is beautiful for a man to grow old," wrote an admirer of Christina Rossetti two years after her death at age sixty-four, "a woman to retain her charm must always remain young. In a deep sense woman may be said to have but one paramount charm, youth." A heroine's body may age, then, but "the youthfulness of the soul . . . in the truly adorable woman, is invulnerable" (Watts-Dunton, "*New Poems*," 208).

Like Mary, the Angel in the House thus reveals multiple aspects. She is mother, sister, and daughter all at once: she is Everywoman—and, of course, no woman (Marina Warner 129–33; Alexander Welsh, 166–79). In Dickens, for example, the face of "the same sweet girl" may reappear throughout a "long line" of family portraits, "never growing old or changing—the Good Angel of the race—abiding by them in all reverses—redeeming all their sins" (quoted in Alexander Welsh 157). Such "convergence of generations in a single heroine" helps Victorian fiction to create the sense of Woman as 'constant and unchanged'" (172, 179), a sense that Comte himself underscored in claiming that "two angels" (his mother and the beloved "Saint" Clothilde de Vaux) harmoniously directed "the beginning and the close of [his] moral initiation," while a third woman, the "daughter of my choice," revived "unconsciously the moral influence of the other two angels" (*Auguste Comte,* 315).

Transmuted into nineteenth-century terms, the pure body of Marian Woman continues to transcend and thus to sanctify not only sex and physicality but history itself. "What one sees symbolized in the Roman churches in the image of the Virgin Mother with a bosom bleeding with love," William Makepeace Thackeray's narrator says in *Pendennis,* for example, "I think one may witness (and admire the Almighty bounty for) every day. I saw a Jewish lady, only yesterday, with a child at her knee, and from whose face towards the child there shone a sweetness so angelical, that it seemed to form a sort of glory round both. I protest I could have knelt before her too, and adored in her the Divine beneficence in endowing us with the maternal *storgé,* which began with our race and sanctifies the history of mankind" (20–21). Like Mary (or the anonymous Comtean holy women), this angelically sweet mother is history's sacred, "unhistorical Other."

Mary approaches the angels in her freedom from carnal weakness, exceeding even them in purity (Marina Warner 237).[21] Such spiritual immunity, like her freedom from bodily corruption, renders her a deeply problematic model for historical women. For if John Mecklin is correct, on a moral level medieval angels are actually the "inferiors of the saints": unlike the characters of angels, after all, saints' "characters were trained in the struggle with very real evils in this world" (44). Thus, a highly ambiguous spiritual innocence was the counterpart of Mary's unearthly physical purity. Like the ideal Victorian woman in Elizabeth Say's study of women's narrative as theological voice, Mary is "morally superior to man and at the same time lacking qualities that are necessary for moral action" (17).

The mother of Patmore's Honoria, for example, is not merely a seraph: she is a peaceful seraph. As a messenger of "calm eternity," she is sent to counter "our erring minds" as well as "time's swift flow." Indeed, she *seems* (the word is crucial) to have been immaculately conceived. "Marr'd less than man by mortal Fall," Patmore's angel does not strive for virtue: she embodies it. "Her disposition is devout, / Her countenance angelical / No faithless thought her instinct shrouds" (68). *Shrouds* is the proper word here: religious doubt could scarcely inhabit the spiritualized, incorruptible body of Patmore's angel. Laura, in *Pendennis,* appears to her future husband to have been no less immaculately conceived. After watching her expressions of "love and purity," "as one might regard them in an angel," he exclaims, "How spotless, and full of love and truth, Heaven made you!"—as if heaven's initial creation alone guaranteed such purity's endurance, with no effort on Laura's part (325; see Alexander Welsh 166).

Set beyond all need for spiritual struggle, the Marian ideal remains tranquil, even in her Victorian incarnation: "She succeeds with cloudless brow, / In common and in holy course," where man (like nonangelic woman) "fails, in spite of prayer and vow / And agonies of faith and force" (79).

If the "virile" female saint is a difficult model, Mary is an impossible one. By definition, she stands "alone of all her sex." Indeed, to use a phrase from Judith Butler's *Gender Trouble,* celebration of Marian virtue as a model for mortal women explicitly establishes the feminine "gender norm" as "finally phantasmatic, impossible to embody" (141). This is a key point. Praise of "natural" womanhood notwithstanding, when nineteenth-century celebrations of true femininity drew upon Marian models, they located that femininity not so much within what Butler calls "the territory of the natural and the real" as within the realm of the supernatural (146). Divinity, not biology, moves the Angel in the House.

The lovely, ageless body; the capacity to redeem through mere presence; the childlike, unconscious mind: such is the "ideal type," writes F. W. H. Myers, judging George Eliot accordingly. "As her aspect had greatness but not beauty, so, too, her spirit had moral dignity but not saintly holiness." Why not? Because "a loftier potency *may* sometimes have been given to some highly-favored woman in whom the graces of heaven and earth have met; moving through all life's seasons with a majesty which can feel no decay; affording by her very presence and benediction an earnest of the supernal world. . . . A deeper pathos *may* sometimes have breathed from the unconscious heroism of some child-like soul" (266; emphasis added). Such a potency may have been given—but to Mary of Galilee, not to the likes of Mary Anne Evans.

Faced with the power and the unattainability of the Marian model, Marina Warner notes, some women may turn to apostasy. Others, however, may find that the Marian model only deepens the "need for religion's consolation" (337). The very Mother who cries with women may be provoking their tears in the first place. The "impossible ideal" of the cult of the Virgin may thus drive female adherents "into a position of acknowledged and hopeless yearning and inferiority" (337). By accepting "the Virgin as the ideal of purity," a corruptible (which is to say historical) woman rejects her own "ordinary female condition as impure," implicitly condemning herself for a flawed state she can never escape on earth: that of being "carnal and female" (77, 337).[22]

As we have seen, the domestic angel follows this pattern in her embodiment of virtues that are as thoroughly feminine as they are humanly unattainable. "Enduringly, incorruptibly good; instinctively, infallibly wise," she models a secondary, feminine glory without heroism (Ruskin 92). Simultaneously, she constitutes both historical women's bodies and their inevitably conflicted consciousnesses as impediments to feminine sanctity. How could one mobilize support for such virtue or hope for its attainment? Once more, a possible answer lies in religious models; for the "character" of ideal Victorian womanhood, no less than the glory of literary genius, draws directly upon constructions of religious sanctity.

Ascetics and Acting Angels:
Marian Virtue and the (Attempted)
Domestication of Feminine Sanctity

A nineteenth-century woman could not become an angel any more than an aspirant to sanctity can become a virgin mother, immaculately conceived. Yet if a dominant tradition of advice to Victorian women was correct, a historical woman could become what I call an Acting Angel. That is, by committing herself to a life of strenuous spiritual asceticism, she could seek both to impersonate and to act as a stand-in for the Victorian feminine ideal. In so doing, she could emulate powerful female saints as well.

Not surprisingly, given the subversive potentials of female sainthood, ecclesiastical authorities conceived of domesticating feminine sanctity at a fairly early date. Indeed, in some regions, attempts at creating a "new type of domestic saint or 'holy housekeeper'" were already underway by the ninth century. Such attempts failed—perhaps in part, Jane Tibbetts Schulenburg suggests, because domestic activities "were less likely to capture the popular imagination and to inspire the enthusiastic devotion required for the making of saints" (117, 119).[23] The domestication of female sainthood did not achieve dramatic success until the late Middle Ages, when the church was prepared to celebrate activities upon which the ninth-century Carolingian bishops had placed "tight controls"—that is, practices of feminine asceticism (Wemple 171).

While the European late Middle Ages gave rise to the growth of many forms of feminine religious life (Goodich 173–85), they mark an increase in asceticism in particular.[24] Not surprisingly, the popular emergence of opportunities for spiritual heroism, arising from or within spaces of acute economic, social, and personal containment, seems to have had a profound impact on the conceptions and practices of female sanctity. As Rudolph Bell puts it in his study of Italian female saints, asceticism made it "evident that woman's holiness was the consequence of sacrifice and willpower": by glorifying "woman as subject, creator of her destiny," it served as "an inspired mode of religious self-assertion" (150, 179). St. Clare of Assisi, the founder of the Poor Clares and companion of St. Francis, provides a famous and highly suggestive example of such ascetic heroism—"a clear, attractive, fascinating model for female piety, one actively encouraged by Franciscan preachers" (127). Confined to their religious house by the Church hierarchy and by Francis himself, Clare and members of her order became famous for extreme asceticism, especially for fasting. In one sense, such dramatic self-denial, played out in close quarters and under the auspices of masculine authority, would seem to embrace Marian womanhood in its domestic and subject aspects—to domesticate the potentially subversive heroism of female sanctity. In another, however, the introduction of sacred heroism into cloistered or domestic settings transformed those settings themselves. "For Clare and her sisters," Bell writes, "there was Francis to guide them, then a male prelacy to order them, and finally only their own bodies to conquer" (124–25).[25]

Although ascetic sanctity might be practiced within severely limited spaces, it was never fully domesticated. Female ascetics did not necessarily limit their activities to their own familial or religious homes (Bynum, *Holy Feast,* 121), and they did not necessarily seek to minister to the creature comforts of fellow family or cloister members. Indeed, the development of holy fasting has suggestive social as well as religious implications. Eventually, it "moved out of the convent and into the home, such that in the fourteenth and fifteenth centuries, nearly half of all female Italian saints never became nuns." By the early sixteenth century, the church itself began to shift its position on such domestic (and, of course, cloistered) sainthood, perhaps in part because of ascetic holy women's "hostility to men." Such women's "sense of fighting actively against patriarchal structures and the male prelacy" and "need to tell their own stories all increased over time" (Rudolph Bell 149). The sanctity of feminine fasting became more suspect: perhaps, authorities considered, self-starvation was a form of disease (172–79).

Such accounts cannot help but call to mind the common process whereby nineteenth-century women metaphorically expanded the boundaries of their own "holy housekeeping" to include domestic affairs on a national and even imperial level. They evoke, too, the first wave of feminism, not only in terms of late-Victorian activists' deployment of the rhetoric of feminine sanctity but also in terms of the history of Holloway prison, where suffragists would soon wield self-starvation as a powerful political weapon. There are promising potential connections between such medieval feminine fasting and Victorian attitudes toward women and food; one might expand the work of Sandra M. Gilbert and Susan Gubar or of Helena Michie, for example, to investigate how secularized fasting both shifts and continues earlier constructions of feminine sanctity.[26] In terms of literary canonicity, however, the most powerful analogy between such medieval "athletes of Christ" (Weinstein and Bell 249) and Victorian ideal figures of feminine virtue is less literal: it is that between medieval feminine asceticism and a strain of nineteenth-century thinking that promised women spiritual glory and redemptive power if only they would refrain from "metaphorically eating *words* and enjoying the taste of *power*" (Gilbert and Gubar 568).

In *Holy Feast, Holy Fast* and elsewhere, Bynum argues that medieval female ascetics' lives and writings seriously challenge modern readers' tendency to ascribe self-starvation simply to internalized misogyny. The counterpart of the holy fast is the holy feast, Bynum demonstrates. The apparent heightening of physicality in narratives of female ascetics' sufferings may be inseparable from the exceptional power ascribed to eucharistic ecstasy in those same accounts.[27] Female saints' hagiographers "spoke of abstinence as preparatory to and simultaneous with true feeding by Christ." It was "identification with Christ's suffering; it was affective, even erotic, union with Christ's adorable self. It was also service of others" (*Holy Feast*, 120). The ascetic pushes her body (and mind) to the limits, Bynum argues, both to resist and to use it: she considers her actions not only to deny or transcend but to glorify its hungers. "Control, discipline, even torture of the flesh is, in medieval devotion, not so much the rejection of physicality as the elevation of it—a horrible yet delicious elevation—into a means of access to the divine" (*Fragmentation*, 182).

The strenuous heroism of medieval female ascetics offers a suggestive counterpart to nineteenth-century glorifications of female strength in suffering. If the sanctity of the Acting Angel had a prophet, it was surely that indefatigable midcentury purveyor of advice to the daughters, wives, and mothers of England, Sarah Stickney Ellis. In popular conduct books that resonate with the passion and urgency of sermons, Ellis calls upon the virtuous Victorian woman to "lay aside" her "very *self*" and assume a "new nature": to adopt, in effect, a kind of sacred mask (*Women*, 15). "All which is most lovely, poetical, and interesting, nay, even *heroic* in women," she writes, "derives its existence from the source I am now about to open to their view" (14)—that is, from a version of feminine domestic influence whose power derives from the ability of woman to become "*individually,* what she is praised for being *in general*," to "lay aside . . . her very *self*—and assum[e] a new nature, which nothing less than watchfulness and prayer can enable her constantly to maintain, to spend her mental and moral capabilities in devising means for promoting the happiness of others, while her own derives a remote and secondary existence from theirs" (15–16).

As a self-created character, a living sacred work of art, Ellis's ideal woman is promised the ability both to annex the power of impossible virtue and to embody a new heroics of feminine asceticism. Like the older asceticism upon which it was based, Ellis's "system of self-sacrifice" attempts to domesticate feminine sanctity, with explosively mixed results. "You have deep responsibilities; you have urgent claims; a nation's moral worth is in your keeping," she urges her readers (*Women,* 6). "Look for a moment at the condition of woman wherever . . . high tone of character has been wanting," she warns. There, misogynist hell yawns: "Identified merely with material things, and, as a necessary consequence, regarded as a soulless and degraded being, [woman is considered] essential to society only in her ministration to the general good of man" (*Daughters,* 46). Ascetic submission forestalls an even grimmer, because soulless, servitude.

If "woman's strength is in her influence," however, that strength must be devoted to more than personal survival (*Daughters,* 6). Feminine self-transformation is the crucial spiritual weapon against that "fierce conflict of worldly interests, by which men are so deeply occupied as to be in a manner compelled to stifle their best feelings, until they become in reality the characters they at first only assumed" (8). Impelled by the brutality of capitalism, Ellis's men are forced to become the "characters they at first only assumed"; inspired by faith, her women must do the same.[28] It is their moral, national, and poetic duty: "If, then, for man it be absolutely necessary that he should sacrifice the poetry of his nature for the realities of material and animal existence, for women there is no excuse—for woman, . . . who has nothing, and is nothing, of herself; whose experience, if unparticipated, is a total blank; yet, whose world of interest is wide as the realm of humanity, boundless as the ocean of life, and enduring as eternity!" (*Daughters,* 43).

Like a sanctified version of George Eliot's Rosamond Vincy in *Middlemarch,* Ellis's ideal woman must uphold "from morning to night her own standard of a perfect lady, having always an audience in her own consciousness" (Eliot 115).[29] Only by acting as angels in their houses might women counter the terrors of misogyny and the ferocity of the marketplace ("I had almost said, this national disease" [*Daughters,* 43]).

Such claims had powerful religious precedents. In terms of sanctity, holy sacrifice means gain, both for the ascetic herself and for those she serves. In Bynum's words, fasting served as "part of suffering; and suffering was considered an effective activity, which redeemed both individual and cosmos" (*Holy Feast,* 207). Female ascetics offered up their fasting, which "was often specifically a response to guilt over the wealth and conspicuous consumption practiced by merchant families" (120), as "spiritual almsgiving" (McNamara 212). Such practices sought "to complement or replace" the "corporal charity" from which many women were restrained (212).

Even more secretly and silently than the holy fasters who are their analogues, Ellis's model women seek to embody a sanctity whose heroic yet externally passive agonies both dramatize and explode the values of domestic femininity. The medieval ascetic risks—and perhaps seeks—death; the Acting

Angel, the disappearance of individual self-awareness. Through "watchfulness and prayer," the Acting Angel attempts to set aside her self, assimilating so completely to a feminine ideal (that which women are "praised for being in general") that her very desire for self-pleasuring "mental and moral capabilities" wastes away (*Women,* 15–16). Such a figure's very "happiness" becomes "remote and secondary" (16). Ellis can be chillingly explicit about such an ethic of sacred self-fictionalization. A woman must be prepared, she writes, to "be nothing, or anything that is not evil, as the necessities of others may require" ("Poetry," 114). Later, Patmore would echo Ellis: "The woman . . . is the glory of [the man's] prowess and nobility . . . and she is able to fulfill this necessary and delightful role, just because she is herself nothing in battle, policy, poetry, discovery, or original intellectual or moral force of any kind" (*Religio Poetae,* 162–63).

Like Jane Tompkins's sentimental heroine—to whom she is intimately related—the Acting Angel seeks to be "empty of self," to become "an invisible transparency that nevertheless is miraculously responsible for the life in everything" (182). Such virtue is brilliantly conceived. Reversing a centuries-old negative equation of femininity and artifice, it provides a subtle and sophisticated means of uniting domesticity and glory, of bridging the disjunction between Marian virtue's simple purity and the messy, complex, inevitably physical existences of historical women. As a sacred imitation angel, a woman might enact the harmonious and often silent grace of Mary. Simultaneously, however, as a secret sufferer—as the ascetic actress behind the Marian mask—she might exert a form of the transcendent control formerly represented by ascetic saints.[30]

It is no accident that one of the most striking visual tropes of the Angel in the House is that of a woman heroically—and futilely—attempting to hide her tears with a Madonna-like smile. "It is thought much of, and blazoned forth to the world," Ellis writes, "when the victim at the stake [a saint? a witch?] betrays no sign of pain; but does it evince less fortitude for the victim of corroding care to give no outward evidence of the anguish of a writhing soul?—to go forth arrayed in smiles, when burning ashes are upon the heart?" ("Poetry," 116).

"Every nerve and muscle" of such a would-be heroine must be "adjusted to the consciousness that she [is] being looked at": she must enact "her own character, and so well, that she [does] not know it to be precisely her own" (Eliot, *Middlemarch,* 80). In her attempt to lead a "remote and secondary existence," she must constantly watch herself; and she must attempt to do so through the eyes of an external observer. As Ann Douglas's groundbreaking *The Feminization of American Culture* puts it, such an ideal woman is "in embryo both a saint and a consumer" (60). Dressed and disciplined to act the angel's part, she "wants her friends' admiration as much as their souls, and she tends to confuse the two" (66).[31] In this, however, she is not a simple narcissist. For Narcissus falls in love with the image he sees through his own eyes; his paralyzing pleasure arises from fascination with his own body and his own vision. The Acting Angel, on the other hand, attempts to see her image through masculine eyes in order to assess its ability to inspire or redeem others. She can take no pleasure in her own gaze, and she need not find grounds for self-congratulation in her body as she imagines it reflected in others' eyes. "Thrown by her natural dependence upon the esteem and affection of those around her," writes Ellis in one of her bleaker moments, "woman learns to regard the smile of approbation as the charmed spell by which the gates of happiness are opened; and to look for the frown of contempt as the signal of her darkest doom. Trembling between these two extremes, there can be no wonder that she should study every means to attain the one, and avoid the other: and this is what the world calls vanity" ("Poetry," 119). Analogous self-absorption had been intrinsic to women's role as art object for centuries (Berger et al. 45–64). Perhaps never before, though, had it been aligned with such powerful self-sacrificial and millennial impulses.

Ellis notwithstanding, the Acting Angel's attempts are inevitably vain in both senses of the term: that is, not only must they mobilize self-absorption but they must do so in the service of an ultimately hopeless endeavor. As Judith Butler asserts, "Failure to become 'real' . . . is . . . a constitutive failure of all gender enactments" (146). Indeed, in nineteenth-century terms, the inescapable failures of "gender as a performative accomplishment" are often precisely the source of the poignancy of feminine heroism (141). Here, for example, is one of the great fictional Acting Angels, Charles Dickens's Esther Summerson:

> (668)
>
> *By and by I went to my old glass. My eyes were red and swollen, and I said, "Oh, Esther, Esther, can that be you!" I was afraid the face in the glass was going to cry again at this reproach, but I held up my finger at it, and it stopped.*
>
> *"That is more like the composed look you comforted me with, my dear, . . ." said I, beginning to let down my hair. "When you are mistress of Bleak House, you are to be as cheerful as a bird. In fact, you are always to be cheerful, so let us begin for once and all."*

For this disturbingly successful Acting Angel, to be "unpretending," even in the privacy of one's own room, is to pretend. No curtain ever drops on the performance of feminine virtue. Esther's supreme exercises of moral self-control tend to consist of facing mirrors and of attempting to transform the image reflected therein from an *I* to an *it*. She claims throughout the passage that she is "very happy, very thankful, very hopeful," but she cannot stop crying (668).

Later, as Esther once more attempts to hide the pain of sacrificing her own happiness to the needs of others, she attains her apotheosis: it is as if an actual angel momentarily possesses her. "Something seemed to pass into my place, that was like the Angel he thought me" (889). Beyond a doubt, this is glory. As Auerbach puts it, albeit in a slightly different context, for the nineteenth century, "The art of translating oneself into a character" has become "an act of devotion to the self's latent, and awesome, powers" (*Woman,* 205). The fast has revealed itself as feast: the successful Acting Angel has "assumed the magnitude of a literary character in life" (205).

Such protean capacity to play a heroine—perhaps even a divine heroine— is central to the power of what Ellis calls the "poetry" of woman's "character" ("Poetry," 112).[32] To the extent that a woman could succeed at this performance, she might annex the power of a holy art object, even as she attained the status of a feminine equivalent to the poet-hero. Granted, Ellis does not promise her readers that they can actually achieve such a character—any more, perhaps, than a candidate for sainthood can attain her goal on this earth. The "ontological locale" of true womanhood, like that of sanctity, remains "uninhabitable" (Judith Butler 146). Yet as earlier ascetics starved their way into sanctity, Ellis's ideal woman may succeed, in Gilbert and Gubar's terms, in the attempt to "kill" herself "into art" (25).

In the world of Dickens's fiction, such Acting Angels as Esther Summerson receive their rewards: Esther attains not only her apotheosis but marriage to the lover she had intended to sacrifice. Elsewhere, however, such is not necessarily the case. Indeed, much as poet worship may shade off into parody, glorifications of Acting Angels may veer into expressions of anxiety or despair. It is surely no accident, for example, that when George Eliot compares herself to one of her own heroines, her metaphor evokes penitential self-flagellation. "Romola is ideal," she writes. "I feel it acutely in the reproof my own soul is constantly getting from the image it has made. My own books scourge me" (quoted in Trudgill 264).

Even from the outside, claims concerning women's ability not only to "adapt themselves to the habits and peculiarities of others," but to "enter into their very beings and penetrate the deep recesses of their souls," were not entirely reassuring (Ellis, "Poetry," 116). Just as medieval female saints could be difficult to distinguish from witches, Woman could be difficult to tell from the Demon (Auerbach, *Woman,* 63–108)—or the Angel in the House from an angel of death.[33] As Caroline Norton suggests in a review of Patmore's work, the counterpart to the Angel in the House is "the Skeleton in the Cupboard" (398).

Despite his celebration of Marian virtues, for example, even Thackeray

voiced acute unease over virtuous feminine self-fictionalizations: "The best of
women (I have heard my grandmother say) are hypocrites. We don't know how
much they hide from us: how watchful they are when they seem most artless
and confidential: how often those frank smiles which they wear so easily are
traps to cajole or elude or disarm—I don't mean your mere coquettes, but your
domestic models, and paragons of female virtue" (*Vanity Fair*, 208). The narrator's tone may be ambiguous: this is *Vanity Fair*, after all. Yet an unnerved reviewer of Ellis's exemplary fiction makes a similar point: "The reader, who is
behind the scenes, will feel that he would not *quite* like to live with a woman,
however excellent and convenient her qualities might be, who was *always* on
her guard—who arranged and contrived *everything*—whose smallest act was
premeditated, shaped to Virtue's plan, if you will, but never unconsidered,
never impulsive" ("Chapters," 52). Even in a good woman, self-annihilating
artifice need not be conducive to domestic comfort. Combine such self-control
with rebelliousness or viciousness, as novel after Victorian novel testifies, and
trouble arises. What renders the performative femininity of a Becky Sharp, a
Lady Audley, or even a Rosamond Vincy so disturbing is precisely their proximity to Acting Angels. Such characters' self-annihilating force may not do them
much good, but it can do a great deal of harm to others, particularly men.

In a Number of Artists' Studios: The Blurring Faces and Vanishing Monuments of Generic Feminine Glory

Though she may enact a "poetry" free of the "disease" of the marketplace,
Ellis's Acting Angel refrains from too much actual writing. Women are "disqualified for great literary attainments" ("Poetry," 113). Although they may
write to "benefit" their "fellow creatures," in so doing they engage in an act
that may levy a high toll. For "literature is not the natural channel for a woman's
feelings." Indeed, "pity, not envy, ought to be the meed of her who writes for
the public" (*Daughters*, 79).

"To be always reading, quoting, or composing poetry" is both "bad taste"
and "the very opposite of poetical." "For it is only in reference to her association
with others that woman can be in herself poetical" (*Daughters*, 45).[34] "Self-
supported, as a sovereign or a sage, she wants all her loveliest attributes" ("Poetry," 114). A woman who insists on exercising rather than enacting literary
power thus runs great risks. "Look at all the heroines, whether of romance or
reality—at all the female characters that are held up to universal admiration,"
Ellis insists. "Have these been the learned, the accomplished women? . . . No:
or if they have, they have also been women who were dignified with the maj-

esty of moral greatness—women who regarded not themselves" (*Women,* 21). Those women who are "endowed only with such faculties as render them striking and distinguished in themselves" are "only as dead letters in the volume of human life, filling what would otherwise be a blank space, but doing nothing more" (48).

Thus, "the volume of human life" may be inscribed only by heroines, whether "of romance or reality." Learning and accomplishment do not a heroine make: only being "dignified with the majesty of moral greatness" will allow a woman to inscribe herself upon her world. One's sole choice, then, is either to be a dead letter or to be what Gubar calls a "blank page": a female figure who makes culture possible through her own silence.

Thus we confront the paradox of canonizing a Victorian woman poet. She must be a heroine, and yet how can she? As an Angel in the House, she would presumably have no need to write: she could act as art directly. And as an Acting Angel, she cannot possibly serve as the protagonist in a story of heroic self-expression. Like Dickens's Esther, she may write, but only under orders and under protest that she is "not clever" (62).

Within the metaphoric hall of literature, attempts to construct Victorian monuments to sacred literary heroines thus tend to be highly problematic. Consider, as an analogue, one of the architectural canon's earthly counterparts, the Library of Congress. "I was sitting in the Main Reading Room," a friend says, "and I started idly looking up at all the busts over my head. I thought, 'Where are all the women?' So I went outside into the antechambers, and there they were: Muses, Graces, everywhere." White men's faces inside, white female Muses and Graces outside, and hardly any people of color anywhere: suddenly, she says, the canon she had been taught took visible form.

Surely, one might object, readers work in some other national (or imaginable) library, benignly overseen by idealized female busts? The very word *busts,* however, might give one pause. And indeed, female bodies seem to have posed grave difficulties for a canonization based upon figurative metaphors. As long as their subjects were male, masculine nineteenth-century canonizers could portray themselves as reconstructing and resurrecting the bodies of writers' work—or, more modestly, as gathering up writers' disjointed limbs into monumental forms of divinity. Not surprisingly, however, such critics often characterized themselves as approaching the body of a woman's text with anxiety.

"It is easy to be critical of men," notes H. N. Coleridge, an early reviewer in whose work the rhetoric of violation is only somewhat muted, "but when we venture to lift a pen against women, straightway . . . the weapon drops pointless on the marked passage. . . . Whilst the mind is bent on praise or censure of the poem, the eye swims too deep in tears and mist over the poetess herself on the frontispiece, to let it see the way to either" (374–75). Like a villain in melodrama, Coleridge finds his "weapon" felled by feminine beauty and purity. Weeping replaces criticism; the "passage" of the text is barred by the tears and mist thrown up by an image of the poetess herself.

In Ellis, the body of the feminine text appears as a potential victim of far less gallant intimate critical contact. "In seasons of depression, or of wounded feeling," when a woman's "spirit yearns to sit in solitude, or even in darkness, so that it may be still," such respite eludes a published writer. "The very essence of that spirit, now embodied in palpable form, has become an article of sale and bargain, tossed over from the hands of one workman to another, free alike to the touch of the prince and the peasant." "How much of what with other women is reserved for the select and chosen intercourse of affection, with her must be laid bare to the coarse cavillings, and coarser commendations, of amateur or professional critics!" (*Daughters,* 79).

Nor did the metaphoric nakedness of textual bodies threaten female authors alone. Witness, for example, an 1837 *Dublin University Magazine* reviewer's approach to works by "the poetesses of our day": "How different the duties of this pink and perfumed page! We breathe the atmosphere of the Boudoir. . . . Ghosts—filmy phantoms of a thousand gentle octavos, flutter into life around us, and as they hover in the caressing air, solicit— roguishly resistless—an approving smile from our venerable visage. There is coquetry in the very play of their leaves, fascination in their gilded bindings, ruin to the peace of man in their vignetted title-pages!" (William Butler 126). Faced with such seductive volumes, a critic could be ruined.

Even when conceived as monuments, the bodies of women's work were not necessarily either safe or safe to touch. An 1890 article by H. H. Gardener, for example, characterizes reviewers' unease with late-century women's writing as follows: "'These young women have no clothes. They stand as nude as a plaster cast of Venus and pose before a pitying world,' writes one critic. 'There are some things in life best left veiled,' says another. Very true. But who is to say just which these things are?" (331). The threat that female monuments may become somehow obscene carries real force, even in the context of Gardener's essay, which challenges conventional feminine representations. To be canonized, after all, a woman must be chaste. ("Never let anybody guess that you have a mind of your own," whispers Woolf's Angel in the House. "Above all, be pure" ["Professions," 59].)

How can critics cast a woman writer as a canonical monument without thereby sculpting a dirty statue? There is a way, as it turns out. First, one must position her as the Virgin Mary. Then one must "cover" her, as a subject, with the sanctifying rhetoric of heroine description. Suggestively, given Victorian critics' task of uniting the *disjecta membra* of a poet's work, the Virgin Mary is "generally believed" to have left no corporeal relics. Assumed into heaven as a whole body, she "leaves behind only fragments of her clothing" (Ward 133). Analogously, critics often assume that the "real" eternal feminine body of the canonic text is elsewhere. As is so often the case, Coventry Patmore articulates such heroine-worship most clearly. Alice Meynell's *Preludes* "breathe, in every line, the purest *spirit* of womanhood," he writes in 1892, "yet they have not sufficient force of the *ultimate* womanhood, the expressional *body,* to give her the right to be counted among classical poets. No woman ever has been such a poet: probably no woman ever will be, for (strange paradox!) though, like my present subject, she may have enough and to spare of the virile intellect, and be also exquisitely womanly, she has not womanhood enough" ("Mrs. Meynell," 762).[35]

Thus, Victorian monuments of feminine canonicity might easily be likened to papier-mâché. Figures whose very forms are coverings for absence, such monuments are designed both to disguise and celebrate vacancy. Their glorious, generic forms embody a Woman who is, by definition, gone. When canonizing critics deal with the "fragments" of their female subjects' poetry, they tend not so much to reassemble or revivify them as to blend them into a suitable pastiche. Sacred as such textual "relics" may be, after all, they are analogous to scraps of the Virgin's clothing: they demand reverence not in themselves but by right of association with one who is gone.

Poet-heroines' sacred fragments thus seem to exert far different powers than those of poet-heroes. Like an ordinary saint, after all, the masculine poet-hero must win canonization through miracles: his literary relics must work wonders on their readers. A literary Madonna heroine, however, is more like Mary. "No miracles are needed to prove her a saint": she is herself a miracle (Ward 133).[36] And thus, repeatedly throughout the century, reverent critics instruct readers that women writers' verses are glorious not so much in themselves as in their association with those sacred heroines who wrote them. Consider, for example, the reception of Felicia Hemans, who was surely the first woman poet to become a Victorian literary monument. Hemans's best poetry is "less to be valued for its own sake," instructs an influential 1880 anthology, "than as the revelation of a delicate and attractive personality. Sprung from a talent expressive not creative, her verses are stamped with feminine qualities" (A. Mary F. Robinson 334). Hemans's "nature," says another essay, thirty years earlier, is "more interesting than her genius, or than its finest productions"; "if not, in a transcendent sense, a poet, her life"—which is over, of course—"was a poem"

(Gilfillan 238). As we shall see, Barrett Browning's and Rossetti's poetry suffered similar comparisons: indeed, at times it seems that everywhere one looks in Victorian criticism, one finds injunctions to "admire [some] poetess still more than her poetry" (Patmore, "Mrs. Meynell," 763).

Such comments are made about male poets as well, of course: Robert Browning's "Transcendentalism," which coined the line, "You are a poem, though your poem's naught," was addressed to a man (line 47). The difference is, however, that the transcendent characters such men represent are not defined (and nearly exhausted) by virtues ascribed solely on the basis of gender. Browning's poet is not a poem written by Eternal Manhood.[37]

Thus shaped by the papier-mâché of feminizing, sanctifying texts, the monumentalized forms of female poets may be blurred or bulky, but they are not immodest. Where a statue of plain Mary Beton or Mary Seton might be obscene, after all, a cast of Venus, or, better yet, of the Virgin Mary, cannot be, even if a historical woman is its model.[38]

As poet Mary Elizabeth Coleridge points out, such "coverage" has a dual resonance. "I believe I am quite capable of being a hero," she writes wryly in 1888, in the context of literary reputations, "but so far as I know, I am not one; and I want to have some good way suggested to me of occupying that desirable position" (177). "Marriage can always make a heroine out of the least heroic of women," she muses a few paragraphs later (179). Coleridge's non sequitur is only apparent, of course. It echoes the perception of other Victorian critics that literary historical "coverage" of women writers might be metaphorically linked to another form of canonical coverage—that is, to the law of coverture.

Years earlier, John Stuart Mill had already made a similar connection. Women's education, he argued, must inevitably provoke challenges to the institution of marriage: "If men are determined that the law of marriage shall be a law of despotism, . . . all that has been done in the modern world to relax the chain on the minds of women, has been a mistake. They never should have been allowed to receive a literary education. Women who read, much more women who write, are, in the existing constitution of things, a contradiction and a disturbing element" (156). Metaphorically, it seems, threats to the mid-century canons of literary and legal coverage could merge.

By late in the century, the intersections of legal and literary canons were attracting explicit attention from writers such as Gardener, who asserts, "It cannot be denied that the canons of literature have, so far, been laid down on strictly masculine lines. . . . What shall and what shall not be discussed, therefore; how the topics may be handled *and for what purposes,* have been established—as have the laws of marriage and divorce—without having first con-

sulted both of the interested parties" (327). Such are the connections between
canons of law and of literature, Gardener insists, that late-century women's experience of gains in marital legal status must lead to a revolution in literary
perspective: "The time has come when 'we' has a wider significance than it
ever had before. It no longer means 'I' in the marriage service. . . . The canons
may be modified womanward in the future. . . . Literature may present life from
an outlook that will greatly astonish those who have believed that there is but
one opinion, but one person, but one thinker, but one observer, but one lover,
but one sufferer—but one *human being,* in short—in a race which is composed
of two sexes" (330–31).

In conflating the "marriage service" with the "canons" of literary "outlook," Gardener points to a crucial tradition within critical responses to Victorian women's verse. As earlier discussions of critical approaches to the bodies of
women's texts suggest, Victorian writing on female poets repeatedly—and often
quite explicitly—applies not only the rhetoric of sanctity but that of courtship
to its subjects. Gallantly, such critics present themselves as ready to constitute
their subjects as real women—and, in analogy to the legal terms of coverture,
to cause them to disappear. For like marital coverture, which technically sub-
sumes a woman's existence within that of her husband, critical and pedagogical
coverage of nineteenth-century women writers seeks to enforce some version
of the "heterosexual contract" (Wittig 33–45). That is, it offers historical females access to the privileges of true femininity, but only at the price of some
form of symbolic annihilation.

In the case of women poets, such annihilation often works through a process of metaphoric absolution whereby a woman poet who is in the process of
being proclaimed quintessentially feminine is both freed from the onus of deliberate artistic creation and rendered a virtually transparent medium for *the* generic genius of Woman. "We do not consider" Hemans "the best" female author of her time, George Gilfillan wrote near the height of Hemans's fame, for
example, but "we consider her by far the most feminine writer of the age. All
the woman in her shines. . . . Spring, in its vague joyousness, has not a more
appropriate voice in the note of the cuckoo than feminine sensibility had in the
more varied but hardly profounder song of the authoress before us. . . . The
songs, hymns, and odes in which this life is registered, are as soft and bright as
atoms of the rainbow; like them, tears transmuted into glory, but, no more than
they, great or complete" (230, 232, 233). "Strictly effusions," and therefore the
result of nature rather than art, Hemans's poems are not written but "rained
around her": they represent not a specific poet's labors but "just audible beatings
of *the* deep female heart" (234, 239, 235; emphasis added). Hemans's truly femi-

nine poetry thus springs straight from the natural heart of Woman. As a human being, she is only its vessel. The composition of truly glorious feminine poetry is thus reduced to a sacred form of automatic writing.

Though his generalizations about gendered interests surely go too far, Paul Elmer More is admirably frank on this score. "Women will judge a poetess by her inclusion of the larger human nature," he asserts (818). "Men, on the contrary, are apt, in accepting a woman's work or in creating a female character, to be interested more in the traits and limitations which distinguish her from her masculine complement. They care more for the *idea* of woman, and less for woman as merely a human being" (819). "Accepting a woman's work" and "creating a female character" thus come to much the same thing.[39] What matters is not the historical, "merely human" female poet; it is her potential embodiment of the critic's "*idea* of woman."[40]

Covered with and by a generic femininity that is simultaneously constituted and erased by a canonical heterosexual contract, women writers' textual nakedness thus receives its shield. Of Hemans, Frederic Rowton writes, "Her works are to my mind a perfect embodiment of woman's soul. The very diffuseness of her style is feminine, and one would not wish it altered. Diction, manner, sentiment, passion, and belief are in her as delicately *rounded off* as are the bones and muscles of the Medicean Venus. There is not a harsh or angular line in her whole mental contour" (386). As they shape their female subjects according to the "contours of [mostly] masculine desire," calling upon the force or divinity of that desire to endow them with literary historical life, such critics become literary Pygmalions.[41] They do not merely resurrect or restore women writers: they give them life as heroines of literary history. "She was a Muse, a Grace, a variable child, a dependent woman, the Italy of human beings," wrote Geraldine Jewsbury of her fictional Egeria, for example (254). Based on Jewsbury's friend Felicia Hemans, Egeria was to attain iconicity in Hemans's reception—so much so, indeed, that at points her glory seems to outshine any conceivable achievements of her mortal model.

In her poem "In an Artist's Studio," Christina Rossetti provides one of the most famous and powerful Victorian evocations of the sinister potential that the protean power of Woman could assume in conjunction with historical women:

> One face looks out from all his canvasses,
> One selfsame figure sits or walks or leans;
> We found her hidden just behind those screens,
> That mirror gave back all her loveliness.
> A queen in opal or in ruby dress,
> A nameless girl in freshest summer greens,

> *A saint, an angel;—every canvass means*
> *The same one meaning, neither more nor less.*
> *He feeds upon her face by day and night,*
>   *And she with true kind eyes looks back on him*
> *Fair as the moon and joyful as the light:*
>   *Not wan with waiting, not with sorrow dim;*
> *Not as she is, but was when hope shone bright;*
>   *Not as she is, but as she fills his dream.*

"In an Artist's Studio" deals with the creation of heroines, and its implications go straight to the heart of Victorian canonization. At the poem's culmination stands a woman "as she fills" the artist's dream. She is a single figure, unified across time. She never directs her true kind eyes at herself or at the world; rather, she turns them back on the artist who made—or dreamed—her. As fair and, by implication, as reflective as the moon, her remote, secondary existence literalizes what Ellis calls the "fair picture which woman's character ought to present" (*Daughters*, 35). While Ellis's ideal historical women attain only an "*almost* spiritual beauty" and an "*almost* superhuman grace," however, this figure succeeds utterly (*Women*, 83; emphasis added). Her face's protean power nurtures the creator of art, who may cast her as a queen, a saint, an angel, or a country girl, and yet still embody in her form "the same one meaning, neither more nor less." That meaning, which fills the artist's dreams and his studio, seems to reach into critical essays, footnotes, and classrooms, not only during the Victorian period but perhaps in our own as well.

Even as it evokes the power of what Auerbach celebrates as the "mythic alliance" between femininity and literary character (*Woman*, 9), however, "In an Artist's Studio" stands as a powerful reminder of how transcendent feminine representations may serve both to mask and to mark historical women's metaphoric and actual absence. With her dream face on the walls, Rossetti's model remains behind the screen. We find her only "hidden": even the mirror that once "gave" back her loveliness may no longer do so. All we know of her is that while the artist feeds on her imagined face, she herself has become "wan with waiting." The poem's final lines implicitly echo her earlier comparison to the moon, but with a bitter difference. Like the moon, she wanes; but time, which will renew the moon, is killing her.

Thus, against the artist's possibly immortal representations of femininity, Rossetti sets the model's irreversible mortality. Behind the screen of art, a corporeal woman ages and changes. Her own eccentric, shifting identity, which is that of a model and not a queen, saint, angel, or country girl, remains as irreducible as it may be unknowable. "As she is": the phrase repeats itself in this brief poem like a memento mori. For the model "as she is" is the model as she dies.

The writer who becomes a heroine of literary history may face an even worse fate; for the dream visions of Rossetti's model are at least lasting works of art. In *The Politics of Literary Reputation,* John Rodden suggests that what he terms "a *face*—the clear image of the literary (and sometimes private) personality—" is an "essential factor" for achieving "a reputation which radiates beyond literary circles and beyond the present moment" (91). In the case of women writers, such faces too often verge on a generic beauty that is doomed to go out of date.

Witness, for example, H. T. Tuckerman's 1845 introduction to Hemans's works. "In the field of letters as well as in the arena of social life," he writes, woman is "man's better angel." It is "irreverent to dictate to genius, but the themes of female poetry are written in the very structure of the soul. . . . The spirit of Mrs. Hemans is essentially feminine. Various as her subjects are, they are stamped with the same image and superscription" (vii–viii). "Essentially feminine," Hemans's spirit conforms to the structure of *the* female soul. Her subjects are stamped with the "image and superscription" of that generic soul; and were they not, it seems, they would be scarcely worth reading.

Rodden finds that Orwell's metaphoric "faces" multiplied as critics and biographers shaped the writer according to their own interests (67–100). Although the reception of nineteenth-century women poets evinces similar patterns, it also demonstrates an opposing process whereby faces are conflated as critics cast their subjects in the form of generic femininity. In a literal sense, for example, the faces of the more famous Victorian women poets do have distinctive and often widely recognized forms. It is no accident, however, that recognition is so often limited to a single romanticized portrait. Students may be able to identify the flattering Field Talfourd drawing of Elizabeth Barrett Browning, for example, but until fairly recently, reproductions of actual photographs were difficult to find. Similarly, to the extent that Christina Rossetti's face has entered popular culture, it is in the form of a youthful image captured in one of her brother's sketches—again, despite the existence of actual (far less flattering) photographs.[42]

Ironically, to the extent that Victorian criticism succeeded in casting women writers as generic feminine ideals, it may have worked, ultimately, to desacralize both their literal and metaphoric "faces." As Walter Benjamin argues, if any ritual "cult value" still inheres in works of art in an age of mechanical reproduction, it does so in images of the specific, historical "human countenance" whose irreducible singularity offers "a last refuge" for the "aura" once embodied by unique artistic creations ("Work," 225–26).

Victorian canonization of literary heroines thus does more than cover its subjects to the point of disappearance: it transforms them into figures that are guaranteed to crumble of their own accord. There may be no better way to date a figure than to assimilate her to universal femininity of any sort. If Woman is "the unhistorical Other of history," after all, she is always the unhistorical Other of a particular history. Although any writer's texts may date themselves, nothing seems to provoke the mockery and nostalgia of successive generations like an era's conceptions of eternal womanhood.[43]

Consider, once more, Hemans's reception. "Her sources of inspiration being genuine, and the tone of her mind feminine in an intense degree, the product has no lack of sincerity," writes William Michael Rossetti, "and yet it leaves a certain artificial impression . . . perhaps through a cloying flow of 'right-minded' perceptions of moral and material beauty. . . . One might sum up the weak points in Mrs. Hemans's poetry by saying that it is not only 'feminine' poetry (which under the circumstances can be no imputation, rather an encomium) but also 'female' poetry: besides exhibiting the fineness and charm of womanhood, it has the monotone of mere sex" ("Prefatory Notice," xxvii). What was once sweet and natural has become cloying and artificial. The generic charms of "feminine poetry" are giving way to "the monotone of mere sex." Similar comments would one day be made about Rossetti's sister.[44]

The crumbling of such monuments may be catalyzed by admirers as well as detractors. Hemans's "genius was essentially feminine," asserts a prefatory memoir to the Albion edition published in 1900 (Hemans, xv). Her "extreme popularity waned some time after her death," however, "through the strange and (we think) lamentable change in the tone of modern society. The age that gave birth to the cry of 'Women's Rights,' and to the unfeminine imitators of masculine habits, was not likely to appreciate the voice of the *true* woman that spoke in Felicia Hemans" (xv–xvi). "It is only the *great* writers who . . . endure the test of centuries, and, as yet, no poetess has thus long retained popularity" (xv). Thus, Hemans speaks not with a specific woman's voice but with that of the true woman, who inevitably devolves into the truly outdated woman.[45]

Ironically, then, in removing the "holy women" from the calendar—in canonizing female poets for their feminine transcendence of history—Victorian critics helped to ensure that future generations would conceive of them as possessing no more than historical interest. Transformation into a sanctified heroine of Victorian literary history thus entails layers of loss. Not only is the metaphoric sinner revised and edited to fit a transcendent character, but that character itself is both definitionally removed from the specificity and physicality of history and cast as an embodiment of feminine silence. Theoretically, any canonical monument may be dislodged. Masculine secular saints, too, are vulnerable to attack as cultural values shift. Yet those figures whose value resides in eternal femininity can remain sacred only by virtue of the fleeting authority of their canonizers' sexual politics. Their papier-mâché is doomed to disintegrate. When it does, moreover, only the barest underlying structure of characteristic literary works may remain available. Thus, for example, Hemans may retain her reputation as an ideal, "calm" mid-Victorian ideal, even as the violent, vehement heroines of her most popular work, *Records of Woman,* fade from critical view.[46] Papier-mâché needs only the lightest of supporting structures: one may revise, edit, and even directly discount a great deal of a female author's works without thereby endangering her position as a monument to generic feminine virtue.

At their most glorious, then, nineteenth-century women writers are canonized by a process that almost inevitably guarantees their downfall: from a long-term literary historical point of view, they are made secular saints and lost at the same time.

These reflections might provide a grim final note. Luckily, however, no account of self-destructing generic feminine glory does justice even to the most "successful" canonical idealization of women writers. For no coverage, legal or literary, is ever complete. Papier-mâché shifts and cracks; the disturbing possibilities of texts and flesh make themselves felt in even the most transcendent constructions. By the century's end, works as divergent as essays by Patmore and Gardener suggest the sense that earlier coverage of ideal feminine forms could not hold. In Patmore's *Religio Poetae,* such a prospect is disastrous. Given "the diminished manliness of men," he writes, "women feel that the external conditions of true womanhood have disappeared; and it is not to be wondered at if many of them, unclothed, as it were, of the sentiment of surrounding manhood, should, in their ignorant discomfort and despair, make as unsightly a spectacle of themselves as does the animal called a hermit crab when, by some chance, it is ejected, bare, comfortless, and unprotected, from the shell of its adoption" (164–65). Stripped of the shell created by the "external conditions of true womanhood"—which is to say the "sentiment of surrounding manhood"—Patmore's "unsightly" modern "women" have no choice but to reveal what lies underneath: pitiful, subhuman misery.

Gardener's essay presents a far different vision of the potential breakdown of true womanhood's coverage. Speaking of the literary women whose metaphoric nudity has shocked critics, she asks, "Is it not just conceivable that the new pictures of life are not more nude, but that the lack of drapery is simply noticed from a changed position—under a new light—and for the first time by those who thought themselves covered because their eyes were turned another way?" (332). As Gardener's "picture" lifts her eyes to the reader, she, too, is a Galatea. She has been given life, however, by the "keen wits, trained minds, and, above all, financial independence" of female writers (333). Unlike a Marian monument, moreover, this figure is not definitively, because unconsciously, pure. She is fully aware of the extent of her own nakedness. Demanding that both metaphoric draperies and feminine virtue itself "come to be adjusted on new lines," Gardener fashions a monumental New Woman who resists traditional canonical "coverage" (332). Still in some sense ideal, still generic, such a creation is nevertheless revolutionary. She is not enough; she does not herald a different form of history altogether. Yet she shakes the foundations of the Victorian canon.

To end on such a note, however, might suggest that the making and losing of generic feminine saints reached some kind of natural end along with the nineteenth century itself. Such an implication would reflect at once too generously upon the twentieth century—which has continued canonical coverage in its own ways—and too harshly upon the nineteenth. For evocative though it is, the sinister beauty of Rossetti's artist's studio suggests only one outcome of the nineteenth century's attempts to transform the bodies of women and the bodies of women's texts into mere figures for absent, transcendent Woman. In *Bleak House,* Dickens's anonymous narrator enters the snug (and smug) confines of another gallery, at Chesney Wold, to reveal Sir Leicester "condescendingly perusing the backs of his books, or honouring the fine arts with a glance of approbation" (457). The narrator imagines cataloguing Sir Leicester's collection of paintings as follows: "'Three high-backed chairs, a table and cover, long-necked bottle (containing wine), one flask, one Spanish female's costume, three-quarter face portrait of Miss Jogg the model, and a suit of armour containing Don Quixote.' Or, 'One stone terrace (cracked), one gondola in distance, one Venetian senator's dress complete, richly embroidered white satin costume with profile portrait of Miss Jogg the model, one scimitar superbly mounted in gold with jewelled handle, elaborate Moorish dress (very rare) and Othello'" (457). True to her name, Miss Jogg remains anchored in the jog-trot of the everyday world. No Muse-like Dulcinea or martyred Desdemona, "Miss Jogg the model" can be—and is—objectified. She cannot be rendered transcendent, however. She remains herself, as material, substantial, and irreducible as the scimitar next to which she stands, and she hangs over Sir Leicester as a dangerous emblem both of the class limits of ideal womanhood and of physical, historical womanhood's resistance to transcendent transformations. For although he is far from suspecting it, Sir Leicester Dedlock's collection contains another work of art capable of aligning him with the painted Don Quixote or Othello: a portrait of his wife, Lady Dedlock, which will ultimately help expose her not "as she fills his dreams" but as she lives out a secret personal history. Beneath her smooth, harmonious facade, Lady Dedlock may be much more like Miss Jogg than her husband could possibly imagine.

Even here, paradoxically, religious models may be illuminating. For in popular legends, even Mary herself could not always be relied upon to hold still and behave. Indeed, she comes to represent the "all-too-human, the irregular, the exceptional" in religion. She takes the place of a favored knight in a tournament; she substitutes for a runaway convent portress (Ward 163–64, 266; Ashe 220). She intercedes for those who turn to her, but she is not above teasing them in the process.

Thus, though static, inhumanly pure Marian virtue may stand as Victorian culture's highest feminine ideal—and a deeply dangerous one both for women writers and for the critics who seek to honor them—it never stands firmly or alone. Where a midcentury feminist such as Jameson praised the Madonna as a secular model, for example, Mary could appear as "the most perfect type of the *intellectual,* tender, simple, and heroic woman" (49; emphasis added); where a late-century sex radical such as Grant Allen did so, Mary's invocation could sanctify the image of "the woman who did" (Trudgill 265, 275–76). No doubt the Angel in the House and her counterparts—among them certain incarnations of "Shakespeare's Heroines," "Felicia Hemans," "Elizabeth Barrett Browning," or "Christina Rossetti"—hovered threateningly over the shoulder of Woolf's imagined woman writer. One might well imagine, though, other figures who hover behind them—historical, all-too-human, irregular forms such as Miss Jogg's—or even, in different guises, Hemans's, Barrett Browning's, or Rossetti's. "Be pure," whisper the angels or the preachers of Acting Angelhood (Woolf, "Professions," 59). "You're wasting your time," whisper the others.

III

Developing Character(s):
Shakespeare's Heroines and
Nineteenth-Century Literary Study

'Tis said that poetry ministers to religion.
The saints in her calendar, are they not holy?
And may they not be blamelessly worshipped
    in spirit and in truth?
Hermione—Imogen—Miranda . . . !

         Anna
         Jameson

THERE IS NO FEMALE SAINT Shakespeare. Even in Virginia Woolf's imagination, Shakespeare's twin, Judith, does not survive to become his peer (*Room*, 48–50). Where no conceivable historical woman could serve, however, "Shakespeare's heroines" succeeded. Joining their author as emblems of sacred literary ideals, the female "saints" in Shakespeare's "calendar" acted as powerful symbolic agents within larger canonization processes. In so doing, they not only served as monuments to vanishing womanhood but helped inspire and authorize an explosion of ambitious critical writing by women. Idealized readings of Shakespearean female characters thus demonstrate both the most annihilating and the most liberatory potentials of nineteenth-century feminine literary canonicity. They also suggest the inextricable bonds between those potentials.

    "In the nineteenth century, as never before," Gary Taylor writes, "women and children shaped the prevailing image of Shakespeare" (209). In one sense, as Taylor himself implicitly acknowledges, this claim is overstated: although expurgations of Shakespearean plays may well have served an "image of Victorian womanhood," actual women (or children) scarcely wrested control of Victorian theatrical productions and publishing houses from the hands of men (210). Indeed, an undercurrent of skepticism concerning even the expurgated Shakespeare's suitability for women readers remained active throughout the century.[1] In another sense, however, Taylor's point is crucial. For however complex and strained their relations may have been, Shakespeare's nineteenth-century "domestication" and actual women's attainment of an "increasingly vocal part in Shakespearean criticism" were intimately connected (205).[2] By the century's end, women were studying Shakespeare in unprecedented numbers, not only in newly opened college and university literature lectures but in a range of more or less ambitious literary societies and study groups (205).[3]

Like the Bible itself, the (suitably expurgated) "family Shakespeare" came to represent a sacred power whose associations were deeply domestic. And as King Shakespeare entered the home, so did his "daughters."[4] Samuel Taylor Coleridge, for example, has gained a certain notoriety among Shakespeare scholars for his assertion that "the Englishman who without reverence, who without a proud and affectionate reverence, can utter the name of Shakespeare, stands disqualified for the office" of critic (Stavisky 10). Less recognized, but no less significant, perhaps, is his analogous requirement of reverence for Shakespeare's women characters—a position grounded in the conviction that only by "entering fully into" Shakespeare's "mode of portraying female characters" could one defend that author "from the most cruel of all charges—that he is an immoral writer" (*Lectures*, 94; *Collected Works*, 1:313).

Coleridge was not alone in linking assertions of Shakespeare's position as a sacred national poet-hero to assurances that "in Shakspeare all the elements of womanhood are holy" (*Collected Works*, 2:269). Indeed, by 1833 a *Blackwood's* article was already announcing the success of such mutual sanctification: "For how long, and by how many, even of the most enlightened, were Shakspeare's women thought poor pictures of the brighter and better half of humanity! . . . But the blind eyes of heresy were couched, and she became a true believer in the angelical being of woman, as revealed from heaven to heaven's own darling genius" ("Characteristics II," 111).

If, as Matthew Arnold put it, by the 1870s the Bible and Shakespeare were "imposed upon an Englishman as objects of his admiration" (quoted in Gary Taylor 167), they were equally, if differently, imposed upon Englishwomen— not to mention the "Shakespearianized" women of America (where, as Raoul Granqvist writes, "Shakespeare's competitor was God himself" [41]).[5] For women, too, had their roles in the "single, coherent, harmonious, long-established, triumphant national culture" celebrated and solidified by Shakespearean study (Gary Taylor 196). "Shakspeare is the writer of all others whom the women of England should take to their hearts," an 1885 work by Madeline Leigh-Noel Elliott quotes Charles Cowden Smith as saying, "for I believe it to be mainly through his intellectual influence that their claims in the scale of society were acknowledged in England. . . . The moral philosophy of Shakspeare, anticipated by another code, which I am perfectly sure he would have been the first to recognise and avow, has exalted our social system above that of the rest of the world" (ii–iii). Shakespeare fulfills the process Christianity began; and what is more, he does so in English. The point was essential, both for

England itself and for the wider linguistic realm over which King Shakespeare was presumed to hold sway.

Where Shakespeare was considered "the best friend and benefactor of womankind that has yet appeared on our earth" (at least "next to the Bible"), women's meditation upon Shakespearean female characters could be understood as an act of devotion (Hudson, "Female Characters," 192). It is no accident that as early as 1809, the publisher of Mary and Charles Lamb's *Tales from Shakespear* was marketing that work as a conduct manual for girls (Wolfson 22–23). By the middle of the nineteenth century, to interpret Shakespeare's heroines meant nothing less than to read the essential, sacred female character itself; to teach them meant nothing less than to teach divine femininity. As critics, scholars, biographers, portraitists, and theater troupes analyzed, reinterpreted, appropriated, and revised the Bard's female fictional characters, readings of Shakespeare's heroines emerged as key sites of conflict and discussion concerning both the construction of femininity and the faith in such femininity as a cornerstone of English or Anglo-Saxon cultural supremacy.

Two divergent but deeply connected strains emerge from the nineteenth century's uneven and inevitably contested attempts to canonize Shakespearean heroines.[6] The first such strain distinguishes itself through insistence upon the transparent unity of female Shakespearean characters. Seeking to shape Shakespeare's heroines as vanishing Marian monuments as well as to establish such monuments' status as eternal revelations of an ultimate—and ultimately Anglo-Saxon—womanhood, it locates Shakespeare's female characters not only within a timeless world of literature but within the even more transcendent world of revelation. It renders them fully ethereal, and it glorifies them as characterless—which is to say, as static, essentially interchangeable representatives of an unchanging, unified holy womanhood. Its literary monuments may also be national; its proclamations of the static harmony of transcendent feminine holiness may both mirror and reinforce hopes for the unchanging, harmonious rule of Shakespeare's actual and metaphoric kingdoms.

Dominated though not entirely defined by women, the second strain also glorifies Shakespearean heroines. In contrast, however, it attempts to locate them, and thus, by implication, the concept of divine womanhood, within history. Multiplicity and historicity are the key values here: Shakespeare's female characters serve as walking compendia of transcendent feminine capacities and as case studies for how personal and historical circumstance affect such capacities' exercise. If these Shakespearean heroines are "real" women, it is because they exist in time—whether narrative time, Shakespeare's time, the time of their nineteenth-century readers, or that of the stage. Almost fully accessible, the monuments shaped to glorify such "characteristics of women" may be befriended, disassembled, or even entered into: they allow readers to imagine not only the women they themselves may be but the women they might have been. Moreover, they may challenge as well as proclaim the supremacy of English culture; as criticism in this mode sometimes insists, though Shakespeare may be quintessentially English, Portia and Juliet are not.

Each of these strains begins with Coleridge and with Anna Jameson; each invokes and elaborates upon watchwords such as *perfection, harmony, naturalness,* and *characterlessness* or upon metaphors such as the mirror of art; and each is often thoroughly, if illogically, interwoven with the other in any given text. Historical and transcendent womanhood never fully merge here, but they often meet.

"Characterless" Characters: Shakespeare's Marian Heroines

As is so often the case with Victorian critical approaches, the search for generic ideal womanhood in Shakespeare's female characters goes back to the Romantics—in this case, most notably to Coleridge. "Lastly the female no character" reads a transcription of Coleridge's notes to a famous lecture on Shakespeare (*Collected Works,* 1:573). This cryptic phrase is further elaborated upon when, in a discussion of Ophelia, Coleridge praises "Shakespear's Charm of constituting female character by absences of characters, = outjuttings—" (*Collected Works,* 2:351). Foreshadowing Sarah Stickney Ellis's suggestion that young women attempt to lay "aside . . . peculiarities of character" ("Poetry," 122), Coleridge's notes speak of "the faults of the sex from which Oph. is so charct. free, that the freedom therefrom constitutes her Character" (*Collected Works,* 2:351).

The "blessed beauty" of "the woman's character" is thus that she has "no character at all": "Shakespeare saw that the want of prominence, which Pope notices for sarcasm, was the blessed beauty of the woman's character, and knew that it arose not from any deficiency, but from the more exquisite harmony of all the parts of the moral being constituting one living total of head and heart" (2:270). In such terms, to call Shakespeare's female figures characterless was "the highest compliment that could be paid to them: the elements were so commixed, so even was the balance of feeling, that no one protruded in particular—every thing amiable as sisters, mothers, and wives, was included in the thought" (1:556).

Thus, Coleridge's criticism attempts to transform one of the preceding century's most notorious statements of misogyny into a form of praise.[7] Even the strongest proponents of the characterlessness theory would never again go so far. Nonetheless, *characterlessness* and *harmony* were to become watchwords of the heroines' literary reputation. "Repeated, emphasized, foregrounded, linked to certain themes," they would serve as a sort of shorthand whose resonance increased through a powerful process of accretion (Rodden 87). When Henry Norman Hudson writes that Shakespeare's heroines are "as thoroughly and intensely individual as any of his characters," or when he celebrates "female character" as capable of evincing "all the intellectual energy and dignity of the other sex, without expelling or obscuring, in the least degree, the essence of womanhood," for example, he may seem explicitly to refute Coleridge's passage on characterlessness ("Female Characters," 200, 194). In fact, however, Hudson quotes and clarifies that very passage, insisting that in the heroines, "all characteristic peculiarities are excluded by their very harmony and completeness of character. . . . It is their perfect evenness and entireness of being in all their movements and impressions that makes them characterless." Hudson's reference to such figures' freedom from "outjuttings or protuberances" only serves to confirm his direct debt to Coleridge (200).

Hudson believed that Shakespearean female characters represented both the "reality and apotheosis of womanhood" (192). In terms of literary canonization, his support was well worth having. One of the nineteenth century's most influential American Shakespeareans, Hudson was known as a teacher, a critic, and as the editor of the Harvard edition of *Shakespeare's Complete Works.* The endpapers of Hudson's 1882 *Shakespeare: His Life, Art, and Characters* advertise not only the complete works but *Hudson's School Shakespeare* ("carefully expurgated"), *Hudson's Three-Volume Shakespeare,* his *English in Schools, Expurgated Family Shakespeare,* and five other English literature textbooks (2–3). As one obituary asserts, "His most important works were designed as educational forces, and they fulfill the intentions of their author to a degree that he could not have anticipated" ("Henry Norman Hudson," 82; Weld 449). Into the twentieth century, new "Hudson" editions continued to appear; and though the notes were cut, significant bits of Hudson's teachings on womanhood often remained. Hudson's editing, expurgations, and explanatory notes thus helped to shape—and gender—uncounted readers' exposure to Shakespeare.[8] They did so firmly within the project of canonizing Shakespearean women as vanishing monuments.

At the base of this project is the insistence that revelation, not history, is the source of Shakespeare's women. If the female figures of Shakespearean plays are "Shakespeare's heroines," they are so not merely because he created them but because he revealed and perhaps revered them as well (Thom, "Shakespeare Study," 101). Such claims would echo throughout the century. While history "gives us powerful delineations of character in its chief agents, that is, in men,"

Thomas De Quincey writes in 1850, Shakespeare is the "absolute creator of female character." Anthony "is found" in history, but Cleopatra is "a pure creation of art" ("Shakspeare," 75). In 1894, Swinburne is still asserting that "Spirits" of a certain sort may trace their "first obscure electric revelation of what Blake calls the 'Eternal Female'" to the effects of "Shakespeare's Cleopatra" (*Study,* 191). In such readings, the "contours of masculine desire" become those of literary creation and of feminine revelation (Ross). De Quincey's godlike Bard, for example, replaces the rigid feminine "marble groups" of Greek tragedy with "real incarnations": he creates "warm breathing realities" with the "fine pulses of womanly sensibilities . . . throbbing in their bosoms" ("Shakspeare," 69–70). Shakespeare is not only femininity's "sole authentic oracle of truth"; he is the "absolute creator of female character" (75). "The possible beauty of the female character had not been seen as in a dream, before Shakspeare called into perfect life the radiant shapes" of his female figures (68). In time, such critical assertions would attain iconicity: though Alfred H. Welsh's 1883 textbook, *The Development of English Literature and Language,* scarcely cites De Quincey, one cannot help but hear echoes of that writer in its bland assertion that Shakespeare's heroines embody "the possible of the female mind, seen, for the first time, as in a dream, yet—unlike Spenser's—warm breathing realities" (1:377).

Vessels for timeless womanhood, Shakespearean heroines convey, in Coleridge's words, "the sweet yet dignified feeling of all that *continuates* Society, as sense of ancestry, of Sex etc— a purity unassailable by sophistry, because it does not rest on the analytic processes . . . in that same equipoise of the faculties during which the feelings *are* representative of all past experience, not of the Individual, but of all those by whom she has been educated and of their Predecessors usque ad Evam" (*Collected Works,* 1:554).[9] Like Dickens's angel-heroines, then—and perhaps like George Eliot's "delicate vessels" in whom "is borne onward through the ages the treasure of human affections" (*Daniel Deronda,* 103) or Henry James's "Juliets and Cleopatras and Portias" and "Hettys and Maggies and Rosamunds and Gwendolens" (*Portrait,* 9)—such heroines are not so much separate entities as conduits for "all that continuates" society (Crosby 24; Gary Taylor 207). "Our child," dreams "Christopher North" in an 1830 issue of *Blackwood's,* "would have seemed—alternately—Una—Juliet—Desdemona—Imogen; for those bright creatures were all kith and kin, and the angelical family expression would, after a sleep of centuries, have broken out in beauty over the countenance of their fair cousin, Theodora North" (John Wilson 267).[10]

Not surprisingly, such figures are free from the need—or the capacity—for growth: "If Shakspere ventured upon any generalization about women, it was perhaps this—that the natures of women are usually made up of fewer elements than those of men, but that those elements are ordinarily in juster poise, more fully organized, more coherent and compact. . . . Shakspere's men have a history, moral growth or moral decay; his women act and are acted upon, but seldom grow and are transformed. . . . Shakspere creates his women by a single strong or exquisite stroke, but he studies his men" (Dowden, *Shakspere,* 97–98).

Indeed, so generic is such goodness that only the accident of circumstance distinguishes one Shakespearean heroine from another. "In all the Shakspearian women," Coleridge writes, "there is essentially the same foundation and principle; the distinct individuality and variety are merely the result of the modification of circumstances, whether in Miranda the maiden, in Imogen the wife, or in Katharine the queen" (*Collected Works,* 2:270). Thus, individual Shakespearean female characters are essentially interchangeable manifestations of womanhood: they are merely, in De Quincey's words, "the shifting phases and the lunar varieties of that mighty changeable planet, that lovely satellite of man" ("Shakspeare," 75).[11] Under the proper circumstances, it would seem, Lady Macbeth might have been Juliet; or Ophelia, Lady Macbeth.

Like Ellis's heroines, Shakespeare's may be "nothing, or anything that is not evil, as the necessities of others may require" ("Poetry," 114). "Pure abstractions of the affections," as William Hazlitt calls them, they "seem to exist only in their attachment to others" (2). Even Edward Dowden, who explicitly rejects characterlessness as an attribute of the heroines, writes that it is "almost an error to study the character of any of Shakspere's heroines apart from the associate with whom she plays her part" (*Transcripts,* 367, 342).

What matters in the interpretation of such characters is less the details of the transitory phase in which they are shown than their ability to influence the others to whom they are attached, by revealing aspects of transcendent womanhood. In assessing the work of Hudson, E. P. Whipple makes a classic statement in this vein: "These ideal creations of the great poet, more truly and vitally natural than most of the women of actual life, he has contrived to reproduce whole upon his page, in the clear sweetness and beautiful dignity of their characters, and has been especially successful in setting forth their innate, unconscious purity of soul, shining through the most equivocal circumstances, and lending a glory to the simplest acts and expressions. It would be vain to look elsewhere for so complete a demonstration of Shakspeare's unrivalled success in exhibiting womankind in women" (236). The implicit hierarchy here is familiar. On the lowest level stand the "women of actual life," most of whom are not so "vitally natural" as fictional heroines. On the next tier stand those "unconscious" and transparent vessels, the "ideal creations of the great poet." And highest of all stands the "innate, unconscious" glory of womankind.[12] What counts is the exhibition of this womankind; in comparison to it, any embodiment of ideal womanhood, even in the ethereal ideal creations of a great poet, appears primarily as a necessary evil. No wonder if the forms of individual heroines themselves are somewhat expendable: their pure textual bodies, like the bodies of women poets' texts, serve only as vessels for a more transcendent, unified truth. It seems fully in keeping, then, that Whipple also praises the "exquisite felicity" with which Hudson "touches without profanely handling the most ideal of Shakspeare's heroines," as well as Hudson's "constant sense of a certain sacredness attaching to the sex" (236). In such contexts, it is only inevitable that nineteenth-century expurgators should have emended or even omitted lines spoken by Shakespeare's female figures as reverence for Woman might seem to require (Gary Taylor 210).

Such canonization of Shakespeare's characterless female characters has a suggestive analogue in Shakespearean heroines' portrayal as "keepsake" beauties. As Othello's proximity to Dickens's Miss Jogg reminds us, the retailing of portraits of Shakespearean heroines was a lively industry throughout much of the nineteenth century.[13] The origins of portraits of Shakespeare's heroines lie in part in the eighteenth-century's so-called fancy portraits, paintings in which fashionable women, costumed as literary figures, simultaneously displayed their charms and their culture (Altick, *Paintings,* 87). (Sir Joshua Reynolds, who painted fancy pictures of well-to-do women as Miranda, Hermione, Rosalind, and Perdita, also cast his subjects as St. Agnes, St. Genevieve, and St. Cecilia: his studio, Allan Cunningham claimed, was filled with sitters who "wished to be transmitted as angels" [quoted in Altick, *Paintings,* 26–27].) Historical models took precedence here: though posed in a balcony above Romeo, Lady J——presumably still wanted to look like a flattering version of herself.

By 1830, however, according to Altick, such paintings were disappearing. Although early nineteenth-century actresses continued to pose as Shakespeare's heroines, "there was a growing tendency to play down the identity of the model and to focus, instead, on the character she impersonated." Historical women were thus replaced by fictional heroines, who were, in turn, often replaced by interchangeable beauties. With time, "the role portrayed, far from remaining a distinctive link between the picture and the play, faded away also" (87). In separate illustrations and in sometimes lavish popular gift books such as Charles Heath's *Heroines of Shakespeare,* dozens upon dozens of "remarkably interchangeable young ladies" appeared as "Shakespeare's Heroines" (Melchiori 121).[14] Recognizable as Shakespearean primarily through their labels with "the name of the character and an appropriate quotation," such figures could be otherwise distinguished primarily by a "readily identifiable attribute, such as a garland of flowers in the case of Ophelia" (Altick, *Paintings,* 86–88). Thus, in parodic parallel to the iconography of sainthood, Rosalind is known by her shepherd's staff, for example, just as St. Barbara is by her city. Lady Macbeth, at least in Heath, distinguishes herself from one of her less sinister sisters by a dagger and a slight frown (figs. 2, 3, and 4). Crowned, with her hands crossed in prayer and her eyes turned upward, Cordelia is barely distinguishable from the Queen of Heaven (fig. 5). "To be tied down to an authentic face of Juliet!" Charles Lamb had raged, "To have Imogen's portrait! To confine the illimit-able!" (quoted in Altick, *Paintings,* 48). In a disturbing sense, perhaps the abstract beauty of most keepsake heroines answered such worries: it tied no one down to any but the most faceless glory.

Nonacting Angels: "Helpless" Sanctity and Shakespearean Study

As the tradition of reading Shakespeare's characters as "natural" (Desmet 42) meets Victorian characterizations of the true woman as a selfless actress, Shake-spearean heroines become central figures in educational schemes aimed at shap-ing the character of ideal womanhood. Female readers are instructed to look into the mirror of art and emulate the higher, holier reality of Shakespearean figures; the act of studying Shakespeare's heroines often comes to appear as a cross between Bible study and primping.[15] "Why not go to a woman to hear about women?" Dowden asks in his 1896 *Transcripts and Studies,* for example. Because, he answers, "each sex can best tell about the other": "Each sex holds the mirror up to the other, and what matter if it be a magic mirror? . . . We may say of Shakspere's heroines, who are women beheld in the most wonderful of magic mirrors, that they are more perfectly feminine than any woman could have found it in her heart or brain to make them" (340). They are also more perfectly feminine than any historical woman could find it in her heart or brain to be. Shakespeare "surely never met his Rosalinds, Mirandas, and Perditas in real life," asserts Thomas Keightley's 1867 *Shakespeare-Expositor,* "though he *may* have had some faint sketches of some of them in his own daughters" (19). Such is the "exquisite harmony" of "woman's character," as displayed by Coleridge's reading of Shakespearean characters, that it may exhibit "distinctive energies of faith, patience, constancy, fortitude," exclusively by "following the heart, which gives its results by a nice tact and happy intuition, without the intervention of the discursive faculty" (*Collected Works,* 2:270). Like the Virgin Mary or the Angel in the House, such figures have no need for the faculty of discourse, for

Fig. 2. Lady Macbeth. Charles Heath, *The Heroines of Shakespeare*, London: W. Kent, 1858. Reproduced with permission of the Hargrett Rare Book and Manuscript Library, University of Georgia Libraries.

Fig. 3. Ophelia. Charles Heath, *The Heroines of Shakespeare,* London: W. Kent, 1858. Reproduced with permission of the Hargrett Rare Book and Manuscript Library, University of Georgia Libraries.

Fig. 4. Cressida. Charles Heath, *The Heroines of Shakespeare,* London: W. Kent, 1858. Reproduced with permission of the Hargrett Rare Book and Manuscript Library, University of Georgia Libraries.

Fig. 5. Cordelia, Charles Heath, *The Heroines of Shakespeare,* London: W. Kent, 1858. Collection of author.

the experience of a speaking self (or selves) whose decisions are reached through articulate (if only internal) struggle. If their "purity" is "unassailable by sophistry," this is because it "does not rest on the analytic processes" (1:554). As Hudson puts it, "In the mind of a true woman there is no division or distraction of aims; no conflicting of impulses; no pulling of different feelings in opposite directions; she 'moveth altogether, if she move at all'" ("Female Characters," 201). "If heroines, therefore, at all, they are so without knowing it, or wishing it to be known. . . . their heroism springs up of its own free will and accord, and because they cannot help it" (204).

Such figures play the "woman's part" perfectly because they do not know it is a part. They are powerless to be anything other than sacred: their chastity lends them "glory," for example, precisely because it is independent of their conscious volition, remaining "innate" and "unconscious" (Whipple 236). (As Hippolyte Taine puts it in a less admiring vein, "You will not then discover virtue" in the souls of women in Shakespeare's plays, "for by virtue is implied a determinate desire to do good, and a rational observance of duty. They are only pure through delicacy or love" [376]).

How central such readings are to midcentury texts on womanhood may be suggested by a glance at John Ruskin's famous "Of Queen's Gardens." Ruskin's first models for the "true dignity of woman" are none other than female Shakespearean characters. Although his account of their innate, protean powers evokes familiar virtues, its vivid specificity still renders it worth quoting. Ruskin's ideal women—Shakespeare's female characters—are immaculately conceived: they are "infallibly faithful and wise counsellors,—incorruptibly just and pure examples—strong always to sanctify, even when they cannot save" (81). Such capacities are beyond Ruskin's female readers, as he implicitly acknowledges. If a woman seeks to attain her sanctifying "true place and power," however, she must attempt to develop these abilities nonetheless. She "must—as far as one can use such terms of a human creature—be incapable of error"; she must learn to exercise the "passionate gentleness of an infinitely variable, because infinitely applicable, modesty of service—the true changefulness of woman . . . variable as the *light,* manifold in fair and serene division, that it may take the colour of all that it falls upon, and exalt it" (92). To be strong always to sanctify is to be as colorless—and as characterless—as white light itself.

It is also to be, of course, "nothing, or anything that is not evil, as the necessities of others may require" (Ellis, "Poetry," 114). And indeed, Ellis herself cites Shakespeare to teach her "system of self-sacrifice" (116–18).[16] "Amongst numerous instances . . . abounding in the works of Shakspeare," however, she identifies one "which bears most strikingly the impress of a master hand" (116–17): the strangling of Desdemona:

Aemilia, her attendant, hears her dying voice, and, beginning to suspect there has been foul play, exclaims,

> "O, who hath done
> *This deed?*"
> "*Nobody; I myself; farewell:*   (118)
> *Commend me to my kind lord; O, farewell!*"

is answered by the wretched victim. Who can read these lines without acknowledging the writer's profound and intimate acquaintance with the heart of woman?

Desdemona's last words certainly seem to speak to the heart of Woman in Ellis's terms: they are emblematic of a virtue in which self-expression and self-annihilation merge.[17]

Such canonization's uses extend not only to the shaping of Woman's (ultimately singular, transcendent) character but to the deep marking of that character by constructions of nation, ethnicity, and race. This phenomenon is probably nowhere clearer than in the works of American educational writer and reformer William Taylor Thom. "We . . . have in Shakespeare an expression of our race-mind," insists Thom, a pioneer in formal Shakespeare study for women and the author of a U.S. Education Bureau pamphlet on African-American education. "To us Americans this can be made—should be made—a potent factor in keeping our vast and rapidly growing nation true to those ancestral instincts that have made it so great. . . . Think of the future of a nation with such elements as ours conformed to the sturdy Anglo-Saxon type, nurtured in the morals of the New Testament, and bred upon the free human spirit of Shakespeare!" ("Shakespeare Study," 102).[18] The "standard" of Shakespeare's "free human spirit" could be applied to those who were not of "Anglo-Saxon" birth, Thom asserted: "Let the Negroes learn good English, if they are to become and to remain good American citizens." For to study Shakespeare and the Bible was to learn citizenship: the "terse, nervous speech of the King James's Bible and of Shakespeare" would teach African-Americans "at one and the same time love of independence and love of law-abiding order."

Such linguistic citizenship took specific, highly dubious forms. Through it alone, wrote Thom, could African-Americans "hope to solve the knotty problem of their relations toward the masterful, superior white race, of whom one of them said recently, with a ludicrously pathetic wisdom of mistake: 'T'ain' no use talkin'; dem *Angry*-Saxons is boun'ter rule anyhow'" (98). Thus Shakespeare's English would form the character of good citizens, even as it taught such citizens the "wisdom" that there was "no use talking" unless one belonged to the "race" that had produced a poet with such a "free human spirit" ("Shakespeare Study," 102). Shakespeare's art remains a mirror here; but it is a mirror designed to reinforce what W. E. B. DuBois called double consciousness.

In Thom's writings, Shakespeare's contribution to the formation of white, middle-class Anglo-American women's characters reveals clear analogies to the promises offered above. "No other man has drawn such female characters," Thom proclaims. For Shakespeare is "true to his race, with whom love of true womanhood is a sort of religion; and his poet's fullness supplements this human side of the Good Book itself." "If, then, the women of our race would know and be what the men of our race love as their ideals, let them study Shakespeare and be what he makes his women." Like African-Americans of both sexes, Thom's national Acting Angels are to learn a language whose ultimate mastery is assumed, by definition, to be beyond their biological reach. They are to have "intercourse" with the "essentially manly type and virile utterance of Shakespeare's thought": they are to learn to revere "the 'literature' of power," the "vigorous thought of men as opposed to women" (101).

Thom wrote a great deal on Shakespearean studies for women. His *Shakespeare Examinations: With Some Remarks on the Class-Room Study of Shakespeare* seems to have been well received, as was the later *Shakespeare and Chaucer Examinations* (including a "special examination on Some Aspects of Womanhood in Chaucer, Shakespeare, and Tennyson" ["Literary Notes," 188]). Although his position statements are unusually direct, they are scarcely without resonance. Indeed, as late as 1929, Shakespearean critic George Gerwig was still echoing and expanding such claims: "Shakespeare may almost be said to have discovered the American girl three hundred years before she discovered herself." "By the very infection of these good examples he rears a race of noble women. . . . The Heroines of Shakespeare present the particular types of heart and soul ideals which have made first the Anglo-Saxon, then the English, and lastly the American woman the embodiment of all that is good and true and wholesome" (9–10). In such terms, for a young woman to study Shakespeare is for her to learn to emulate an Anglo-Saxon womanly "self" whose ideal form was revealed or set three hundred years before she was born. The best she can hope is to approximate an ideal whose fictionality ensures her failure—that is, if its ethnicity has not already done so. In a different way, then, she, too, is to study Shakespeare in order to discover that for her, as a specific, historical subject, there is "no use talking."

Like Mary or the Angel in the House, such Shakespearean heroines represent an impossibly pure and transcendent womanly virtue, a "real" gender that is "finally phantasmatic, impossible to embody" (Judith Butler 141). With such "mirrors" as their tools, female readers are thus doomed to a sort of agonized cosmic primping, an unescapable and yet futile attempt to enact a fixed and

unattainable purity. At points, moreover, glorifications of characterless Shakespearean heroines render the duties of their mortal counterparts even
more vain; they rely precisely upon the extent to which such heroines do
not act, even as Acting Angels. George Gilfillan goes so far as to employ Shakespeare's heroines in an attack on Ellis: "What a gallery of Shakspeare's female
characters would the author of the 'Mothers, Daughters, and Women of England' have painted! . . . Perdita! Would she have sent her to boarding school?"
(235).

Thus, even the Acting Angel's self-abnegation is too active, too self-
conscious to be that of a "right-minded woman," at least as exemplified by
Hudson's reading of Shakespearean heroines. "Such is the proper influence of
a right-minded and right-mannered woman on those about her," Hudson
writes of Cordelia. "She knows it not, they know it not; her influence is all the
better and stronger that neither of them knows it: she begins to lose it directly
she goes about to use it" (*Shakespeare*, 2:379). Such a figure's power, which is
precisely not that of Acting Angelhood, "lies not in which she values herself
upon, and voluntarily brings forward, and makes use of, but in something far
deeper and diviner than all this, which she knows not of and cannot help"
(2:379). Deliberate exercise of power—even the "selfless," indirect power of
influence—brings with it a fall from the grace of right-minded Shakespearean
women, whose "good actions seem not done to be seen, but in the belief that
they are not seen; and therefore we feel assured that they are equally good when
out of sight" (Hudson, "Female Characters," 204).

If the characterless Shakespearean heroine is no Acting Angel, even less is
she an actress. Perhaps Shakespeare "hit the true perfection of the female character," Hazlitt had already suggested in 1817, because he did not have to worry
about actresses playing his roles (2–3). "Women in those days were not allowed
to play the parts of women," and this "state of manners itself," which prevented
historical women "from exhibiting themselves in public, and confined them to
the relations and charities of domestic life," allowed their fictional counterparts
to avoid "theatrical display." Thus, the "tender and artless" women of Shakespeare "are certainly very unlike stage-heroines; the reverse of tragedy queens"
(3). "Always feeling, and thinking, and speaking *as women*," writes Hudson,
Shakespeare's heroines are "moved by the real interests of life, *not as authors or
actors,* moved by playhouse vanities; their heroism springs up of its own free will
and accord, and because they cannot help it" ("Female Characters," 204; emphasis added.) The conjunction of *author* and *actor* is revealing: quarantined from
professional women, whether writers or actresses, the heroines are equally protected from deliberate agency.

If feminine heroism must be heroism whose representative "cannot help"
it, then the way to link Shakespearean womanhood to historical women is to

render historical women's performances involuntary. This, at any rate, seems to be the strategy pursued by George Gilfillan in praising Felicia Hemans: "You are saved the ludicrous image of a double-dyed Blue, in papers and morning wrapper, sweating at some stupendous treatise or tragedy. . . . the authoress appears only the lady in *flower*" (234–35). Hemans sweats not; neither does she roll her hair. She is like Shakespearean heroines, the graces of whose "minds and persons always come from them involuntarily and unconsciously, like the expiration of their breath" (Hudson, "Female Characters," 203). Indeed, her greatest achievement is to merit comparison with Shakespeare's fictional women—those nonexistent authors who would, of course, have been the finest women writers of all: "All the woman in her shines. . . . The finest compliment we can pay her—perhaps the finest compliment that is possible to pay to woman, as a moral being—is to compare her to 'one of Shakspeare's women,' and to say, had Imogen, or Isabella, or Cornelia become an author, she had so written" (Gilfillan 231).

No author could compete with such figures; no actress can compete with Shakespeare's heroines. As Oscar Wilde suggests in *The Picture of Dorian Gray*, such faith in Shakespearean heroines was potentially deadly. Notorious for his challenge to nineteenth-century Shakespearean scholarship in the "Portrait of Mr. H," Wilde no less brilliantly evokes the power, paradoxes, and deadly bad faith of Shakespearean heroine worship in the *Picture of Dorian Gray*.

The heroine in question is, of course, the Shakespearean actress Sybil Vane. Love of Dorian has taught Sybil Vane that Juliet's speeches, "the words I had to speak were unreal, were not my words, were not what I wanted to say." As a result, she has faltered in her art. "I have grown sick of shadows," she tells Dorian (76). In thus echoing that quintessential Victorian heroine, the Lady of Shalott, she not only defends but dooms herself. For Dorian Gray does not want to hear Sybil Vane's "own words." "Ordinary women never appeal to one's imagination," he has already explained. "They are limited to their century. No glamour ever transfigures them. . . . But an actress! . . . Why didn't you tell me that the only thing worth loving is an actress?" (47).

As an incarnation of protean Shakespearean womanhood, Sybil Vane "is sacred!" (47):

> "*Tonight she is Imogen . . . and tomorrow night she will be Juliet.*"
> "*When is she Sybil Vane?*"
> "*Never.*"
> (49–50)   "*I congratulate you.*"
> "*How horrid you are! She is all the great heroines of the world in one. She is more than an individual. You laugh, but I tell you she has genius. . . . My God, . . . how I worship her!*"

As an "ordinary" woman, however, she is "nothing" to him (77). Where Dorian once revelled in her enactment of Shakespearean tragedy, he now dismisses her open despair at the loss of his love as "absurdly melodramatic" (78). She commits suicide; and when Dorian seems to be in danger of giving way to remorse, his mentor Lord Henry Wotton offers as consolation a reading whose assumptions parodically echo claims that Shakespeare's women are "more truly and vitally natural than most of the women of actual life" (Whipple 236). "To you at least she was always a dream, a phantom that flitted through Shakespeare's plays and left them lovelier for its presence, a reed through which Shakespeare's music sounded richer and more full of joy. The moment she touched actual life, she marred it, and it marred her, and so she passed away. Mourn for Ophelia, if you like. Put ashes on your head because Cordelia was strangled. . . . But don't waste tears on Sybil Vane. She was less real than they are" (91). What's Sybil Vane to him, or he to Sybil Vane? The heroines, and the heroines alone, are "real."

Thus, Sybil Vane's tragedy is silenced by, or subsumed into, those of "real" fictional women; and yet her rivals scarcely seem to have won any victory worth having. For at the end of such readings, even the Shakespearean heroines themselves may be enveloped by silence. Like her great model, for example, Hudson's Cordelia stands alone among her sex and vanishes: "An impersonation of the holiness of womanhood, herself alone is her own parallel. . . . We see her only in the relation of daughter, and hardly *see* her even there; yet we know what she is, or would be in every relation of life, just as well as if we had seen her in them all. . . . the vision sinks sweetly and quietly into the heart, and in its reality to our feelings, abides with us more as a remembrance than an imagination." "After all," Hudson continues, "I am not sure but it were better to have emphasized her character with the single remark of Schlegel: 'Of Cordelia's heavenly beauty of soul I do not dare to speak'" (*Shakespeare*, 2:379–80). Similarly, it "seems almost a profanation to praise" Desdemona. "There is a holiness in her mute resignation, which ought, perhaps, to be left where the Poet has left it, veiled from the eyes of save those whom a severe discipline of humanity may have qualified for duly respecting it" (2:488). Having accorded its feminine subject full transcendence, criticism runs out of things to say.

Womanly Character and
the Characteristics of Women:
Anna Jameson's Feminine Models

Even where fictional nineteenth-century womanhood was concerned, to be thoroughly venerated was, in many respects, to vanish. This is scarcely the whole story, however. For those very critics who came closest to evoking female

Shakespearean characters as interchangeable vessels failed to practice their own theories with any consistency. After all, there is something a bit disconcerting about praising the instinctive purity and selflessness of a group that includes Cleopatra and Lady Macbeth (Melchiori 121).[19] Moreover, when it came to actual readings of the plays, even on the most superficial levels, specific Shakespearean figures emerged as the foci of strong, highly personalized criticism. In practice, the same writers who praised Shakespeare as the prophet of generic Woman often responded as if to distinctly individual women. Coleridge himself betrays a fondness for specific characters, for example (*Lectures,* 553). Ruskin could dismiss Goneril, Regan, and Lady Macbeth as "frightful exceptions" (80–81), but when it came to describing Ophelia, he broke with his own theory of infallible womanhood. She was, he wrote, a "weak" woman who failed Hamlet "at the critical moment," and she did so because it was in her "nature" (80).[20] If the published essay examinations of Thom's female students are any indication, moreover, his teaching practices, too, may have been more complex than his theory: the examinations certainly suggest not only admiration but appropriation of the "language of power" (Ragland; *Shakespeare and Chaucer Examinations*).[21]

Canonization of fictional characters, like other canonization, thus remains an unpredictable process. As Isobel Armstrong remarks, "A release into language, imaginatively and intellectually, is something that the complexities" of Shakespearean texts "can achieve in a powerful way" (7). In a complex, mournfully funny story about recitations in church, contemporary African-American writer Maya Angelou drives that remark home and follows a lively nineteenth-century tradition in the process. As a child, Angelou reports, she was driven into silence by sexual abuse. Around the time she was beginning to speak again, she decided to deliver Portia's "quality of mercy" speech before her congregation one Sunday. Over the protests of adults who wanted her to honor an African-American writer instead, she succeeded in doing so. She knew, she explains, that the part had been written for her. She had taken it, and no one was ever going to take it away.[22]

In this sense of possession, as well as in her fondness for Portia, Angelou echoes the most successful female Shakespearean critic of the nineteenth century, who, in turn, echoes Coleridge. When Coleridge "heard it said that Shakespeare wrote for men but the gentler Fletcher for women," reports one listener at his lectures, "it gave him great pain and when he remembered how much our characters were formed from reading pourtrayed, he could not deem it a slight subject to [be] passed over as if it were a mere amusement like a game at Chess. Coleridge could never tame down his mind to think Poetry a Sport." Coleridge's "great pain" at Shakespeare's denigration as a writer for women springs not merely from reverence toward the Bard but from an explicit sense that if "our characters [are] formed from reading," then criticism fails in its moral duties if it discourages women from studying Shakespeare's "mode of displaying female characters" (*Collected Works*, 1:313). To use his own metaphor: if poetry is not a sport, then women may not be safely excluded from the playing fields of Shakespearean studies.

Anna Jameson agreed, and largely as a result, she became both the most influential woman writer of nineteenth-century Shakespearean criticism and one of the most influential nineteenth-century critics of Shakespearean characters.[23] The nature of this achievement is suggested not only by Jameson's childhood memories of having fed a "great taste" for "forbidden books" by slipping Shakespeare off "the forbidden shelf" (*Commonplace Book* 137–38), but also by the fact that in 1855, more than twenty years after *Characteristics of Women* had won her international renown as a Shakespearean critic, she could still write, "There exists a Shakespeare Society at this present time, but I do not know that any ladies are members of it, or allowed to be so" (305).[24] By the century's end, women played significant roles in organized Shakespeare study groups, and they did so in ways that rendered their debts to Jameson unmistakable.

Characteristics was central to Jameson's lifelong investigations of the iconography of sacred womanhood.[25] The book's emphasis on sanctity was no doubt central to its success: although a woman who practiced literary criticism per se might be suspected of overweening intellectual ambition, one who wrote about Shakespeare's heroines could easily be understood as engaging in both an act of reverence and a feminine duty. Once a culture has argued that studying fictional heroines builds character, after all, it has authorized women to undertake a form of literary criticism. What better way to train oneself to emulate ideal, fictional womanhood than to study Shakespeare? In *Characteristics*, Jameson attempts— and at points attains—powerful accommodations between the poles of heroine worship and historical readings, between elevating the generic character of woman and investigating the specific "characteristics of women." The delicacy of such a balance is suggested by her very title. First published as *Characteristics of Women, Moral, Poetical, and Historical,* the volume was frequently reprinted, and perhaps most often cited, as *Shakspeare's Heroines*. And frequently cited it was: for *Characteristics/Shakspeare's Heroines* could serve both to authorize and to undercut the sanctity of vanishing Marian womanhood. Perhaps no other critic's works would ever achieve the same peculiar, precarious balance, though many would try.

The explicit, revealing aim of *Characteristics* is to "illustrate the various modifications of which the female character is susceptible, with their causes and results" (4–5). As this description suggests, Jameson asserts the existence of an essential, innate feminine character. Indeed, much as Coleridge had tried to recuperate Pope's dictum on women's characterlessness, Jameson attempted to explain or rationalize Coleridge's. "When Coleridge said antithetically, 'that it was the beauty of a woman's character to be characterless,'" Jameson wrote, "I suppose it is as if he had said, 'It is the beauty of the diamond to be colorless;' for he instances Ophelia and Desdemona; and though they are colorless in their pure, transparent simplicity, they are as far as possible from characterless, for in the very quality of being colorless consists the character" (*Studies*, 37–38).

The "elementary principles" of such diamondlike feminine character are "modesty, grace, tenderness": "*Without* these a woman is no woman, but a thing which, luckily, wants a name yet; *with* these, though every other faculty were passive or deficient, she might still be herself. These are the inherent qualities with which God sent us into the world: they may be perverted by a bad education—they may be obscured by harsh and evil destinies—they may be overpowered by the development of some particular mental power, the predominance of some passion; but they are never wholly crushed out of the woman's soul, while it retains those faculties which render it responsible to its Creator" (*Characteristics*, 154). Femininity remains divine here, and its attributes are familiar. All the same, Jameson has turned conventional feminine canonicity on its head. Rather than representing an impossibly ethereal ideal, the elemental feminine character becomes an essential(ist) dower, a vulnerable but divine biological gift.

Years later, Jameson would give such discussions yet another twist by asserting her firm belief that "as the influences of religion are advanced, and as civilisation advances, those qualities which are now admired as essentially *feminine* will be considered as essentially *human*, such as gentleness, purity, the more unselfish and spiritual sense of duty, and the dominance of the affections over the passions." It is a mistake to believe that there are "essential masculine and feminine virtues and vices" (*Commonplace Book*, 85). At this point, however, the "inherent qualities" of femininity are women's; and as Jameson makes clear, *Characteristics* is preeminently directed at female readers.

Jameson's reading of Miranda in *The Tempest* suggests certain key implications of her insistence on femininity as a constellation of inherent rather than inimitable virtues. Miranda's character, she writes, "resolves itself into the very elements of womanhood. She is beautiful, modest, and tender, and she is these only; they comprise her whole being, external and internal. She is so perfectly unsophisticated, so delicately refined, that she is all but ethereal" (*Characteristics*, 170). If one feels oneself in the presence of a Marian monument to vanishing femininity, one is correct: "Let us imagine any other woman placed beside Miranda—even one of Shakspeare's own loveliest and sweetest creations—there is not one of them that could sustain the comparison for a moment; not one that would not appear somewhat coarse or artificial. . . . What, then, has Shakspeare done? . . . He has removed Miranda far from all comparison with her own sex; he has placed her between the demi-demon of earth and the delicate spirit of air. The next step is into the ideal and supernatural" (170–71).

In Jameson, however, Miranda never takes that next step. Instead of emptying Miranda's canonical figure out into transcendence, Jameson lays it open, revealing a "distinct and individual character" whose "peerless grace and purity of soul" are direct effects of her upbringing, her exposure to uniquely ideal "supernatural and poetical circumstances" (171–72). Miranda "has never caught from society one imitated or artificial grace." Her approximation to the "pure ideal" of womanhood may thus be "not only the credible, but the natural, the necessary" result of "such a situation." As such, it seems scarcely to be expected of anyone not raised on an enchanted island (172). Miranda stands as a Marian model, then, not because she was immaculately conceived but because she has been lucky: "Shakspeare then has shown us that these elemental feminine qualities, modesty, grace, tenderness, when expanded under genial influences, suffice to constitute a perfect and happy human creature;—such is Miranda. When thrown alone amid harsh and adverse destinies, and amid the trammels and corruptions of society, without energy to resist, or will to act, or strength to endure, the end must needs be desolation. Ophelia—poor Ophelia!" (154). On Prospero's island, elemental womanhood alone may suffice to render a woman—a "human"—"perfect and happy." In a world such as Ophelia's, it may leave her "far too soft, too good, too fair, to be cast among the briers of this working-day world" (154). If one is not to "fall and bleed upon the thorns" of everyday life, then, one would do well to supplement elemental womanhood with additional characteristics such as energy, will, or the strength to endure.[26]

As the above should indicate, Jameson's is hagiography of a very special order. For in *Characteristics,* as her mouthpiece Alda asserts, Shakespeare's "men and women" are "complete individuals, whose hearts and souls are laid open before us." "We can unfold the whole character before us, stripped of all pretensions of self-love, all disguises of manner" (13–14). "In this respect," responds Medon, another mouthpiece, "they may be compared to those exquisite anatomical preparations of wax, which those who could not without disgust and horror dissect a real specimen, may study, and learn the mysteries of our frame, and all the internal workings of the wondrous machine of life" (14).

Such figures are far from the "radiant shapes" invoked by critics such as De Quincey. If their characterization sounds cold blooded, it should: as Christy Desmet points out, despite Jameson's insistence upon empathy with Shakespeare's women, she positions herself, emphatically, as an objective critic (42–

46). Her heroines are models in an experimental as well as an ideal sense. She dissects and reconfigures them, sometimes computing the results in almost mathematical terms. Thus, for example, "Portia, Isabella, Beatrice, and Rosalind, may be classed together as characters of intellect." Intellect plus "poetical imagination" equals Portia; plus "religious principle," Isabella; plus "spirit," Beatrice; plus "sensibility," Rosalind (41).

Manipulated like an "exquisite anatomical preparation of wax," Miranda thus plays a crucial role in Jameson's constructions of feminine literary character: that of a control in the experimental transposition of the pure "elements of womanhood" from one environment to another. The implications of such experimentation become clearer when Jameson juxtaposes Miranda with yet another quintessentially feminine heroine, Desdemona. "As a character," Desdemona comes "nearest to Miranda." Where "all is pure poetic nature within Miranda and around her," however, "Desdemona is more associated with the palpable realities of every-day existence." Thus, although "no two beings can be more alike in [abstract] character," none could be "more distinct as individuals" (199).

"I know a Desdemona in real life," Jameson insists, "one in whom the absence of intellectual power is never felt as a deficiency, nor the absence of energy of will as impairing the dignity, nor the most imperturbable serenity, as a want of feeling: one in whom thoughts appear mere instincts . . . and virtue itself seems rather a necessary state of being than an imposed law." This is backhanded praise, indicative of a canonization that shifts critical standards for reality. Jameson tests—and proclaims—the possibility of Desdemona's virtue not against an abstract ideal, but against her own presumably expert knowledge of actual women.[27] The virtue of an actual woman thus validates that of a Desdemona, even as the vulnerability of a Desdemona leads one to contemplate her nineteenth-century counterpart with anxiety as well as admiration: "No shade of sin or vanity has yet stolen over that bright innocence. No discord within has marred the loveliness without—no strife of the factitious world without has disturbed the harmony within. The comprehension of evil appears for ever shut out, as if goodness had converted all things to itself." Jameson's "yet" is unsettling, as is her reminder that in the context of the play, Desdemona is a "victim consecrated from the first" (209). As such criticism proves the possible, historical existence of Marian virtue's "angelic refinement," it also suggests, however delicately, that an Angel in the House may be an accident waiting to happen.[28]

In their combination of transcendent and highly specific virtues, Miranda and Desdemona may stand for a number of Jameson heroines. Repeatedly and explicitly, for example, Jameson compares Cordelia, in *King Lear,* to the Madonna (234, 251) or to "a saint ready prepared for heaven" (245). Jameson even anticipates Hudson by ascribing to the beauty of Cordelia's character "an effect too sacred for words" and by quoting Schlegel's refusal to "venture to speak" of Cordelia's "heavenly beauty of soul" (233, 234). Speak she does, however, to ascribe to Cordelia not only kinship with Antigone but a character that is at once too complex to "resolve" purely into the "elements" of womanhood and too strongly marked to be determined by her social or personal relations (235, 247–51). Even "if Cordelia had never known her father," Jameson asserts, she "would not have been less Cordelia, less distinctly *herself*" (246). Cordelia's "internal power" and "wonderful depth of purpose" derive not from the needs of others, in Ellis's terms, but from her "peculiar and individual disposition" (235, 241). Feminine virtue, as represented by Jameson's Shakespearean characters, is both inevitably contingent and transcendently multiple.

Possessed of abstract, transcendent characteristics, the heroines are also deeply vulnerable both to human influence and to the weight of circumstance. One must consider not only their component elements ("modesty, grace, tenderness"; "energy, will, strength"), but the specific personal and historical framework that shapes such elements' workings in time. It is wrong to judge characters out of context, Jameson insists, but one must refrain as well from judging them entirely within context. Just as it would be foolish to expect Desdemona to behave like Miranda simply because both their characters reduce to the elements of womanhood, it would be senseless to expect either to behave as if she possessed the additional characteristics of Imogen or Portia.

Jameson's female Shakespearean characters are thus far from interchangeable. "The gentle Desdemona would never have dispatched her household cares in haste," Jameson writes, to listen to Hamlet's "philosophical speculations." "Such a woman as Portia would have studied him; Juliet would have pitied him; Rosalind would have turned him over with a smile to the melancholy Jaques; Beatrice would have laughed at him outright; Isabel would have reasoned with him; Miranda could but have wondered at him; but Ophelia loves him" (*Characteristics*, 161). After Jameson, such substitutions were to become a favorite critical game. "Can we imagine the play of *Hamlet* with Ophelia replaced by Portia? Would Othello's deed have been possible if Imogen had been the wife instead of Desdemona?" asks one writer. "I think not" (C. H. Gould 105). "Who could imagine Portia being so cowardly as to commit suicide?" asks another ("Our Prize Competition," 381). "Our great poet-teacher" has "given us 126" heroines, each "clearly drawn and thoroughly individual," insists Mary Cowden Clarke ("Shakespeare as the Girl's Friend," 355).

In *Characteristics*, Shakespeare's heroines emphatically include villainesses. Jameson's emphasis on both transcendent and historical qualities grounds an insistence upon respect and even sympathy even for Lady Macbeth, who might have been a good woman under other circumstances. "What would not the firmness, the self-command, the enthusiasm, the intellect, the ardent affections of this woman have performed, if properly directed?" Jameson asks of Shakespeare's murderess (386).[29] At the same time, consideration of the force of circumstance suggests the need for a long, hard look even at characters—Shakespearean and nineteenth-century—who have remained virtuous. For "the world contains many Lady Annes and Cressidas, polished and refined externally, whom chance and vanity keep right, whom chance and vanity lead wrong, just as it may happen" (19). Who knows whether one might not look into such a mirror of nature and recognize oneself? Shakespeare's wicked women do not leave us the "resource" of being able to "hug ourselves in our secure virtue," Jameson writes. "They frighten us into reflection—they make us believe and tremble" because "we cannot claim for ourselves an exemption from the same nature" (19, 18). "True it is," she writes, "that the ambitious women of these civilized times do not murder sleeping kings: but are there, therefore, no Lady Macbeths in the world? no women who, under the influence of a diseased or excited appetite for power or distinction, would sacrifice the happiness of a daughter, the fortunes of a husband, the principles of a son, and peril their own souls?" (369; see also Desmet 49–51).

By conceiving of Shakespearean characters as anatomical figures, Jameson alters not only their significance as feminine models but their capacity, metaphorically, to shape critical practices. Indeed, as her introduction to *Characteristics* makes clear, Jameson positions her readers as cultural surgeons in training. They are to begin by dissecting "exquisite anatomical preparations of wax," but if their training is successful, they may end by approaching "real specimens," even at the risk of "offence to others" and "pain to [them]selves" (14).[30]

Indeed, Jameson's concern with the effect of circumstances on character logically commits those who revere Shakespeare's heroines both to a form of literary criticism that is closely tied to social and historical analysis and to the support of women's demands for practical social reforms. Although *Characteristics* attempts a certain delicacy in its insistence upon the point, one of Jameson's central assumptions is that "the condition of women in society, as at present constituted, is false in itself, and injurious to them" (5). Granted, women's characters are not all that they might be. Individuals' emulation of transcendent feminine virtues will not solve the problem, however. Writing of *The Merchant of Venice,* for example, Jameson notes that "many women have possessed many of those qualities which render Portia so delightful. She is in herself a piece of reality, in whose possible existence we have no doubt: and yet a human being, in whom the moral, intellectual, and sentient faculties should be so exquisitely blended and proportioned to each other—and these again, in harmony with all outward aspects and influences—probably never existed; certainly could not now exist" (58). Shades of Coleridge: here, one might think, is the old "exquisite harmony." Yet Portia is significantly characterized as a "human being," not a woman. Moreover, history, rather than transcendence, is the ontological ground upon which she stands. Her claim to be a "piece of reality" rests upon those qualities that she shares with actual women. What history confirms as possibility, however, history precludes as actuality. For Portia's "divine self" requires not only external but internal harmony; and "a woman constituted like Portia, and placed in this age and in the actual state of society, would find society armed against her" (58). Indeed, "instead of being like Portia, a gracious, happy, beloved, and loving creature, [she] would be a victim, immolated in fire to that multitudinous Moloch termed Opinion. With her, the world without would be at war with the world within" (59).[31] The sacred heroine would be burned like a witch. Although earth can and does produce potential Portias, "Opinion" still ensures that "heaven" remains the only sanctuary for "such a mind" (59).

Thus, for Jameson as for the critics of characterless characters, Shakespeare's reality has suddenly become utopian. Instead of ascribing Portia's superiority to the impurities of actual women's spirits or the inadequacies of their mortal female flesh, however, *Characteristics* points elsewhere, to "that multitudinous Moloch termed Opinion." Just as the "characteristics" of Jameson's title pass from "moral" to "poetical" to "historical," so the question of Shakespeare's relation to sacred female character modulates from questions of generic womanliness to readings of multiple, contingent poetic womanliness, to interpretations of historical women's relation to both and thus to the Woman Question itself.

In this, as in so many other ways, *Characteristics of Women* is a suitable introduction to that strain of readings that blends with, parallels, and also challenges or rejects critical constructions of Shakespearean characters as representatives of generic ideal womanhood. Predominantly, although not consistently or entirely represented by female critics, and most widely represented during the final third of the century, this strain was significantly linked to the literal acting of Shakespeare's heroines onstage. Positioning themselves as neither angel/archaeologists of textual bodies nor heroically doomed emulators of the divinely ethereal "character of Woman," its proponents followed Jameson's lead by metaphorically transforming themselves into both the analysts and the heirs of Shakespearean womanhood—into intimate experimental investigators of the transcendent characteristics of women. Even while they asserted faith in the sanctity, heightened reality, and naturalness of at least certain Shakespearean female characters, such critics insisted upon characters' flaws, multiplicity, and historicity not as accidents but as determining, authenticating factors, as the sources both of their vitality and of their claims to stand for "real" womanhood altogether.[32]

"I Might Have Been Cleopatra": Characteristics of Heroines in History

In 1887, the English *Girl's Own Paper* announced a contest. Taking as inspiration Mary Cowden Clarke's essay "Shakespeare as the Girl's Friend," ("published in No. 388 of this magazine"), readers were asked to submit essays on "My Favorite Heroine from Shakespeare." Winners would receive cash prizes and membership in the "Girl's Own Order of Merit" ("Essay Writing"). As a later issue reported, the results were surprisingly good: competitors' papers showed "an amount of excellence far exceeding anything the examiners were prepared for" ("Our Prize," 380). Other surprises may have been in store as well, however. For though striking depictions of Ophelia's and Juliet's corpses illustrate the announcement of contest results, these heroines scarcely play a major role in contestants' choices. "Desdemona and Cordelia have, it is true, been chosen by a number of the girls," the article establishes. Then, as if mourning the unsuitability of its own illustrations, it continues, "but Ophelia, one of the most exquisitely drawn of all Shakespeare's creations, has had but little recognition, while Juliet is the favorite of some half dozen girls only" (381). Indeed, by the magazine's own count, "the heroines who successfully overcome their troubles have been just six times more popular than those whose ends are tragic" (381).[33]

The Girls' Own Heroine was later to become Maya Angelou's own heroine: Portia attracted more than one-third of the essayists' votes. She also attracted the admiration of several contestants who were scolded for having departed from the contest's point. Portia would have been "deeply . . . interested in the great subject of women's rights," insisted one. Another wrote, "My heroine would not support any of those fanciful opinions, advocated by some women of the present day—opinions which, if carried out, would result in our clever girls becoming second-rate men" instead of first-rate women (380–81). "Could anything be more inapropos than this?" the *Girl's Own Paper* asks (381). In fact, such readings actually accord with the contest's premises. In the critical tradition represented by Mary Cowden Clarke herself, Shakespearean heroines cannot help but be brought into their admirers' nineteenth-century lives: indeed, they serve as ideals precisely because they are proclaimed suitable for such appropriation.[34]

"In Shakspeare's page, as in a mental looking-glass," Clarke opens her "Shakspeare Study Series" in the *Ladies Companion* of 1849, "we women may

contemplate ourselves" ("Shakspeare-Studies," 25).[35] Like Dowden's characterization of the sexes as mirrors for one another, Clarke's metaphor irresistibly
recalls Virginia Woolf's claim that "women have served all these centuries as
looking glasses possessing the magic and delicious power of reflecting the figure
of man at twice its natural size" (*Room*, 35).[36] It also reminds one of the difference between the position of a Victorian woman and a Victorian man rever-
ently contemplating Shakespeare's heroines. The man is looking at an ideal; the
woman is looking at a mirror that may or may not reflect her back at something
close to her own size. "As, in the tall glass called a '*Psyche*,' a lady gains a full-
length view of herself," Clarke continues, so, "in Shakspeare's mirror, a woman
may obtain a psychological reflex of her nature that may aid her to its spotless
array. . . . She may learn how to preserve its intrinsic graces of purity and innocence, at the same time that she is instructed how to deck it with becoming
ornament of accomplishment and refining culture" (25). Enter the Acting
Angel: incapable of the "naturalness" embodied by fictional heroines, Clarke's
model reader studies Shakespeare to gain its "psychological reflex." As quickly
becomes apparent, however, Clarke counsels women to look into the psyches
of Shakespearean characters in more than one sense. If she seeks to "point out
how female character has been set forth by the immortal Poet," she also seeks,
no less, to "invite women to examine themselves . . . to lead them to imitation,
emulation, and a desire to compete in excellence with his most charming specimens of their kindred womanhood." These Shakespearean characters are not
inimitable revelations but "dear friends . . . by whose help and example we may
hope to model ourselves." In this evocation of intimacy, as in her presentation
of Shakespearean female characters as both types and individuals—as "all as
markedly contrasted as day and night; but . . . all in themselves and in their
action and circumstance true to the spirit of *womankind*" (25)—Clarke follows
Jameson. In so doing, Clarke enrolls herself within a vital tradition.

Repeatedly, late-century women critics cast Shakespearean heroines as
"creatures . . . whom we can take to our hearts, whose influence ministers to
us in a thousand ways, and for whom we feel a genuine friendship" (Elliott ii).
Such intimacy went hand in hand with historical specificity. In Nina Auerbach's
words, criticism that expands female Shakespearean figures' contexts beyond
the scope of the plays—whether by speculating about their pasts, delineating
their internal conflicts, or linking them to historical figures—accords them "a
larger life than their plays allow" (*Woman*, 211). It also allows them, paradoxically, a less fictional life, at least insofar as they are models of feminine virtue. Now read as possessed of complex and perhaps opaque internal lives,
Shakespearean characters become neither more nor less natural or unconscious
than the women who were cast as their models, critics, and—in the terms of

the time—"impersonators." In books, articles, and reports of study groups, nineteenth-century accounts of Shakespeare's heroines thus burst the confines of their plays and enter history. Sometimes heroines move into history proper as representations of specific figures from the past or as embodiments of the (time-bound) femininity of their own fictional worlds.[37] Sometimes they develop personal histories—complex or traumatic childhoods, say, or other psychological problems capable of explaining unclear motives.[38] Occasionally, such heroines challenge not only conventional readings of Shakespeare but even their own characterizations within the plays themselves.[39]

At points—as, most famously, with Clarke's *Girlhood of Shakespeare's Heroines*—critics in this vein openly shift from the realm of criticism to that of fantasy: they do not so much revise or edit canonical monuments as supplement them with accessible domestic icons. At other points, they may elaborate with abandon, all the while asserting the most objective of critical stances. In *Shakespeariana*, for example, E. S. Emery follows a sober call for historical relativism with a description of Lady Macbeth's "wealth of tawny yellow hair" (221). They may also offer carefully substantiated readings, based on thorough familiarity with unexpurgated editions. In another *Shakespeariana* article, Fanny Davenport addresses the importance of scenes generally left unacted and lines omitted from "doctored, altered, and revised editions" (276). Whatever their pretensions to serious Shakespearean criticism, however, such readings tend to share a crucial project: they enroll historical women, along with Shakespeare and female Shakespearean characters, in narratives of mutual sanctification or authentication. Shakespeare is glorious, the underlying argument goes, because his women characters embody transcendent qualities whose psychological as well as moral veracity is proven by history. Historical women are glorious because their own characteristics (at least potentially) correspond to those of Shakespearean heroines. To quote Dowden, "These ideal figures cannot fail to quicken our sensibility for what is beautiful in real life; there are hidden or marred ideals all around us in the actual men and women, in the commonplace lives of the street, the market, and the fireside. If we knew every motion of an Imogen or a Cordelia, it might be possible to detect the heart of one of these beating under a modern gown" (*Transcripts,* 339). If we knew other heroines so well, might we not also recognize a St. Theresa, foundress of nothing?

Far from being at a second remove from the transcendent femininity embodied in Shakespearean heroines, then, "the women of actual life" (to use Whipple's term) share in that femininity's power, which thus comes to be paradoxically located both within and beyond all boundaries, whether of the plays or of daily life. Such a shift in perspective was inextricably connected to consideration of Shakespeare in performance. Although abstract Shakespearean characters might be read as "always feeling, and thinking, and speaking as women, moved by the real interests of life, not as authors or actors" (Hudson, "Female Characters," 204), matters were different onstage. Here, even the most divine Shakespearean heroine could appear only in the body of a mortal actress—which is to say, of a woman not only known to calculate her every move but one who, at least to many Victorian minds, might be no better than she should be. Thus "impersonated," the Shakespearean character became, at least for the duration of the performance, something altogether more specific, more carnal, more mortal. She gained a "person" in the Victorian sense of a body; she entered history. Moreover, to the extent that actresses were successful in creating memorable interpretations, they impersonated Shakespearean characters in a more lasting sense as well, ensuring that audiences would strongly identify such characters with the professional players who had incarnated them.

Actresses who inspire such associations are critics. From early in the century, the dramatic interpretations of, say, Sarah Siddons or Harriet Smithson exercised a powerful influence upon analysis of Shakespeare's characters. Players such as Ellen Terry, Helena Faucit Martin, and Fanny Kemble, however, were able to go a step further: they not only offered public talks and readings on the subject of Shakespeare's female characters, but they entered into a rich, lively field of women's criticism by publishing successful works that analyzed the heroines they had "personated." By the 1880s, actresses' written contributions were both expected and eagerly anticipated ("The Drama: Modjeska"; Ziegler). Actresses read critics; critics watched and read actresses. It is no accident, for example, that Jameson dedicated *Characteristics* to Fanny Kemble or that the book's second edition notes that its author had "contemplated writing the Life of Mrs. Siddons, with a reference to her art" (viii).

The heroines celebrated by such readings are a far cry—literally and metaphorically—from the interchangeable beauties of Heath. Consider one of the most famous visual representations of these figures: John Singer Sargent's famous portrait of Ellen Terry as Lady Macbeth (fig. 6). Poised for one shimmering moment, Sargent's figure sways back and holds a heavy crown over her chainlike, serpentine braids, which catch the circlet's gold and draw it to the ground, over a dress of barbaric beauty. *Macbeth* contains no such scene. Whose "face" is this? Terry's? Lady Macbeth's? It is, as Auerbach says, "the apotheosis of Ellen Terry as she crowns herself with Shakespeare's character" (*Woman,* 207).

Sargent paints Lady Macbeth, Auerbach writes, "by isolating her from Macbeth, from Irving, from the stage, and even from Shakespeare" (*Ellen Terry,* 261). He does not, however, separate her from Ellen Terry. As a result, the portrait both echoes and condemns the aesthetics of "fancy pictures." For though this figure may bear no closer relation to the text of *Macbeth* than does

Fig. 6. Ellen Terry as Lady Macbeth. John Singer Sargent. Reproduced with permission of the Tate Gallery, London, Great Britain.

one of Heath's interchangeable beauties (charmingly posed with her attribute, the dagger), this particular Lady Macbeth could be confused with no other Shakespearean character. What is more, this actress, impersonating her, could be confused with no other player.[40]

Theatrical portraiture remained alive throughout the century. If Jameson's *Characteristics* is any indication, however, Sargent's Lady Macbeth may symbolize a process whereby the faces of actual women increasingly emerged within the "faces" of Shakespeare's heroines. At first illustrated by Jameson's own drawings, *Characteristics* went through a number of editions accompanied by more or less generic heroines' portraits. In 1897, however, G. Bell and Son's "modernized" edition replaced "earlier steel engravings with photographs (or occasionally with photographs of paintings) based on actual productions" (Melchiori 121–22).

At some points, such blending seems to have endowed models with the glory of canonicity (Auerbach, *Ellen Terry*, 222); at others, it rendered the heroines fully historical. Charles E. L. Wingate's 1895 *Shakespeare's Heroines on the Stage,* for example, may mark one of the nineteenth-century limits of attempts to historicize the canonicity of Shakespearean heroines. Here, Shakespeare's heroines are actresses. Seen from the outside only, such figures are neither transcendent nor textual entities. Their photographed faces, which appear as fully historical and fully corporeal, may be the faces of Shakespeare's heroines. If so, however, it is only in a secular sense. Where the canonicity of Shakespeare's characterless heroines disappeared into unified transcendence, that of his historical heroines may thus disappear into specificity. These may be great actresses, but they are no saints.

In what Auerbach has identified as a key moment in Virginia Woolf's *Between the Acts,* (*Ellen Terry,* 247), Mrs. Swithins, who has been watching Miss LaTrobe's pageant, attempts to explain what the performance has meant to her. "You've given me . . ." she begins. "Ever since I was a child I've felt . . . [. . .] This daily round; this going up and down stairs; this saying 'What am I going for? My specs? I have 'em on my nose.' . . . [. . .] What a small part I've had to play! But you've made me feel I could have played . . . Cleopatra!'" "I might have been—Cleopatra," Miss LaTrobe repeats. Then she thinks, "'You've stirred in me my unacted part,' she meant." This praise, which heralds Miss LaTrobe's "moment . . . her glory" (Woolf, *Between the Acts,* 152–53), might well have been a female Victorian reader's tribute to Jameson—or to Lamb, Clarke, Elliott, Kemble, Martin, Terry, or even Dowden—not to mention other, less-known writers who contributed to the tradition of reading the glories of Shakespeare's heroines as those of specific, historically contingent women.

Such writing may seek not only to enlarge the moral, poetic, and historical range of abstract, ideal womanhood but to effect a radical subversion of feminine canonicity. Female critics and actresses may get "into the skin" of models of sacred Womanhood somewhat as if they were entering a Trojan horse. At its most effective, such a strategy is akin to what Carol Neely terms "compensatory criticism" (242–43). Smoothly conventional at first glance, upon closer look heroines who have been thus possessed are potentially inflammatory. Portia becomes a suffragette; Lady Macbeth, a middle-class woman who pushes her husband to ruthless business practices. In their claims to transcendent but deeply individual characters, such figures prepare the way for claims that heroines may possess the kind of distinctive individual genius that Romanticism accorded to men. They ground attempts to establish a (far from unproblematic) process of equal opportunity canonical monumentalization. While not breaking entirely with generic womanly virtue, they may seem to retain merely a few shreds of feminine glory, suitable primarily as decorative features.

Thus, as Auerbach puts it, a "literary character embraces and fuels the self-glorification" of the historical woman who portrays her (*Woman,* 209). At their most ecstatic, as in passages from Martin, accounts of historical women's relationships to female Shakespearean characters evoke a merging whereby actresses become not only the vessels through whom Shakespeare speaks,[41] but beings capable of momentarily entering and "possessing" the figures of Shakespearean heroines. "My heroines—they were mine, a part of me," writes the actress Martin (51). "I have had the great advantage of throwing my own nature into theirs, of being moved by their emotions: I have, as it were, thought their thoughts and spoken their words straight from my own living heart and mind" (viii). Far from emulating the ideal "nature" of fictional characters through any "system of self-sacrifice," women in Martin find it "a glory to throw the best part of their natures into these ideal types" (4).

As *New Shakspere Society* member Grace Latham underscored, critics could and must share in such glory. To understand a Shakespearean character, she writes, "we must sink as far as possible our own individuality in it, make its joys and sorrows our own, see with its eyes, and (to use a French theatrical expression), so get into its skin" (402; see Ziegler 94–96). Here, as so often, *Characteristics* had taken the lead: Jameson praises Shakespeare's heroines as not only "what we could wish to be, or ought to be," "but what we persuade ourselves we might be, or would be, under a different and a happier state of things, and perhaps some time or other *may* be" (19).

Though a number of Victorian actresses and female critics, from Jameson on, identified their ability to "throw" themselves into Shakespeare's female characters as liberatory, there is probably no more vivid evocation of such a

process than the following notes from a flyleaf of Ellen Terry's reading copy of
Romeo and Juliet:

> *You must have a sensitive ear, and a sensitive judgment of the effect on your
> audience. But all the time you must be trying to please yourself.*
>
> *Get yourself into tune. Then you can let fly your imagination, and the
> words will seem to be supplied by yourself. Shakespeare supplied by oneself!
> Oh! . . .*
> (Terry
>
> *To act, you must make the thing written your own. You must steal the*   15)
> *words, steal the thought, and convey the stolen treasure to others with great art.*

"Shakespeare supplied by oneself"—the phrase sums up both the dangers and
the delights of many Victorian women's canonizations of Shakespeare's heroines. In many Victorians' eyes, Terry was Ophelia; having "thrown" herself into
the role, she was in many senses trapped by it (Auerbach, *Ellen Terry*, 237).
Martin, too, discusses childhood identifications with Shakespeare's brutalized
tragic heroines in terms of a terrified fascination with suffering and suffocation
(50–51, 93). One might read such identification as a form of subjection intimately related to what Judith Fetterley terms "immasculation" (xiii–xxvi), and
in many respects one might be right.[42] Actress and writer Kemble, for example,
claims the honor not only of having had *Characteristics* dedicated to her but of
having written the following poem:

To Shakespeare

> *Shelter and succour such as common men*
> *Afford the weaker partners of their fate,*
> *Have I derived from thee—from thee, most great*
> *And powerful genius! whose sublime control*
> *Still from thy grave governs each human soul,*
> *That reads the wondrous record of thy pen.*
> *From sordid sorrow thou hast set me free,*
> *And turned from want's grim ways my tottering feet,*
> *And to sad empty hours, given royally,*
> *A labour, than all leisure far more sweet.*
> *The daily bread, for which we humbly pray,*
> *Thou gavest me as if I were a child,*
> *And still with converse noble, wise, and mild,*
> *Charmed with despair my sinking soul away;*
> *Shall I not bless the need, to which was given*
> *Of all the angels in the host of heaven,*

Thee, for my guardian, spirit strong and bland!
Lord of the speech of my dear native land!

Disturbingly reversing and expanding the tripartite Comtean divinity of sister, mother, wife, Kemble thus invokes a Bard who is at once husband, father, puppetmaster, guardian angel, national "lord," and God. The poem's representation of heartfelt gratitude deserves attention. If the speaker's position as daughter and Bride of the Bard—and her submission to the exercise of "sublime control" from beyond the grave—sound a bit sinister, however, perhaps they should. For one might do more than possess a heroine; one might be possessed by her as well. As Elaine Showalter's painful account of "Ophelias" in Victorian madhouses reminds us, the relations whereby fictional and historical or experienced characters constitute one another may be endlessly circular ("Representing Ophelia," 85–87).

By raising crucial, vexed issues concerning historical women's identification with fictional characters—including and especially characters created by male authors—texts such as those quoted above also suggest the problems involved with the very project of historicizing ideal womanhood. Through their construction of "real" femininity as an innate characteristic of historical women rather than an inimitable state, Jameson and others expand the possibilities for representing feminine virtue, and thus feminine literary canonicity. They may even express awareness of how they themselves, as readers, writers, and players, create and appropriate heroines to specific ends (*Characteristics,* viii; Neely 249). Like actresses, they may thus "possess" their subjects—using Helena in *All's Well That Ends Well,* for example, to enroll "moral courage, perseverance, and steadfast faith in the power of self-help" among women's ideal characteristics. They do not, however, fully shift the rules of the game. Helena's assimilation to a conventional model of "womanly self-abnegation and self-diffidence," for example, comes at the cost of omitting reference to the bed-trick (Clarke, "Shakespeare as the Girl's Friend," 365). Such canonization thus sacrifices both the means of Helena's triumph within the play and the source of much of her fascination for critics (Wolfson 31–33).

Often revising and editing with abandon, critics in this vein may historicize and multiply the terms of feminine transcendence, but they still glorify fictional characters' roles as standards of ideal female character(istics). What is more, they underscore assumptions that criticism's essential function with respect to female characters is the elucidation and elaboration of those standards. Witness, for example, Edith M. Thomas's 1900 characterization of one woman poet: "Elizabeth Barrett Browning is a 'daughter of Shakespeare' in the sense that she is own sister, in the spirit, to all those exquisite creations we think of in the naming of 'Shakespeare's heroines'; or rather say she is herself identical with the dearest of those oft-doubted types of quintessential womanhood: Portia for the subtlety and adroitness of her reasoning; Rosalind for nimblest wit on the lips of woman; Juliet for the all-adorning idolatry of love; Imogen for most constant tenderness; and an Isabella for worship!" (516). Like Gilfillan's praise of Hemans, Thomas's praise still deploys the heroines' canonization to create of Barrett Browning an idealized monument. Granted, this is a personalized monument whose glories are more than reflected. Where Hemans rated only comparison to the heroines, Barrett Browning is intimately established as their "own sister, in the spirit." Moreover, where Hemans is made to shine with the generic glory of woman, Barrett Browning embodies her own glory—composed, of course, of the sacred characteristics of Shakespearean women. Nonetheless, "quintessential womanhood" remains the ultimate value: E. B. B.'s glory is still that of "exhibiting womankind in women" (Whipple 236).

Thus, the poet's worth is proved by her relation to quintessential womanhood, a relation that must always be problematic. Even in Jameson, no woman is guaranteed retention of those inherent feminine qualities without which "a woman is no woman, but a thing which, luckily, wants a name yet" (*Characteristics*, 154). The specter of the unnatural woman is never laid; virtuous historical women are still located within a "real" femininity whose "ontological locale" remains "fundamentally uninhabitable" (Judith Butler 146).

Indeed, the attempt to integrate revealed femininity into everyday life may even bring with it an altered, intensified pressure for historical women to perform (or be glorified as performing) such femininity. In Jameson's terms, one cannot simply cede real womanhood to fictional characters and leave it at that. Paradoxically, then, attempts to historicize the character of ideal femininity may actually expand the cultural authority of such femininity by dissembling its phantasmatic basis. In fact, criticism such as Jameson's may play a central role in shaping nineteenth-century female critics' frequent preoccupation with celebrating their subjects as embodiments of ideal femininity and thus attempting to assimilate them to ultimately inhuman virtues.

Thus, just as historicizing canonization of Shakespearean heroines served as a site both for female critics' ambitious forays into literary and cultural criticism and for powerful attempts to expand and demystify ideal feminine "characteristics," such canonization also created its own sort of vanishing monuments. Not surprisingly, late-century and turn-of-the-century writing offers a wide range of irreverence toward Shakespeare's heroines, often combined with suggestions that their "natural" or "eternal" femininity was no such thing.[43]

In 1910, Ford Madox Hueffer (later Ford Madox Ford) offered a rueful masculine contribution to such reassessments of nineteenth-century feminine canonization: "The woman that we know is fused at last into the Woman of the Novelists. This invariably happens, for we woo a Portia who has neither a past nor a future, and life welds for us this Portia into an ordinary woman. This combination of the Woman of the Novelists who is always in one note with a creature of much the same patiences, impatiences, buoyant moments, reactions, morning headaches, and amiabilities, as our own—this hybrid of a conventional deity and a quite real human being is a very queer beast indeed. We wonder if you ever quite realise what you are to the man on your hearthstone?" (163). Hueffer continues by imagining a specific male believer in historicized ideal womanhood: "His own wife was *Diana of the Crossways*. She still, if she would only be serious for a minute—is Diana of the Crossways. Mrs. Hunter, however, is only Mrs. Hunter. . . . He does not know that Mrs. Hunter was once St. Catherine—is still St. Catherine" (166). In time, Hueffer asserts, the man in question is bound to notice that his wife is behaving irrationally (as we all do). He will take her to task; and if, instead of accepting responsibility, she excuses herself by claiming kinship to sacred heroines, he is bound to tell her to "give up talking and try to be the womanly woman" (167). "And by the womanly woman he means the Woman of the Novelists. And if you achieved this impossibility, if you became this quite impossible you, she, he would still squash you with the unanswerable question: 'What does St. Catherine, what on earth does St. Catherine of Siena, want with the vote?'" (167). "You see," Hueffer instructs his female readers, "this terrible creation, the Woman of the novelists, has you both ways. Man has set her up to do her honour, and you, how foolishly and how easily you have fallen in the trap!" For "you, women, too, have aided and abetted in the setting up of this empty convention" (167). Even within the framework of Hueffer's fiction, one cannot help wondering about the unnamed husband's—and Mr. Hunter's—responsibility in all this. Still, there is more than a grain of truth here. Pastiche is pastiche, no matter who mixes it.

As the following chapters illustrate, a number of nineteenth-century female critics and supporters turned canonical revision and editing to the radical project of creating figures in whom the glories of "true poet" and "true woman" might be combined, with results similar to those sketched above. In the twentieth century, particularly early in the second wave of feminist criticism, another project has supplemented, if not fully supplanted, such attempts at creating a revolutionary or at the very least subversive secular sainthood: that of uniting the "true poet" with the "true feminist." Like their nineteenth-century precursors, the resulting idealized figures offer themselves as more than simple forms for silence: they deploy long-standing systems of reverence to specific political ends, one of which is often the authorization of intellectual work by women. In so doing, they seek to perform valuable cultural work. Indeed, students of recent feminist thought could do worse than to consider how supporters of the women's liberation movement have molded our own papier-mâché monuments. Like other such figures, however, feminist heroines go out of date. And thus, it may be time to expand feminist literary recovery work yet once more—to extend it, that is, to the fragmented, intransigent texts of those writers whom we ourselves have subjected to the monumental glories of "true" feminist womanhood. It may not be too late to unmake a few "saints"—and, in the process, to help ensure that certain of our generation's poets are not lost.

IV

Canonization through
Dispossession: *Elizabeth Barrett
Browning and the "Pythian Shriek"*

"How do I love thee? Let me count the ways." Surely no line of Victorian poetry is quoted so frequently, or in such dichotomous contexts, as the opening of Poem 43 in Elizabeth Barrett Browning's *Sonnets from the Portuguese*.[1] Under most circumstances, the line raises a smile. "How do I love this job?" snarls a puffy Boynton cartoon cat, printed on reminder notes; "Let us count the ways," reads a slogan for Arby's fast food. Occasionally, the parody is more pointed. In a *New Yorker* cartoon, for example, an exhausted, beringletted Miss Barrett accepts an abacus—and a reminder to carry the fives—from a bearded Browning. In certain cases, however—in wedding ceremonies, for example, and in Valentine's Day readings—"How do I love thee . . . " evokes a reverent, if edgy, hush. Moved, perhaps in spite of themselves, audiences participate in the ritual invocation of Barrett Browning's verse as a pure and absolute expression of romantic love. Sentimental the *Sonnets* may be, popular culture acknowledges, but they are also sacred.

Are the *Sonnets* sacred as literature, however, or as something else? Moreover, what does their dual canonization as standing jokes and ritual readings have to do with the canonization of Barrett Browning or of her other works? The two questions are interconnected: although the *Sonnets* have long defined E. B. B.'s fame, they themselves have not been defined as suitable objects for critical attention. Most of us think we know the *Sonnets,* but how many of us, even students and teachers of English literature, have actually studied them? Like their author, they have come close to being simultaneously canonized and lost.[2]

For a sense of the shape of this paradox, one need only turn to a self-described "living monument in the field of American Letters": Houghton Mifflin's 1974 Cambridge edition of Barrett Browning's *Poetical Works*, which has served many students in the United States as an affordable standard resource. The dustjacket of this volume promises to "meet all the needs of the general reader and student." Its introductory essay, by Ruth M. Adams, clearly numbers canonical revision and editing among those needs: "Who reads Elizabeth Barrett Browning? More people, but not a vast number. Historians . . . will read selectively in *Casa Guidi Windows* and *Poems before Congress. Aurora Leigh* has been rediscovered by those who appreciate its vignettes of society, high and low, its concentration on women, their aspirations to independence and self-sufficiency, and its rejection of mid-Victorian taboos on subject matter. But the audience that is most assured and most numerous consists of those in love or in love with love, who find the *Sonnets from the Portuguese* a full and satisfying expression of their emotions. Certainly some of these sonnets are destined for a modest immortality, but immortality nonetheless" (xiii).

True to the dustjacket's promises, Adams thus "identifies the [relatively few] poems of Mrs. Browning that have proved of lasting value or interest," assigning to each an authorized audience.[3] With *Casa Guidi Windows, Poems before Congress,* and a few other verses relegated to the historians, lovers of literature are left only *Aurora Leigh* and the *Sonnets*—that is, insofar as they seek only a first reading. For after that, "it is not to *Aurora Leigh,* effective as parts may be, that the reader will return. It is too discursive, too tedious, too platitudinous in most of its sentiments, too much on the level of melodrama in its basic narrative to command respect or liking" (xxii). Thus, this standard edition of Barrett Browning firmly admonishes against any temptation to reread *Aurora Leigh:* the "living monument" is inscribed with a keep-off sign. Only the *Sonnets* remain, to "give Elizabeth Barrett Browning her modest but secure place as a true lyric poet" (xxii).

The *Sonnets,* that is—and something else. Having reduced Barrett Browning's canonical claims to a single work, Adams proceeds to locate the cultural value of that work not only in its capacity to offer a "full and satisfying expression" of the "emotions" of "those in love or in love with love" but in its service as clear documentation for the poet's love story: "Directness of communication, plus the legend of her own life, assures that [Barrett Browning] will be read both for the pleasure the poems give and from curiosity about her own romantic love affair with Robert Browning" (Introduction, xiv). The *Sonnets'* glory is that of the legend.

Adams's introduction first appeared in 1974. By 1977, William S. Peterson was writing that "the chief obstacle to an intelligent understanding of Mrs. Browning's poetry is the mythological fog which envelops her life" (Introduction, vii). That cloying fog, which was thickest in the vicinity of the *Sonnets,* was already beginning to lift. In the slow-moving world of standard pedagogy, as represented by the Cambridge edition, however, it has yet to dissipate. Conservative at its first printing, the Adams introduction still stands—and with it a long-standing tradition that both limits E. B. B.'s claim to literary recognition to the *Sonnets* and sets up obstacles even to the *Sonnets'* critical study.

In such a context, Peterson's description of the *Sonnets* as a "dark, allusive work irradiated with occasional visionary glimpses" might come as a surprise (xvi). So, too, might the *Sonnets* themselves, however. Indeed, so natural has it become to value—and devalue—the Portuguese sonnets as a simple, transparent, and thus "full and satisfying expression" of the emotions of those who are "in love or in love with love," that it is worth pausing here to reconsider the sequence that Robert Browning termed his "strange, heavy crown" (*Robert Browning and Julia Wedgwood,* 99). For recognition of the *Sonnets'* strangeness, heaviness, and eccentric richness is an indispensable prerequisite for understanding their virtual loss as works of art.

To gain a sense of what is at stake, one need only focus on the first action in the sequence. To quote the sonnet in full:

> I thought once how Theocritus had sung
> Of the sweet years, the dear and wished-for years,
> Who each one in a gracious hand appears
> To bear a gift for mortals, old or young:
> And, as I mused it in his antique tongue,
> I saw, in gradual vision through my tears,
> The sweet, sad years, the melancholy years,
> Those of my own life, who by turns had flung
> A shadow across me. Straightway I was 'ware,
> So weeping, how a mystic Shape did move
> Behind me, and drew me backward by the hair;
> And a voice said in mastery, while I strove,—
> "Guess now who holds thee?"—"Death," I said.
>   But, there,
> The silver answer rang,— "not Death, but Love."

In a sense, this sonnet offers what Adams's introduction and conventional literary tradition promise: a moving evocation of the power of love and a verse record of the Brownings' courtship. The speaker here is no Everywoman, however. Not only does she believe herself to be near death, but she seeks consolation by quoting Theocritus in the "antique tongue." One has to revise and edit a great deal to render such a lover generic. Even then, if one expects the speaker to offer a "full and satisfactory expression" of one's own emotion, one may tend not only to read her peril of death as overblown but to flatten the poem's eroticism.[4] The image of Love drawing back the speaker's hair is one whose passionate precision arises from historical specificity. Love's mystic shape is of the speaker's time, not ours. His gesture not only refutes a genuine expectation of death but establishes an intimate claim whose erotic power is deeply, thoroughly Victorian.[5]

Victorian, that is, in the sense of arising from a specific moment in time—but not necessarily Victorian in the sense generally associated with the *Sonnets*. For if the *Sonnets'* speaker is too individual, too historically determined to sing the praises of generic love, her speech itself is surely too abstract, too inwardly focused, and too transgressive or ambivalent to suit readers in search of a representatively quaint historical romantic love affair. Here, too, the drawing back of the hair suggests how such expectations not only overlook the *Sonnets'* very sources of power but block their recognition. For though the *Sonnets* have become justifiably renowned for reversing the courtly tradition of love poetry by speaking romantic desire in a woman's voice, they radically rewrite another famous encounter as well: the courtship of Death and the Maiden.

Much as the lovely, doomed Maiden awaits her lover, only to be overwhelmed by the sinister gallantry of another guest, the *Sonnets'* faded, weeping speaker sits in apparent expectation of Death's "mystic Shape." When Love arrives in his place, the erotic, gothic struggle that ensues is both new and uncannily familiar. As the medieval maiden insists upon life, Barrett's speaker struggles for death. Love has made a mistake, she insists, or is offering one final test of faith. For God has laid the "curse" of "Nay" on her eyelids, like pennies on the eyes of a corpse (ii, 4–9). If God offers her a saving "baptism" through the sweetness of Love, he must be presenting it in a self-sacrificial "cup of dole" (vii, 7–8). Death's dew has anointed her forehead, the speaker implies: she is doomed and shriven, promised elsewhere (iii, 13). No (mere) earthly lover should attempt to intervene in the performance of such a promise. Brandishing that equivalent of a "sepulchral urn," her smoldering heart, she warns her would-be lover to back off, lest fire "scorch and shred" him (v, 2, 9–14). Her very breath, she assures him, is poison fit to shatter his "Venice-glass" (ix, 12).

Like her predecessor, the *Sonnets'* speaker ultimately accepts the substitution of suitors. In place of the heavenly reward she had believed promised by her own "ministering life-angel," whose eyes were fixed "upcast" to the "white throne of God" (xlii, 3–5), she accepts an earthly lover, "not unallied / To angels" (xlii, 6–7)—a lover who is a worker of lifegiving miracles as well as a poet: "budding, at thy sight, my pilgrim's staff / Gave out green leaves" (9–10). Now ranked among "God's gifts" (xxvi, 14), her lover proves that "Love, as strong as Death, retrieves as well" (xxvii, 14). The speaker's eventual submission to the "mastery" of this "new angel" is paradoxical, however (i, 12; xlii, 14): she has been crushed low as if by "sword," and yet her conqueror has lifted her up from "abasement" (xvi, 8–9, 13). Saved and vanquished at once, she abandons not the conventional modesty of maidenhood but the heroic discipline of divinely ordained asceticism:

> *my soul, instead*
> *Of dreams of death, resumes life's lower range.*
> *Then, love me, Love! look on me—breathe on me!*
> (xxiii, 11–14)   *As brighter ladies do not count it strange,*
> *For love, to give up acres and degree,*
> *I yield the grave for thy sake, and exchange*
> *My near sweet view of Heaven, for earth with thee.*

Perhaps one form of sainthood has been replaced by another. Once "a poor, tired, wandering singer . . . leaning up a cyprus tree," she had told her lover, "The chrism is on thine head,—on mine, the dew,— / And Death must dig the level where these agree" (iii, 11–14). Now, anointed by a kiss, "the chrism of love, which love's own crown, / With sanctifying sweetness, did precede" (xxxviii, 10–11), she no longer "sings" while weeping. She longs, toward the poem's close, to shoot "My soul's full meaning into future years, / That *they* should lend it utterance, and salute / Love that endures, from Life that disappears!" (xli, 12–14). The patient ascetic has become a noisy prophetess; the deathly ash of her "heavy heart" has been transformed into the fertile (if weedy) "heart's ground" from which the *Sonnets* themselves have been drawn (v, i; xliv, 5–14).

"Romantic" this may be—and expressive, no doubt, at least at points, of the emotions of those in love (or in love with love). One cannot help wondering, however, how often close reading may have thwarted readers' recourse to the *Sonnets* for "a full and satisfying expression" of their own emotions. To a reader such as Christina Rossetti, the *Sonnets'* ambivalence about restoration to life and to earthly love may well have been deeply resonant, for example, but what of other readers? As Dorothy Mermin points out, there is a long history of "embarrassment" over the *Sonnets* ("Female Poet," 351–52). Although such embarrassment no doubt has many origins, one may well be the text's capacity to transform would-be condescension into confusion. Expecting a Victorian valentine, one finds instead the "strange, heavy crown" of a difficult, ambitious, and deeply personal art—not to mention the passionate idiosyncrasies of a speaker whose angelic lover, in one version of the *Sonnets,* makes her feel "as safe as witches" (Barrett Browning, *Sonnets,* ed. Peterson, 25). If the *Sonnets* are embarrassing, it may be because the experience of reading them reveals the extent to which we, and not they, rely upon dreams of simple, innocently sentimental Victorian love. We must question our faith in that love—in that safe form of secular sanctity—if we are to come to terms with the *Sonnets'* strangeness and power.

Styles of Sanctity:
Barrett Browning's
Early Canonic Crises

Though Elizabeth Barrett Browning came closer to achieving full literary canonicity than any of Victorian England's other female poets, hers was always an unstable cultural presence. Decades of criticism agreed with the *Eclectic Review* that Barrett Browning's existence had done something "in a very emphatic way" to "settle the question" of the "intellectual relation of the sexes" ("Elizabeth Barrett Browning," 189). The question was, what? Metaphoric monuments to Barrett Browning's glory tended to teeter between extremes— between evocations of a Comtean honorary "Great Manhood" and of the "eternal," generic category of femininity, for example; or between emphasis on poetic wonder and feminine virtue. Although such instabilities were inherent in any attempt to canonize a woman poet, in Barrett Browning's case they were exacerbated both by the poet's own active role in shaping feminine canonicity and by the complex and at points paradoxical relations between her public and private personae.

Surely few women poets can have been more deeply and explicitly concerned with issues of feminine canonicity than Elizabeth Barrett Browning— or more challenging, during their lifetimes, as subjects for critical attempts at stabilizing the poet-heroine's role. E. B. B. worked actively to enter and shape that role; but first for biographical and then for political reasons, she rendered her position as a would-be poet-heroine an extraordinarily difficult one.

By fourteen, the "Poet Laureate of Hope End" had already composed an *autobiographia literaria,* "Glimpses into My Own Life and Literary Character." By twenty, she had written the "Fragment of an 'Essay on Woman,'" a work that not only rejected conventional praise for preceding generations of women poets but enrolled its author in a sacred feminine literary canon of her own naming (12). Indeed, although Deirdre David surely goes too far in implying that responsibility for the Barrett Browning legend lies primarily with the poet herself (98–99), E. B. B.'s career could be read as one long succession of attempts to accommodate—and to alter—the shape of feminine literary canonicity. Though only highlights can be sketched here, her career provides an indispensable context for understanding the canonization/decanonization process that started as soon as Barrett Browning died.

In her second signed volume of verse, the 1844 *Poems,* Elizabeth Barrett entered Victorian literary historiography as not only a strikingly ambitious and intellectual poet but an explicit candidate for feminine literary sanctity. It was an auspicious debut. Throughout much of the nineteenth century, long after her elopement had rendered its inclusion deeply ironic, editions of her complete works still opened with E.B.B.'s dedication of that volume to her father: "Somewhat more faint-hearted than I used to be, it is my fancy thus to seem to return to a visible personal dependence on you, as if indeed I were a child again; to conjure your beloved image between myself and the public, so as to be sure of one smile,—and to satisfy my heart while I sanctify my ambition, by associating with the great pursuit of my life its tenderest and holiest affection" (*Complete Works,* 2:142–43).[6]

Sanctifying literary ambition was already a central project for the poet, as the remainder of the volume reveals. In her preface, Barrett speaks as a poet-heroine whose domestic devotion converges with self-abnegating Christian devotion—and blends, almost imperceptibly, with the "patience angélique du génie." Aligning herself with holy visionary predecessors, she celebrates her own multifaceted suffering as the source of glorious "knowledge" and "song" (147–48). She also insists that she has been "hurried into speech" by "adoration" for divinity, driven to attempt a sacred subject that "fastened on" her "rather . . . than was chosen" (146, 143). "Life," she writes, is a "continual sacrament," and "poetry has been as serious a thing to me as life itself" (146, 148).

Such prose opens the way for "A Vision of Poets," a poetic work in which Barrett not only explicitly addresses "the necessary relations of genius to suffering and self-sacrifice" (147) but evokes an eerie architectural canon whose monuments simultaneously celebrate Romantic genius, Pythian inspiration, and the agonies of Christian sanctity (lines 220–50). Instructed by a female figure who comes "forth / To crown all poets to their worth," the masculine poet of the "Vision" imbibes first "starry water" that separates him from humanity, leaving him "holy and cold," and then the vile bitterness of "world's use," "world's love," and "world's cruelty" (lines 56–57, 140–41, 149, 158, 183). He awakens within a "great church" in which, "Pale and bound / With bay above the eyes profound," he finds a "strange company" of poet-saints (lines 221, 271–73): "Deathful their faces were, and yet / The power of life was in them set— / Never forgot nor to forget" (lines 274–76). "Glorified," their faces remain "still as a vision, yet exprest / Full as an action—look and geste / Of buried saint in risen rest" (lines 282–85).

Only one woman is named among the "poets true, / Who died for Beauty as martyrs do / For Truth—the ends being scarcely two" (lines 289–91). She is, of course, Sappho; and she is crowned not only with bay but "with that gloriole / Of ebon hair on calmèd brows—" (lines 318–19). To her as to no other poet, Barrett Browning's narrator speaks directly and in a tone of reassurance: "O poet-woman! none forgoes / The leap, attaining the repose" (lines 320–21).

Poetic, Christian, and perhaps Marian monuments, the figures in this cathedral of art stand

> *All, still as stone and yet intense;*
> *As if by spirit's vehemence*
> *That stone were carved and not by sense.*
>
> *But where the heart of each should beat,*
> *There seemed a wound instead of it,*   (lines 424–32)
> *From whence the blood dropped to their feet*
>
> *Drop after drop—dropped heavily*
> *As century follows century*
> *Into the deep eternity.*

Soon, however, they sing a harmony that makes them "burn in all their aureoles"—until (in another line that resonates with Browning's "Childe Roland"), "the blood which fell / Again, alone grew audible, / Tolling the silence as a bell" (lines 504, 508–10).

An angel breaks the silence. In his challenging question, the agonies of the female Pythia, the passion of saints, and the "angelic patience of genius" meet:

> *"If to speak nobly, comprehends*
> *To feel profoundly,—if the ends*
> *Of power and suffering, Nature blends,—*
>
> *"If poets on the tripod must*
> *Writhe like the Pythian to make just*
> *Their oracles and merit trust,—*
>
> *"If every vatic word that sweeps*
> *To change the world must pale their lips*
> *And leave their own souls in eclipse,—*
>   . . . . .
> *"If ONE who did redeem you back,*
> *By His own loss, from final wrack,*
> *Did consecrate by touch and track*
>
> *"Those temporal sorrows till the taste*
> *Of brackish waters of the waste*   (lines 523–58)
> *Is salt with tears He dropt too fast,—*

"If all the crowns of earth must wound
With prickings of the thorns He found,—
If saddest sighs swell sweetest sound,—

"What say ye unto this?—refuse
This baptism in salt water?—choose
Calm breasts, mute lips, and labour loose?

"Or, O ye gifted givers! ye
Who give your liberal hearts to me
To make the world this harmony,

"Are ye resigned that they be spent
To such world's help?"
                            The Spirits bent
Their awful brows and said "Content."

Content to writhe like the female Pythia and to drink in suffering and bitterness as if they were the tears of Christ, Barrett Browning's "strange company" accepts not only suffering but suffering in potentially feminine form.

Not incidentally, the strange company also implicitly accepts E. B. B., who stands metaphorically ready for any number of crowns of thorns. Such associations were not lost upon several of the volume's initial reviewers, in whose pages the poet appeared not only as a sacred model whose "pain-perfected" voice offers "Revelations," but as a "Margarita or Perpetua of the Christian mythology" (Wicksteed 445; Grant 322; "Poems of Elizabeth Barrett Barrett," 132).[7] E. B. B. was already beginning to succeed as a sacred poet-heroine of resignation and suffering.

Around a month after the 1844 volume appeared, however, Barrett received her first letter from Robert Browning. She responded; and by so doing, the woman who had publicly aired her "fancy . . . to seem to return to a visible personal dependence" on her father set into motion a series of events that would drive her to an act of filial disobedience of the first order (*Complete Works*, 2:142). Barrett had cast herself as seeking to embody the highest traditional values both of feminine submission and of poetic ambition, without openly redefining either in the process. The task would have been impossible to fulfill; her life made it impossible to undertake.

A woman who chooses to take a lover and marry can no longer draw upon the symbolic power of ascetic sanctity. With Barrett Browning's marriage, one kind of saint was lost, though another might be found. Dinah Mulock expressed a sense of both possibilities in her 1851 response to E. B. B.'s "later sonnets," the *Sonnets from the Portuguese:*

To Elizabeth Barrett Browning on Her Later Sonnets

I know not if the cycle of strange years
  Will ever bring thy human face to me,
Sister!—I say this, not as of thy peers,
  But like as those who their own grief can see
In the large mirror of another's tears.

Comforter! many a time thy soul's white feet
  Stole on the silent darkness where I lay
With voice of distant singing—solemn sweet—
  "Be of good cheer, I, too, have trod that way;"
And I rose up and walked in strength complete.

Oft, as amidst the furnace of fierce woe
  My own will lit I writhing stood, yet calm,
I saw thee moving near me, meek and slow,
  Speaking not, but still chanting the same psalm,
"God's love suffices when all world-loves go."

Year after year have I, in passion strong,
  Clung to thy garments when my soul was faint,—
Touching thee, all unseen amid the throng;
  But now, thou risest to joy's heaven—my saint!
And I look up—and cannot hear thy song,

—Or hearing, understand not; save as those
  Who from without list to the bridegroom-strains
They might have sung—but that the dull gates close,—
  And so they smile a blessing through their pains,
Then, turning, lie and sleep among the snows.

So, go thou in, saint—sister—comforter!
  Of this, thy house of joy, heaven keep the doors!
And sometimes through the music and the stir
  Set thy lamp shining from the upper floors,
That we without may say—"Bless God and her!"

Barrett Browning was to write that this poem had touched her "to the quick" (*Letters of Elizabeth Barrett Browning*, 2:68). One can imagine why. Its subject remains a saint, yet she is also a treacherous sister who has left those she once comforted to freeze outside the "dull gates" of her private heaven. The "music and the stir" of her "bridegroom-strains" create only songs in which they cannot share. The speaker's blessing may be genuine, but her pain seems no less so.

Nor were metaphoric sisters the only ones Barrett Browning left behind. Viewed from the distance of some 150 years, through the glorious haze of the Browning legend, E. B. B.'s elopement looks like high romance. From the poet's own perspective, and perhaps from the viewpoints of many of her contemporaries, it was nothing of the sort. A necessity it might have been; a suitable story for public narration it was not. Presumably, those who knew enough to be able to recount the circumstances of the Brownings' courtship in the 1850s and 1860s understood the depth of the familial trauma involved and refrained from adding to the Brownings'—and the Barretts'—pain through violations of confidentiality. In any case, articles published in the years leading up to and directly following Barrett Browning's death reveal that even the Americans, who were notoriously enthusiastic reporters or fabricators of biographical information (Altick, *Lives,* 133), tended to focus on the Brownings' happy marriage and not on their courtship. The general operating consensus seems to have been that the less said about the whole business, the better.

Legendary lore to the contrary, then, in the decade just after Barrett Browning's courtship, critics initially received the *Sonnets* with muted praise (see, for example, "Poetesses," *English Review,* 332).[8] Individual readers, including poets, may well have been susceptible to the *Sonnets'* "explosion of sealed sensation" than reviews indicated (Moers 165),[9] but the fact remains: reticence, not overwhelming enthusiasm, marked the *Sonnets'* initial public reception. Barrett Browning's canonization would now turn to the public persona, just as the writer herself turned to public poetry. Sonnets (and sainthood) aside, by the time she was suggested for Poet Laureate in 1850, Barrett Browning often emerged in periodical literature not only as a major poet but as a form of national heroine—as what the *English Review* celebrated as England's "Queen of Song" ("Poetesses—Mrs. Browning and Miss Lowe," 332).[10]

To the extent that her personal life played a major role in such midcentury idealizations, the focus was often on E. B. B.'s person—or rather, on her near lack of corporeal presence. In 1853, for example, American author George Stillman Hillard wrote, "I have never seen a human frame which seemed so nearly a transparent veil for a celestial and immortal spirit. She is a soul of fire enclosed in a shell of pearl" (1:178). Hillard's "soul of fire enclosed in a shell of pearl" was to attain an iconicity rivalled only by Mary Russell Mitford's earlier tribute to the young E. B. B.'s "sunbeam" smile (170).[11]

The power of such characterizations is poignantly suggested by a journal entry of Sophia Hawthorne, Nathaniel Hawthorne's wife. "I was afraid to stay long, or to have Mrs. Browning talk," she notes, "because she looked so pale, and seemed so much exhausted. . . . I do not understand how she can live long, or be at all restored while she does live. I ought rather to say that she lives so ardently that her delicate earthly vesture must soon be burnt up and destroyed by her soul of pure fire" (362). Dutifully revising her own impulsive human worry about Barrett Browning's health into a ritualized evocation of radiance, Hawthorne goes on to call E. B. B. "angelic" and a "seraph in her flaming worship of heart," asserting that "how [Barrett Browning] remains visible to us, with so little admixture of earth, is a mystery" (401–2).[12]

No sooner was E. B. B. rendered a model Englishwoman and a disembodied "soul of fire," however, than she began to publish works such as *Aurora Leigh, Casa Guidi Windows,* and *Poems before Congress,* and thus to induce a new canonic crisis. Drawing at points deliberately upon her status as a cultural model, Barrett Browning explicitly intensified the instabilities and subversive potential of her early conceptions of feminine sainthood.[13] In *Poems before Congress,* the last volume she prepared for publication, the powerful (and once notorious) antislavery poem "A Curse for a Nation" may stand as a kind of counterpole to the earlier "A Vision." Both invoke the imitation of Christ; but where the former focuses upon the crucifixion, the latter aligns itself with the Sermon on the Mount. "From the summits of love a curse is driven, / As lightning is from the tops of heaven," the speaker's Angel urges her (lines 15–16). Divine guidance, which had once led the male poet of "A Vision" out of the world and into a pure, canonical realm of passive saints anointed and immobilized by Christ's tears, now leads the female poet of "A Curse" in the opposite direction:

> "Therefore," the voice said, "shalt thou write
>   My curse to-night.
> Some women weep and curse, I say
> (And no one marvels), night and day.
>
> And thou shalt take their part to-night,
>   Weep and write.
> A curse from the depths of womanhood
> Is very salt, and bitter, and good."

(lines 41–48)

This is visionary poetic sainthood at its most subversive and autonomous, both on the level of sexual politics and on those of national and racial politics as well. It signals the grounds for a second canonic crisis. E. B. B.'s abolitionist speaker does more than direct her curse at the United States; at first she attempts to excuse herself from that duty by arguing that as an Englishwoman, she scarcely speaks from a position of strength in criticizing other countries as unjust: "My heart is sore / For my own land's sins" (lines 19–20).

When the "saint—sister—comforter" eloped, critics had honored her by extending their reticence to her work as well as her biography. When England's

Queen of Song created a divinely inspired speaker who criticized her own country and cursed its ally, criticism often had recourse to a vocabulary of demonic possession. Metaphorically attempting to exorcise the visceral, often bitter passion of *Poems before Congress* from the glorious figure of England's poetic queen, reviewers invoked a canonical counterheroine capable of momentarily possessing their ideal. W. E. Aytoun, for example, explains E. B. B.'s "poetic aberrations" by insisting that like a "Pythoness . . . under the influence of her Cacodaemon," Barrett Browning has been "seized with a . . . fit of insanity" (492). "Balak," not an angel, has inspired "A Curse for a Nation" (494). Even the poet's friend Henry F. Chorley (who misreads the subject of "A Curse") asserts that she has taken "to its extremity the right of the 'insane prophet' to lose his head, and to loose his tongue" ("Poems before Congress," 372). Indeed, as Barrett Browning reported with rueful pleasure, William Howitt actually published a *Spiritual Magazine* article insisting that ever since the publication of *Casa Guidi Windows,* the poet had been "biologised by infernal spirits" (*Letters of Elizabeth Barrett Browning,* 2:406–7).[14] Thus, the chanting of the priestess became what Edmund Gosse was to condemn as the "Pythian shriek,"—and, in the process, *Poems before Congress* was set well on its way to being marginalized as "uncharacteristic."[15]

Thus, by the time Barrett Browning died, her significance as a poet and a national, cultural, and political figure was deeply controversial. Her succeeding, highly charged canonization was as conflicted and uneven as any other. Working through an irregular process of accretion, it encompassed a range of watchwords and iconic anecdotes whose combinations could take unpredictable, even contradictory forms. As phrases that achieved iconicity in one decade sifted into the revisionary narratives of another, the poet-heroine's form in one year's schoolbooks radically diverged from her appearance in that same year's literary magazines, lecture halls, or private letters. Here as elsewhere in canonization history, then, periodization is a difficult and often misleading issue. Nonetheless, since shifts in the poet's reception tended to be connected to biographical revelations, that reception may be broken down into several clear, if rough stages. After E. B. B.'s death, she emerges first as a Promethean intellectual; then as a still-powerful "wife, mother, and poet"; then as a great lover whose glory may no longer depend upon her poetry; and finally as an Andromeda (or Peau d'Ane) in Wimpole Street, whose physical and mental frailty adds poignancy to her role as a heroine of nostalgically conceived romance (see Lootens). Each of these figures supplements or competes with rather than fully supersedes her predecessors. Each exercises her own powers; each requires her own silences.

The Poet as Boundary Goddess:
E. B. B. as Monitory Model

At first, reverence and perhaps even respect seemed to demand biographical reticence. Fearful of being rendered the "heroine of a biography," Barrett Browning herself had been prepared to balk readers' curiosity long before her marriage (Barrett Browning, *Mrs. E. B. Browning's Letters*, 124–25). That approach was reinforced not only by the poet's reluctance to discuss her elopement but by her widower's famous insistence upon privacy. It would be years before a full-scale biography appeared and even longer before public release of any significant collection of E. B. B.'s letters. Early on, when controls on biographical revelation were tightest, a number of narratives conceive of E. B. B. almost exclusively as a poet. Though often muted, they echo throughout the century. In such accounts, if the *Sonnets* are not "revised and edited" out, they are discreetly tucked away, often into dependant clauses, beside or behind the likes of *The Seraphim*.[16] Indeed, given later assumptions about the *Sonnets'* Victorian popularity, it is crucial to note how many articles recount Barrett Browning's entire career without so much as a reference to them.[17]

The Barrett Browning of such writing is preeminently the "author of *Aurora Leigh*": her literary achievement consists not primarily of lyrics or ballads but of epic, religious, and political verse. She is still England's Queen of Song. What is more, she is often the "ultimate" woman poet—sometimes in the sense of "most characteristic" or "greatest so far," but sometimes, too, in the sense of "final." In this latter role, she is not so much sacred as Promethean: she serves as a female canonical Terminus, a glittering boundary goddess who marks, in the words of an 1862 *Saturday Review* article, "the uniform limits of the female intellect" ("Last Poems," 473).

"If Destiny and Nature had intended that a great poem should be written by a woman," asserts the *Saturday Review*, "*Aurora Leigh* would perhaps have proved the creative equality of the sexes" ("Last Poems," 473). As it is, however, the same journal had already asserted, *Aurora Leigh* "furnishes . . . the most conclusive proof that no woman can hope to achieve what Mrs. Browning failed to accomplish" ("Mrs. Browning," 42). "Such a combination of the finest genius and the choicest results of cultivation and wide-ranging studies has never been seen before in any woman, nor is the world likely soon to see the same again," writes William Stigand in the *Edinburgh Review*, submitting E. B. B.'s "career" as "some proof of the impossibility that women can ever attain to the first rank in imaginative composition" (533). If a woman of such "singular genius and accomplishments, who devoted herself heart and soul to one of the loftiest of human pursuits" could not succeed at writing great poetry (532), why should any other woman try?

Thus, E. B. B. has tested and proved the limits of generic womanhood: the more unique her gifts and privileges, the more clearly must her ultimate failure serve as definitive proof of female poetic incapacity. At its most concrete, as in C. B. Conant's 1862 *North American Review* essay, such writing casts Barrett Browning as a woman in spite of herself, a charming overreacher whose "great success is in her failure" (344). E. B. B. attempted to hew out a monumental poetic work, Conant acknowledges; but she remained comparable to a "tender-handed woman" who dared to enter "her husband's shop and mimic his handicraft . . . until, weary of the uncongenial work, she threw down the implements, and stood in the grace of her sex,—lovelier for the pantomime" (345). Thus frozen, Conant's E. B. B. embodies the glories not of poetry but of the feminine—the feminine, that is, as perceived by the critic who looks through (and beyond) a female poet's works: "The fair sculptor 'builded better than she knew.' She has left a perfect statue of herself, a service to womanhood and to the world which cannot easily be over-estimated. Whatever inconsistencies belong to woman, and whatever are incidental to the conflicting position in which Mrs. Browning placed herself, between the impulses of her sex and the avocations of the other, are transparently exposed in her own creations" (341). Properly interpreted, E. B. B.'s futile attempt at "competition with men" hence becomes a "glorious [if inadvertent] success, as a higher illustration than was ever otherwise afforded of what a woman is, and of what she may do in her own exalted and luminous sphere" (345). A monument to True Womanhood glimmers behind Barrett Browning's verse, refuting the poet's own articulated feminism.[18]

At its least flattering, such criticism retains E. B. B.'s role as a marker of feminine poetic limitations without according her even the honor of the noble overreacher. Mortimer Collins, in the *Dublin University Magazine,* for example, equates poetic and sexual license in offering a "weighty lesson for literary ladies" (159). Barrett Browning is "one whom many will doubtless rank the greatest poetess the world has ever known," not only because "morally and intellectually, her life was complete" but because "she also found—how different from her predecessors—the right husband" (157). "She would never have reached so high a point if she had not married a great poet" (158). Barrett Browning's "achievements," he summarizes succinctly, are "her own"; her "faults" are "of her womanhood" (162; see also Conant 340). Indeed, even she could not escape the "strange destiny" whereby "women of genius" are "ever impelled to treat topics which men avoid; they must give us 'Jane Eyres,' 'Consuelos,' 'Aurora Leighs.' Perhaps after all, though we have some poetesses whom we should be loth to spare, the production of poetry is not precisely woman's mission. Perhaps, after all, the best poem she can offer us is a crowing child, with beautiful bright hair, pillowed upon her loving breast" (158). Compelled by a strange destiny, even so pure a woman as Barrett Browning is helpless to avoid "erotic speculations" and "grossness" (158, 159). How much more dangerous might poetry writing be to a woman whose life was not "morally and intellectually complete?"

"Wife, Mother, and Poet":
E. B. B. as Secular Trinity

Barrett Browning's supreme status, both as woman and as poet, could render her a female canonical Terminus: it could doom her to stand as a glittering monitory figure, hand outstretched toward a dead end at best and a gross erotic swamp at worst. It could also cast her as an inspiration or a prophetess, however. In the first decade after E. B. B.'s death, celebration and silence often merge in paradoxical canonization attempts. Even as admirers celebrate the poet's marriage, they leave her courtship and elopement unmentioned; even as they glorify her poetic fame, they downplay her verses' controversiality. Powerfully and illogically, such accounts often merge the poet's Promethean power with the holiness of domestic angels as well as of warrior-saints.

At points, such combination required extreme measures. James Russell Lowell, for example, was Professor of Belles Lettres at Harvard when he recorded his condemnation of "the physically intense school . . . of which Mrs. Browning's 'Aurora Leigh' is the worst example, whose muse is a *fast* young woman with the lavish ornament and somewhat overpowering perfume of the *demi-monde,* and which pushes expression to the last gasp of sensuous exhaustion. . . . An overmastering passion . . . must be fleshly, corporeal, must 'bite with small white teeth' and draw blood, to satisfy the craving of our modern inquisitors" (*My Study Windows,* 212). Like critics during E. B. B.'s lifetime, Lowell quarantines Barrett Browning, the pure poet-heroine, from the corruption represented by her own work. Metaphorically exorcising E. B. B. from possession by the vampire passions that inspired *Aurora Leigh,* Lowell later insists that he has been far from wishing to injure "the pure and fragrant memory" of Barrett Browning—even as he continues to condemn the "hectic flush" and "unpleasant *physical* excess" of *Aurora Leigh* in visceral terms: "It gives me the same kind of shock I felt once in a dissecting room" ("Hectic Flush," 344).

If testimony to Barrett Browning's power as an inspirational figure reaches its most paradoxical in Lowell, it reaches its most poignant in American novelist

Elizabeth Stuart Phelps's *Story of Avis*. Here, Barrett Browning's work is divine sustenance, while the poet herself is not only a "saint—sister—comforter" but a herald of the future. Early in the novel, young Avis, who has fled her domestic chores, climbs the highest tree in an orchard and opens *Aurora Leigh,* "that idyl of the June, that girls' gospel, which will be great as long as there are girls in the world to think it so." She experiences a revelation: "Full of the vague restlessness which possesses all healthy young creatures, and the more definite hungers natural to a girl of her temperament, Avis . . . was not without capability of relishing a certain quality of poison, not too fully flavored. . . . But it was silent as a convent in the apple-boughs; the growing day drew on a solemn veil of light; . . . and so the manna fell" (31).[19]

Like her mother before her, Avis is ultimately driven to sacrifice her art for her family. Nonetheless, she retains "her conviction that she might have painted better pictures—not worse—for loving Philip and the children; that this was what God meant for her" (447). This conviction has been inspired by her reading of *Aurora Leigh* and her knowledge of its author's biography (447). Generations of failed attempts must go into the making of a woman artist, Phelps insists. In the meantime, "In the budding of all young gifts, in the recognition of all high graces, in the kindling of all divine fires, we feel a generous glow. . . . When the passion of our lives has long since wasted into pathos, and hope has shrivelled to fit the cell of care, we lean with increasing ardor on the hearts of those in whom purpose and poetry were permitted to be as one" (57).

Leaning "with ardor on the heart" of Barrett Browning, a whole series of writers, mostly from the 1870s, read the poet's life and works as revelations of a feminine literary sanctity whose glories are both heroic and conventionally domestic. Taken individually, their accounts often pull in different directions; taken as a group, they attempt—and at points attain—a dazzling if ultimately untenable equilibrium between celebrating E. B. B.'s individual poetic genius and her embodiment of the generic glory of Woman.

No single work of this sort is more emphatic or more suggestive than the *Atlantic Monthly* obituary by Barrett Browning's friend and admirer Kate Field. To Field, E. B. B. was "Wife, mother, and poet, three in one, and such an earthly trinity as God had never before blessed the world with." Field's is an active, public, sacred heroine: her "life was one long, large-souled, large-hearted prayer for the triumph of Right, Justice, Liberty" ("Elizabeth Barrett Browning," 368). "Wrong was her enemy; against this she wrestled, in whatever part of the globe it was to be found" (371). Yet she is also saintly in a more private sense. Presenting Barrett Browning's personal life as a matter for public celebration, Field combines veneration for the poet's "great love" with admiration for her great verse (369). She justifies E. B. B. on all counts, explicitly answering criticism of "A Curse for a Nation" by citing an explanatory letter and implicitly defending the Brownings' elopement by asserting its miraculous effects, both personal and poetic. (It was "destiny" that brought Barrett and her future husband "face to face," Field insists—"a destiny with God in it" [369].) "Association with the Brownings . . . made one better in mind and soul," she writes. "It was impossible to escape the influence of the magnetic field of love and poetry that was constantly passing between husband and wife" (373).

In its rush to sanctify both the poet's life and her works, however, Field's essay sometimes loses the balance that renders the canonization of woman and poet fully reciprocal. Granted, even when she is cast as "the glory of all" Casa Guidi and as "that which sanctified all," Field's Barrett Browning still retains some humanity. She is a specific, embodied Glory who prefers an armchair near the door and strews newspapers on the table. When Field asserts that the poet's character was "well-nigh perfect," however, or that she was "so humble in her greatness that her friends looked upon her as a divinity among women," one cannot help becoming uneasy (370). Is this a woman or a Marian monument?[20] By the end of Field's essay, one scarcely wonders at hearing that the dying poet's "spirit could see its future mission" or even that an "an unexpected comet" glared across the sky the night after her death ("Elizabeth Barrett Browning," 374–75). The only surprise is that E. B. B. should have died at all. "Sinless in life," why should she not have simply been assumed into heaven?

As the "shadow of Mrs. Browning's [sinless] self," E. B. B.'s poetry is as indispensable here as the Holy Ghost whose place it takes in Field's secular trinity (375). At points, however, it already threatens to become equally insubstantial. Indeed, as the *Sonnets* emerge from the obscurity to which they are still relegated by many of Field's contemporaries, they do so less as texts than as transparent veils over their author's heart: "What wealth of love she could give is evidenced in those exquisite sonnets purporting to be from the Portuguese, the author being too modest to christen them by their right name, Sonnets from the Heart. None have failed to read the truth through this slight veil, and to see the woman more than the poet in such lines as these: —'I yield the grave for thy sake, and exchange / My near sweet view of heaven for earth with thee!'" (369).

Where Field's obituary hovers on the edge of creating Barrett Browning as a Marian model, Samuel B. Holcombe's *Southern Literary Messenger* obituary dives straight into the process. Condemning Field's essay as what one might expect from "an avowedly pantheistic publication" such as the *Atlantic Monthly,* Holcombe nevertheless follows Field's lead in celebrating the *Sonnets* (415). As he makes clear, Holcombe intends no "elaborate" critical engagement with "Mrs. Browning's idiosyncratic merits and foibles as a poet": his concern is with her "womanly character as exhibited in her writings" (413–14). That character, we are told, renders her "truly the Shakspeare among her sex" (414). Far from being concerned with Field's "Right, Justice, Liberty," however, Holcombe's female Bard is scarcely dedicated even to the art of poetry. "For her," Holcombe writes, "love was the element of life; her soul was pure and chaste as fire; but the wondrous music of this immeasurable passion penetrated her whole being, and kindled it into an ardent and beautiful flame. In her poems, the passions of love in the maiden heart, the devotion of the wife and the affection of the mother, are severally and fully portrayed" (414).

As Love's music "penetrates" the "whole being" of Holcombe's divinely relative Comtean trinity, it "kindles" her into a kind of poetic virgin motherhood. With her "ardent" soul, "pure and chaste as fire," E. B. B. thus speaks for the ideal "maiden, wife, and mother"—and apparently for no one else. What happens, one might ask, when the same poet adopts the voice of masculine or androgynous angels? Of a runaway slave who strangles the child she conceived through rape? Of the great god Pan? Of an Italian patriot declaring war? Of a factory child? In many of her most daring and influential poems, then, Holcombe's Barrett Browning would seem to have been out of her element.

In a dramatic literary Assumption, Holcombe ends by envisioning the "spirits of Beauty, of Love, of Purity, of Virtue," gathering "around the dying couch of the peerless Daughter of Poesy . . . to convey the soul of their faithful priestess and interpreter into a sphere of being better adapted to her inexpressible tenderness, her generous sympathies, and her richly-gifted mind" (417). The "womanly character" of E. B. B. thus attains full status as a vanishing figure of feminine virtue—at the modest price of being implicitly purified of both fleshly desire and much of the body of her work.

By 1868, accounts of the "shrine" at Casa Guidi had already been trickling in for some time.[21] A poem in the 1868 *Atlantic Monthly* brings E. B. B.'s secular sanctity to new heights, however. Lying near death within Casa Guidi itself, the poem's speaker is "returned to warm existence" by nothing less than a vision of Barrett Browning:

> *A fate like Farinata's held me fast*
> *In some devouring pit of fever-fire,*
> *Until, from ceaseless forms of toil that cast*
> *Their will upon me, whirled in endless gyre,*
> *The Spirit of the house brought help at last.*
>   . . . . .

She came, whom Casa Guidi's chambers knew,
And know more proudly an immortal now;
The air without a star was shivered through
With the resistless radiance of her brow,
And glimmering landscapes from the darkness grew.

Thin, phantom-like; and yet she brought me rest.
Unspoken words, an understood command
Sealed weary lids with sleep, together pressed
In clasping quiet wandering hand to hand,
And smoothed the folded cloth above the breast.
. . . . .

The quiet brow; the face so frail and fair
For such a voice of song; the steady eye,
Where shone the spirit fated to outwear
Its fragile house;—and on her features lie
The soft half-shadows of her drooping hair.
. . . . .

(Bayard Taylor,
"Casa Guidi
Windows")

Who could forget those features, having known?
Whose memory do his kindling reverence wrong
That heard the soft Ionian flute, whose tone
Changed with the silver trumpet of her song?
No sweeter airs from woman's lips were blown.
. . . . .

The tablet tells you, "Here she wrote and died,"
And grateful Florence bids the record stand:
Here bend Italian love and English pride
Above her grave,—and one remoter land,
Free as her prayers would make it, at their side.

I will not doubt the vision: yonder see
The moving clouds that speak of freedom won!
And life, new-lighted, with a lark-like glee
Through Casa Guidi windows hails the sun,
Grown from the rest her spirit gave to me.

Released from the physical torments of delirium and the spiritual torments of "the Tuscan Master's hell" by a vision of the "spirit" of Casa Guidi, the speaker seems inclined to believe in divine intercession: if poet-worship heals, why question it?

In the end, though, if anyone outfitted Barrett Browning with a full critical

halo, it was Edmund Clarence Stedman. "There are some poets whom we picture to ourselves as surrounded with aureolas, who are clothed in so pure an
atmosphere that when we speak of them—though with a critical purpose and
in this exacting age—our language must express that tender fealty which sanctity and exaltation compel from all mankind" ("Elizabeth Barrett Browning,"
101). First published in *Scribner's* in 1873 and then reprinted as a chapter in his
Victorian Poets, Stedman's "Elizabeth Barrett Browning" clearly attained iconicity: it remained central to Barrett Browning studies throughout the rest of the
century and beyond.[22] Ironically, the essay's popularity may even have eclipsed
that of many of Barrett Browning's actual works. Open an 1877 volume entitled
Elizabeth Barrett Browning, for example, and one finds that Stedman, not
E. B. B., wrote the contents; check the National Union Catalog for the years
just after 1900, and although new editions of *Aurora Leigh* are absent, *Victorian
Poets* continues to appear until 1917.[23]

　　In fact, in certain respects, Stedman literally defined Victorian poetry. As
Christopher Ricks has noted in the *New Oxford Book of Victorian Verse,* "The
word 'Victorian' had from the start been . . . associated with writers; the *OED's*
first instance of the adjective is Stedman's *Victorian Poets,* and the first sense of
the noun is 'a person, especially an author, who lived in the reign of Queen
Victoria', where especially an author means very especially a poet: [Robert]
Browning as the 'strongest, truest poet of the Victorians' (1876), and [Alfred]
Tennyson as, 'alone of the Victorians', having 'definitely entered the immortal
group of our English poets'" (xxvi). As *Victorian* entered the language of literary
criticism, then, Robert Browning came along as "strongest and truest," Tennyson, as "alone" among the immortals, and Barrett Browning as "the representative of her sex in the Victorian era" (*Victorian Poets,* 148).

　　In Stedman's terms, the honor could not have been higher. "We men are
fallen tyrants," Stedman once wrote to a female friend. "What plea I can enter
for myself I don't know—unless it be to let my article on Mrs. Browning count
in my favor" (Stedman and Gould 2:520). According to his biographers, "'A
man dictates his faith, or illustrates it, by the opinion he has of woman' was
Stedman's version of an old truth. One of the most perfect essays ever written
by Stedman was that on Mrs. Browning, and he said it was his tribute to
Woman" (2:517). The Barrett Browning essay is indeed a tribute to Woman, at
least insofar as Woman is a lost, sacred literary heroine.

　　As "tender fealty for sanctity" overrides literary analysis in Stedman's work,
the familiar sentimental haze of refused critical engagement settles: "We are not
sure of our judgment; ordinary tests fail us. . . . Fire is fire, though shrouded in
vapor, or tinged with murky hues. We do not see clearly, for often our eyes are
blinded with tears;—we love, we cherish, we revere" (101). Stedman's fealty,

which seeks to honor both a poet and a woman, thus canonizes a "soul of fire" (Hillard 1:178)—a figure whose "memory and career appear to us like some beautiful ideal." Indeed, so ethereal is Stedman's vanishing monument that she almost disappears before the essay begins: "Nothing is earthly, though all is human." he writes. "A spirit is passing before our eyes, yet of like passions with ourselves" (101).

With Stedman, Browning's biography reached fruition as a full-scale "sacred life." Much like its medieval forerunners, this narrative is a pastiche. Casting Barrett Browning as "England's greatest female poet" and the "most inspired" woman poet of history (102), Stedman brilliantly rings the changes on her earlier portrayals. The devout invalid with her "cloister-life" (104); the queen (110); the "fragile" feminine overreacher (107); the singer of "liberty, aspiration, and love"(112); Mazeppa (112); the chrysalis (102); the Sibyl (102, 112); and even the Lady of Shalott (108) are all here—and all subsumed by the portrayal of E. B. B. as a perfect, flamelike secular saint (101).

Metaphorically linking his subject both to Mary ("all these things she 'kept in her heart'") and to Christ (she gives "Cry of the Children" from on "the Mount" [107]), Stedman articulates an almost complete paradigm for accounts of Barrett Browning's biography as a secular saint's life. First, there is the "chrysalid state," the intellectual "novitiate" of her "cloister-life" (102–4), in which the physical isolation and suffering that once won E. B. B. popular reverence are underplayed or condensed and concretized by the dramatic (if apocalyptic) story that she witnessed her favorite brother's death at sea.[24] Next, there is the turning point, the "chief event in the life of Elizabeth Barrett": her marriage, which brings motherhood and the "ripe fruition of a genius that hitherto, blooming in the night, had yielded fragrant and impassioned, but only sterile flowers" (108). Then come the poet's final years in Italy, which pass in a kind of sanctified haze. Her "beautiful character" is now "exhibited" in letters and in friends' tributes (112)—not, it must be noted, in her unnamed final volumes, whose contents sound like "sweet bells jangled" (104). As E. B. B.'s "exhausted frame" becomes "now, more than ever, . . . 'nearly a transparent veil for a celestial and immortal spirit,'" her poetic life, too, declines (112). Finally, in hagiographic tradition's great deathbed scene, the "enraptured seer of celestial visions" rises to her sure reward (114).

Stedman's account crystallizes popular watchwords into a coherent narrative; it is echoed in turn by his successors in the project of legend-making. Such echoes may not only encompass Stedman's glorification of E. B. B. but also repeat and extend his dismissal of that poet's later writing. To quote William T. Herridge, "In faltering, hurried accents, over which criticism will draw a kindly veil, she spoke her last words for universal liberty, and then awaited with calmness the divine emancipation of death"—not to mention ascent from the "Mount of Transfiguration" (620, 623).

In contrast to accounts of the poet's final volumes, those of her final hours are explicit and celebratory. After living her final years in "a pure atmosphere of love," Marion Couthouy's dying heroine finds that "supernal Beauty . . . now opened upon her. . . . Was it not a foreshadowing of the Beatific Vision?" (753). On a less elevated note, Elizabeth Porter Gould proclaims Barrett Browning victor of what might be called the female writers' deathbed competition. George Eliot's last moments could not possibly have been as inspirational, Gould insists. The best death had clearly gone to the best woman ("Supremacy," 44).

Stedman's work did more than consolidate earlier watchwords into a relatively consistent narrative, however. It also helped catalyze crucial shifts in his time's paradigms of feminine literary sanctity. As his biographers put it, Stedman "cared less for literary than for matrimonial women," perhaps particularly when the literary women were fractious.[25] Confronted with Barrett Browning, who was both literary and matrimonial, he shaped of her life—and of her work, especially the *Sonnets*—a testament to the indispensable "relations of art and marriage, where the development of female genius is concerned" ("Elizabeth Barrett Browning," 109). It was by "one of Nature's charming miracles," he writes, that marriage gave Elizabeth Barrett both "a precious lease of life" and a "fellow-artist whose disposition and pursuits were in absolute harmony with her own" (109). Through this naturalized "miracle" alone did the "exalted" Barrett Browning rise "to her height" (110).

Stedman's timing was crucial, both in terms of the developing institution of literary study and in terms of the institution of marriage. According to Raymond Williams, Terry Eagleton writes, "The only sure fact about the organic society . . . is that it is always gone" (36; see Williams, "A Problem," 9–12). There is probably another "sure fact": such a society is one in which women know, and are happy in, their places (Doane and Hodges 3–4, 8). When "all the laws that governed sexual identity and behavior seemed to be breaking down" (Showalter, *Sexual Anarchy*, 3), a number of anxious late-century critics turned to mid-Victorian England as such a lost society—and, somewhat ironically, to Barrett Browning as its heroine. Stedman's essay heralds this development. In a tone that is not merely evaluative but elegiac, it casts E. B. B. as "the representative of her sex in the Victorian era," endowing her with qualities (including "abnegation, hope and faith") that once "seemed the apotheosis of womanhood." Since her death in 1861, Stedman implies, the "passion flower of the century" has vanished; the "conscious medium of some power beyond the veil" has been silent ("Elizabeth Barrett Browning," 113). As Victorianism came to an end, it seems, womanhood began to go downhill.

With Barrett Browning and her father both dead for more than ten years, references to the Brownings' elopement were becoming less risky. Stedman weighs Edward Barrett Moulton-Barrett's probable reasons for opposing E. B. B.'s marriage, even going so far as to speak of Moulton-Barrett's "utter selfishness" in attempting to forbid the poet and her sister to marry (108). Still, Stedman alludes to rather than addresses the elopement. Moreover, he suggestively counters E. B. B.'s association with filial disobedience through a familial vision that turns long-standing metaphoric patterns to new uses. "The English love to call her Shakespeare's Daughter," he writes, "and in truth she bears to their greatest poet the relation of Miranda and Prospero" (113). Few literary heroines can have been proclaimed the dutiful metaphoric child of more or greater patriarchs than was Moulton-Barrett's disobedient daughter. "What more beautiful subject for a modern painter," Stedman suggests, "than the girl Elizabeth . . . than this ethereal creature seated at the feet of the blind old scholar [Hugh Stuart Boyd], her face aglow with the rhapsody of the sonorous drama, from which she read of Oedipus, until 'the reader's voice dropped lower / When the poet called him BLIND!' Here was the daughter that Milton should have had!" (103). George Barnett Smith, who was to quote and extend much of Stedman's portrayal of Barrett Browning, would be lured into asserting that she should be termed Shakespeare's daughter rather than Tennyson's sister, thus earning from Henry James the withering suggestion that "it might do to try 'Wordsworth's niece' or 'Swinburne's aunt'" (475, 480; James, "George Barnett Smith," 331).

To be sure, for Stedman there are still "three masterworks": *Aurora Leigh, Casa Guidi Windows,* and the *Sonnets* ("Elizabeth Barrett Browning," 109). Not surprisingly, however, the *Sonnets* play a newly central role in this account of miraculous marriage. For "he is but a shallow critic who neglects to take into his account of a woman's genius a factor representing the master-element of love" (108). Just as the "chief event in the life of Elizabeth Barrett was her marriage," the "height" of her literary achievements was the *Sonnets.* Indeed, the *Sonnets* are not only E. B. B.'s greatest works, but they are the definitive works of women's poetry altogether: "The Portuguese Sonnets . . . are the most exquisite poetry hitherto written by a woman, and of themselves justify us in pronouncing their author the greatest of her sex,—on the ground that the highest mission of a female poet is the expression of love" (110).

As centerpieces of a hierarchical, emphatically gendered aesthetics, the *Sonnets* once more establish E. B. B. as a boundary goddess. Now, however, the boundaries have shrunk. Women poets' "highest mission" is not the writing of epic, religious, or political poetry—not the utterance, in Field's terms, of "one long, large-souled, large-hearted prayer for the triumph of Right, Justice, Liberty" ("Elizabeth Barrett Browning," 368). It is, rather, "the expression of love"—and of a love, moreover, that inspires critics with the desire to reciprocate in kind. "When an impassioned woman, yearning to let the world share her poetic rapture or grief, reveals the secrets of her burning heart, generations adore her, literature is enriched, and grosser beings have glimpses of a purity with which we invest our conceptions of disenthralled spirits in some ideal sphere" (Stedman, "Elizabeth Barrett Browning," 113).

Such reading recognizes not the labor of art but the passion of confession. As a transparent vehicle for "pure" passion, the woman poet becomes both angel and muse: if "we," who are "grosser beings," adore her, it is in great part because the unveiling of her "burning heart" is a medium for our own visions, our own "conceptions of disenthralled spirits in some ideal sphere."

Poet-Heroine to Romantic Heroine: Barrett Browning's Canonical Transformation and the *Sonnets'* Emergence as Relics

During the time when Stedman's sacred life of E. B. B. was first composed and read, Barrett Browning appears repeatedly as "one of the saints": she is both the "apostle of the true woman's poetry" and a prophet who has conveyed into her sex's "hands what might be called a perfect decalogue of womanly virtue" (Stevenson; "Some Recent Women Poets," 101; "Poetry of Mrs. Elizabeth Barrett Browning," 377).

Typically, where E. B. B. thus appears as both first among women poets and "supreme among women," the miracles of her verse and of her marriage stand equally balanced (Elizabeth Porter Gould, "Supremacy," 49). In time, however, this balance was to shift. As the century progressed and Robert Browning's poetic reputation rose, glorifications of Barrett Browning began to be subsumed, albeit slowly and unevenly, by celebrations of "the Brownings." Already caught up by what Richard D. Altick calls "the steady drift of nineteenth-century critical attention . . . away from the work and toward the writer" (*Lives*, 96), the attention of Barrett Browning's critics drifts even further, away from the writer and toward Robert Browning's wife.

The project of canonizing a Victorian woman as poet had always been deeply problematic. To create a "sacred life" a narrator must combine wonder and virtue, and in nineteenth-century terms, the wonder of true poetry accorded ill with the virtue of true womanhood. Now, however, celebrations of

Barrett Browning's courtship and marriage began to offer an escape from this dilemma—a canonical third term. Replace the wonder of true poetry with the wonder of true love, and the problem is solved. Where E. B. B.'s glory became that of a sacred heroine of romance rather than a poet, critics could easily accord her even the most traditional feminine virtues. Moreover, they could retain her as a literary heroine of sorts: for was her reputation not encompassed by Robert Browning's brilliant fame?[26]

Once, the Brownings' love had been celebrated for its contribution to Barrett Browning's poetry; now, the poetry would come to be celebrated for its documentation of the Brownings' love. Rhetorically, the shifts involved are subtle. Symbolically, they could not be more dramatic. It is suggestive, for example, that Emily Hickey and Frederick J. Furnivall, who co-founded the (Robert) Browning Society in 1881, both came to Browning's works through those of E. B. B. (Peterson, *Oracle*, 25). Robert Browning had long been "Mrs. Browning's husband"; Elizabeth Barrett Browning was now becoming Robert Browning's wife.

Robert Browning's wife, that is, and "Pen" Browning's mother. In his famous introduction to the 1899 edition of *Aurora Leigh,* Algernon Charles Swinburne outdid himself in praise for the description of Marian Erle's baby (16:7–8). His glorification of E. B. B. as maternal poet was scarcely original, however. In 1890, Sarah Warner Brooks had written that "in Casa Guidi windows, tender and serious as the Madonna folding in her arms the sinless Child," E. B. B. was "enshrined forever" (428). The pattern is familiar. When, in 1899, E. Windgate Rinder listed the "solicitous tenderness of maternal passion" among those "elemental things" that would supplement "literary beauty" in giving *Aurora Leigh* continued life (vi–vii), for example, the division was implicit: womanly virtues from art; motherhood from poetry.

Thus, eagerness to number the poet's "maternal spirit" among her work's more enduring qualities did not necessarily lead critics to privilege those works composed after E. B. B. became a mother (Meynell, "Elizabeth Barrett Browning," 161). Indeed, by the late 1880s, Anne Thackeray Ritchie had already provided a crucial lead in sanctifying Barrett Browning as a mother at the expense of *Aurora Leigh*. In a *Dictionary of National Biography* article published between 1886 and 1887, Ritchie reports that in the late 1850s, as the Brownings were en route to London, both the manuscript of *Aurora Leigh* and Pen Browning's new clothes were temporarily lost in Marseilles. "Mrs Browning's chief concern was not for her manuscripts, but for the loss of her little boy's wardrobe, which had been devised with so much tender motherly care and pride" (81).[27]

Reprinted and widely quoted, sometimes in juxtaposition to the poet's claim to Leigh Hunt that she took more pride in her son than in "twenty Auroras," Ritchie's story would be repeated as a vindication of Barrett Browning's womanly priorities, a confirmation, in the words of one *Dial* review, that Barrett Browning had been a "'little woman' who loved 'little things,'" an old-fashioned "fond mother and home-keeping wife" who was "neither a shrill debater nor a clamorous mover of the previous question nor a seeker to delve where she should spin," yet who had earned "her place among the immortals" ("Memories," 341).[28] Such vehement praise marks a canonical model who is only one step away from going out of style. By 1892 Ritchie herself anticipates later criticisms of E. B. B.'s mothering by revising the narrative to add a criticism of Pen Browning's clothes ("Robert and Elizabeth Barrett Browning," 842; *Records,* 253).

Despite celebrations of Barrett Browning's maternal purity, however, it is as a lover, not as a mother, that E. B. B. is most dramatically canonized toward the century's end. In such contexts, the *Sonnets* began to take center stage. Marriage might be in crisis, many critics asserted or implied, but the Brownings' love could still symbolize the endangered yet eternal values of that institution at its best. Moreover, as a heroine in such accounts, Barrett could wield the sacred powers both of chastity and marriage. For she had kept "the citadel of her womanhood pure and strong until it was conquered once and forever"; and a miracle had been her reward (Elizabeth Porter Gould, "Supremacy," 45). "Never such love-evolving life found answer so complete this side the Kingdom of Love" (Stevenson 236).[29]

"Whatever cynicism may say of the folly of matrimonial ideals," writes William Herridge in an 1887 *Andover Review,* Elizabeth Barrett's "choice—unhappily with so few parallels in the annals of literature," needs "no justification before the gaze of an admiring world" (613). Her "matchless" *Sonnets* are more than the "work of a poetess": they are "the psalm of a priestess" of matrimonial love (613–14). No one could read them "without being stimulated to a truer chivalry and a more profound appreciation of the sacred mystery of a woman's love" (614).[30] Thus,. turning "from the work to a noble personality in the worker," critics could read Barrett Browning's career as recording "in letters of gold those eternal laws which lie behind the changing movements of society, and are the foundations upon which the universe is laid" (607, 623). And turn from the work readers did. If, to many readers, the Brownings seemed invincible during this period, it was clearly because they were "classics in perfect married love, as well as in the realm of poetry." Robert Browning himself, that "patron saint of a study group," basked in a dangerous glory partly derived from his association with Barrett Browning (Altick, *Lives,* 122; 119). Even his verse would not remain entirely immune from unfavorable comparisons to the romance of the Brownings' courtship (Stephen 28).

No single essay is more crucial in this context than Edmund Gosse's famous introduction to an 1894 edition of the *Sonnets from the Portuguese*. Gosse's touching, if slightly inaccurate, account of a tremulous Barrett Browning slipping up behind her husband to place her love poems in his hands is a moment of true romance: it quickly attained iconicity. Widely quoted and reprinted, both in later editions of the *Sonnets* and in Gosse's own popular *Critical Kit-kats*, the scene still appears, in excerpt, in the notes to Porter and Clarke's scholarly edition of Barrett Browning's *Complete Works* (3:391–92).

As Gosse's introduction demonstrates, glorifications of the Brownings' courtship could spring from sexual anxieties extending well beyond the "marriage question." In the 1870s, Stedman himself had discreetly hinted it "no sacrilege to say" that the *Sonnets*' "music is showered from a higher and purer atmosphere than that of the Swan of Avon" ("Elizabeth Barrett Browning," 109).[31] By 1894, when Gosse wrote, a new vocabulary stood ready: not only *feminism* but *homosexuality* had entered the general vocabulary (Showalter, *Sexual Anarchy*, 3). That "Edwardian development," the "homosexual Shakespeare," had arrived, and with him a new explicitness about the cultural implications of intersections between sexual and literary reputations (Stavisky 52).[32]

One year before Oscar Wilde's arrest on charges of sodomy, in an era in which "many Englishmen regarded . . . homosexual scandals . . . as certain signs of the immorality that had toppled Greece and Rome" (Showalter, *Sexual Anarchy*, 3), Gosse proclaimed that E. B. B.'s "voluble, harsh, and slight" sonnets had a "curious advantage" over those of her great predecessor ("Sonnets," 10). Although "it is probable that the sonnets written by Shakespeare to his friend contain lovelier poetry, . . . those addressed by Elizabeth Barrett to her lover are hardly less exquisite to any of us, and to many of us are more wholesome and more intelligible" (10). If Gosse terms Barrett Browning's "wholesome" *Sonnets* more "intelligible," it is clearly because—to adapt a phrase coined about this time—they express a love that dares to speak its name (Alfred Douglas 264).

Perhaps, Gosse implies, there is no point in undertaking what Simon Shepherd has termed "the tidying-up of the National Bard's sexuality" (98): "Many of the thoughts that enrich mankind and many of the purest flowers of the imagination had their roots, if the secrets of experience were made known, in actions, in desires, which could not bear the light of day, in hot-beds smelling quite otherwise than of violet or sweetbriar" (Gosse, "Sonnets," 16–17). Still, consolation exists. The *Sonnets* offer an "accredited chronicle" of chaste marital love, "lifted far out of any vagueness of conjecture or possibility of misconstruction" (16). "Built" as they are "patently and unquestionably" on an authorized heterosexual "union in stainless harmony," the *Sonnets* become not so much texts as inspirational edifices, bulwarks of a literary city on the hill (17).

Significant for setting the *Sonnets* as the culmination of Barrett Browning's career and for establishing heterosexuality as a central source of their redemptive power, Gosse's introduction is no less important for its role in the *Sonnets'* literal and metaphoric transformation into relics, a process that simultaneously raises them to glory and relegates them to the status of objects. As a whole series of charming gift volumes attests, by the century's end, when separate editions of *Aurora Leigh* were going out of print, the *Sonnets'* combined canonization and commodification was well under way.

There is no prettier presentation of E. B. B.'s verse than a certain British Library book whose printed text Gosse mentions in his introduction. Cushioned in its own morocco box, this gilt-edged, tooled volume is a full-fledged reliquary. Inside its front cover, beside the golden text of Sonnet XIX, is a lock of brown hair behind glass; inside the back cover, a white lock whose contrasting color is somehow moving. Both locks, a note in the volume attests, came from Robert Browning on his deathbed. The white one was his own; the brown one was given to him by Elizabeth Barrett Browning before their marriage. He carried it with him (in a carefully displayed bit of paper) as long as he lived. Next to a letter from Browning's daughter-in-law to Thomas J. Wise stands the volume's centerpiece: the "1847 Reading Edition" of the *Sonnets*.

The brown lock of hair seems to be the real thing, though it was clipped from the wrong Browning's head. If so, it will surely not be the first time that true and false relics have been housed together. For the "Reading edition," with its anonymous "octavo of 47 pages," which Gosse asserts to have been printed through the assistance of Mary Russell Mitford, is a fraud ("Sonnets," 2–3). As Philip Kelley and Betty A. Colley tell it, after Robert Browning's death, the Brownings' daughter-in-law, Fannie, removed a lock of hair from "one of the love letters where it had remained since it had been cut from Robert Browning's head," and presented it to Thomas J. Wise (xxxiv). The honor seemed well merited: "sometime President of the Bibliographical Society, honorary Master of Arts at Oxford, member of the exclusive Roxburghe Club of book collectors, and one of the most learned bibliographers in England," Wise had been an active member of the Browning Society, a correspondent of Robert Browning's regarding the authenticity of Barrett Browning publications, and the compiler of the standard bibliography of Barrett Browning's works (Altick, *Adventurers*, 37–50). By the 1930s, however, bibliographers John Carter and Graham Pollard had begun to suspect the authenticity of certain publications listed in that bibliography, and had followed a trail of clues straight back to Wise (8–86, 167–68). As it turned out, Wise was a forger. He had actually used the Browning Society's own printer, Richard Clay and Sons, to create his fakes (45, 50).

Fannie Browning told Wise the hair had come from her father-in-law. Wise, however, "convinced himself it was that of Elizabeth Barrett Browning.

He had a box built which was inscribed 'This lock of Elizabeth's hair was held by Robert Browning in his hand while he was dying.' On one of her visits to Hampstead, Fannie—who was at Robert Browning's deathbed—saw the inscription and corrected Wise. He smiled and exclaimed, 'If he was not holding a lock of her hair in his hand, he ought to have done so!'" (xxxiv, n.15; 510).[33] So much for the power of history to defuse legend. Once more, in literary as in religious canonization, reverence and falsification have gone hand in hand.

Gosse's role in Wise's forgery remains unclear (Altick, *Adventurers,* 37), as does the extent to which one should accord him responsibility for another, more abstract kind of falsification: the process of canonizing the *Sonnets* as chaste, nostalgically conceived Victorian valentines. Since Gosse's essay began as an introduction to the *Sonnets,* there is some justification for his abandoning E. B. B.'s verse after their publication, for example; and though Gosse praises the *Sonnets* as relics, he also analyzes them as verse. Nonetheless, his essay contributes powerfully to a larger pattern of accounts in which the "supreme" *Sonnets* dramatically overpower and marginalize the remainder of E. B. B.'s verse, in great part through claims to a glory that seems at least as much documentary as artistic.

If the *Sonnets* were the "perfection of song," the "very spirit of human love made visible," they were so because they were the "matchless series . . . through which Mrs. Browning has chanted her life's apotheosis" (George Barnett Smith 488; Elizabeth Porter Gould, "Supremacy," 45; Rowland 555). "We are unable to tell by which we are most affected," wrote one frank author in the *Literary World,* "the poetry itself, or that wonderful 'apocalypse of soul,' than which no revelation could be more beautiful" ("Poetry of Elizabeth Barrett Browning," 153).

Thus, the *Sonnets* came to be reified as relics of Barrett Browning's "life's apotheosis." The interplay of such canonization and commodification finds its most dramatic and poignant monument in Baylor University's Armstrong Browning Library. At the library's "architectural focal point," the "Cloister of the Clasped Hands" (Herring 23), Harriet Hosmer's bronze cast powerfully renders its subjects' physicality. Spare, small, and irreducibly individual, the Brownings' hands lie in a grasp whose very strength evokes the transience of mortal love. These living hands are lost. To one side of Hosmer's sculpture, a marble wall holds the "O Lyric Love" passage from *The Ring and the Book,* engraved in gold; inevitably, the paired sonnet on the other wall begins, "How do I love thee?" Above and behind the glass case is a painting by John Carroll—a wifty, sentimental scene in which a glamorized Elizabeth leans on Robert's arm. The painting's source? The Eaton Paper Company, purveyors of the perfect stationery for love letters.

Commodified, metaphorically chastened, and offered as antidotes to sexual anarchy, Barrett Browning's love poems became sacred objects; but in the process, in many cases, they may have ceased to be read as poems. As relics of a great love, they were perfect. Like other relics, however, they need not even be particularly attractive in and of themselves. Even when Gosse himself termed them the "purest" of Barrett Browning's works, for example, such praise merely established them as the "least imperfect," the "most free" from "laxity" and "license" ("Sonnets," 6). The body of the poet's verse was thus metaphorically rendered as less pure than the spirit of her love. Love, not art, created the *Sonnets'* supremacy; the value of the verse was coming to depend on the power of the heroine.

Biographical Revelations and the Hysterical Heroine: The Browning Letters

Both in terms of reverence and reticence, Robert Browning was a key agent in his wife's canonization, whether as a woman or as a poet. As a popular figure, he came to radiate a cultural glory that blended with and augmented that of his wife;[34] on a personal level, his devotion to E. B. B.'s memory only intensified her already powerful connections to sainthood. The most famous instance of such reverence, which occurred in 1889, was sparked by the following passage, printed in the newly published letters of Edward FitzGerald: "Mrs Browning's Death is rather a relief to me, I must say: no more Aurora Leighs, thank God! A woman of real Genius, I know: but what is the upshot of it all? She and her Sex had better mind the Kitchen and their Children; and perhaps the Poor: except in such things as little Novels, they only devote themselves to what Men do much better, leaving that which Men do worse or not at all" (2:280–81). Quick to respond, Browning printed the following scathing reply in the *Athenaeum:*

To Edward FitzGerald

I chanced upon a new book yesterday;
I opened it, and where my finger lay
  'Twixt page and uncut page, these words I read
—Some six or seven at most—and learned thereby
That you, Fitzgerald, whom by ear and eye
  She never knew, "thanked God my wife was dead."

Ay, dead! And were yourself alive, good Fitz,
How to return you thanks would task my wits:

> *Kicking you seems the common lot of curs—*
> *While more appropriate greeting lends you grace:*
> *Surely to spit there glorifies your face—*
> *Spitting—from lips once sanctified by Hers.*

From the standpoint of the poet-heroine's canonization, the incident is painful and deeply ironic. For what FitzGerald attacks is not so much the "woman of real Genius" as the author of *Aurora Leigh;* and what Browning understandably defends is not so much the author of *Aurora Leigh* as his wife, whose very kiss confers sanctity.[35]

Browning died the same year—and with him, not only a certain quality of reverence for his wife's memory, but a certain level of biographical reticence. For Barrett Browning's widower had remained as adamantly devoted to the privacy of his wife's memory as he was to its sanctity: as long as he lived, he ensured that few of Barrett Browning's private papers could appear in print, and he resisted publication of her unpublished verse.[36] When E. B. B.'s letters began to appear, then, they bore the glamor of long-cherished secrets.

"Sweet poet! sweetest lover! unto thee / The great world bows in fond idolatry," wrote Allen Eastman Cross in 1889. The great world was soon to echo his evaluative hierarchy. As Alice Meynell instructed readers one year before the 1898 publication of Frederic G. Kenyon's two-volume edition of the *Letters of Elizabeth Barrett Browning,* Barrett Browning was already coming to represent "a moral, and an emotional excellence, rather than a poetical excellence." She was expected to "live in history" as "a nobly passionate personality rather than as a poet" ("Introduction," 452). Barrett Browning's "character" was now "her greatest legacy to the world" ("Elizabeth Barrett Browning," *Outlook,* 380). Though their estimates of Barrett Browning's poetic achievement vary, reviewers of the Kenyon volumes tend to agree: they praise the woman over her works and the love story over all else.

Stedman's moral had been that if a true woman revealed the secrets of her burning heart in song, generations would revere her. The moral of many stories told toward the century's end was that if such a woman consummated one of the great marriages of all time, that glory would never fade—even though remembrance of her poems might. "A greater gain to humanity than the picture of a good and noble life is the view we obtain of the most perfect example of wedded happiness in the history of literature," one 1897 article ruled. "This, even more than her poems, was the legacy which Mrs Browning left to her fellow-men" ("Married Life," 529). To quote William Cameron, "If her novitiate of suffering was severe, her married life was throughout a period of almost indescribable happiness. . . . Her poetic work is the truest and fairest expression of what she was, and of what she felt. All that was womanly in [E. B. B.'s] work will live, despite every defect of art, in virtue of its womanhood. . . . In the least inspired of [her poems] there was a graciousness of fancy, a sweetness of nature, a tenderness of feeling, a rectitude of intention, which entitles them to respect if it does not ensure them permanence in memory" (45, 46).

The woman must save the work, if it is to be saved at all. "Her spiritual fire and her moral courage will probably redeem in the eyes of posterity her artistic defects," a *Spectator* review predicted ("Mrs. Browning's Letters," 686). When Carlyle asserts that "no Poem is equal to its Poet," his claim concerns the relations between humanity and art (Altick, *Lives*, 99). When Barrett Browning's critics make apparently analogous claims during this period, they tend to be addressing the relations between femininity and art; and they tend to conclude that though it may be fine to be a woman poet, it is better to be the heroine of a romance. As one author optimistically put it, "All Barrett Browning's readers [were] her lovers"; and lovers may adore a heroine without revering her verse ("Mrs. Browning Complete").

When R. B. Browning published his parents' love letters in 1899, he unleashed a storm of controversy over rights to privacy; but he also did much to end a long-standing, if muted, scandal of another sort. As the *Saturday Review* put it, justification for Browning's decision to publish was "easily found in the favourable light it throws upon the one dubious act of his father's life. Those who admired Robert Browning most have always wished, in the corner of their hearts, that he had not snatched his wife by a clandestine arrangement from the house of her unconscious father. This wish will never be felt again." Now, irrevocably, what remained of public silence surrounding the Brownings' elopement came to an end. As the details of their courtship finally emerged, the two poets entered "into their glory" as definitive figures of romance ("Letters," *Saturday Review*, 243).

There is no judging the extent of earlier readers' unease over the Barrett-Browning elopement, of course. Still, the tenor of reviews of the love letters indicates that it may have been strong. Despite the letters' revelations, for example, the best that *Fortnightly Review* writer Eleanor Towle could say was that the Brownings' elopement had been carried out "upon the highest if not the soundest principles" (231). A *London Times* article, reprinted in the *Eclectic Magazine*, was even less sympathetic: "Judging from the evidence of these letters alone, it would seem that the Barrett-Browning story offers no exception to the good common sense rule that in nine cases out of ten a secret engagement is a foolish mistake" ("Browning Love-Letters," 736). Browning should simply have asked for Barrett's hand "as soon as she might recover her health," the review naively suggests (737). The *Church Quarterly Review* goes even further.

The "runaway match" might have turned out "to be the greatest possible blessing to both parties," it acknowledges. Still, only the courtesy of the reviewer prevents "another side to the question of the relationship between the lover and the lady's father" from being aired (153, 159).

Though the heyday of the poet-heroine (and of poet-heroes) was nearing its end, in the face of such disapproval, romantic sanctification flourished once more in its most extravagant forms. Spurred by heated critical controversy over whether the letters should have been published at all, admirers insisted upon their redemptive power. Could anyone expect R. W. Browning to imprison "a visitant angel"? (Porter, "Browning Love Letters," 302). "Of course," H. M. Sanders wrote, "we all agree as to the supreme sacredness of love" (116). Still, it never hurt to have new proof, especially where marital love was concerned. "Marriage as an institution has been under some sharp censures of late," noted a writer for the *Academy*, and "it had in that volume for the most pessimistic readers its sure defense" ("Memoirs," 489–90). "When there *are* such depths and heights in a world of sin and limitation," Elizabeth Porter Gould wrote in *Education*, "why should they be hidden, while weak, adulterated and sinful actions are spread out on the housetops?" ("Browning Letters," 214). It would have been no less than "sacrilege to have destroyed such a revelation when it is so much needed to-day" (215).

As more than one writer stressed, literary historiography had particular need of such revelations. "In the unlovely wilderness of much literary biography," the "life of the Brownings" could be "set like an oasis" (Sanders 117). Thus, "though the publication of such letters goes far to establish a really regrettable precedent, yet with the squalid story of Byron's love affairs paraded in half-a-dozen volumes, with Shelley's scarcely less unhappy marriage-ventures [and George Sand and De Musset's 'liaison'] become public property, . . . it is all but imperative for the credit of humanity that this story should be told" (Gwynn 428).

The Brownings' love story had become a great romance of literary history—and perhaps a greater gift to that history than any mere text could be. As Charlotte Porter put it, "The spiritual beauty of the love revealed in these 'Letters of Robert Browning and Elizabeth Barrett' is so magnetic that it makes their reader, too, this more than half-century later, fall in love with the writers" ("Browning Love Letters," 301). The Brownings were ideal lovers (Canton 286; Abbott 486; Sanders 120), the "hero and heroine of the most wonderful love story . . . that the world knows of" (Gwynn 426). Whether cast as "true drama," or as the "poem" that they "devised out of their own lives," their love story became an ultimate, unwritten text, a sacred revelation against which no mere written work could ever hope to compete (Wentz 237; Porter, "Browning Love Letters," 301). Greater than mere history, and as glorious as written romance, it was a "manifestation of true love—a manifestation such as history has never and fiction has rarely if ever paralleled" (Abbott 490).

Against such a text, the *Sonnets* had little chance. For alongside (or perhaps underneath) the increasing purification and etherealization of E. B. B.—and, by extension, of her verse—there had always been an undercurrent of anxiety about the dangerous bodies of the poet and her texts. "Sonnets they are not," an 1889 *Nation* essay had already asserted, for example, "for they err against all the canons; but they are passionate expressions of love" (Schuyler 7). Compelled to fault the actual writing of "these glorious poems" in that same year, critic John Dennis abandons his generally calm, academic tone to become painfully personal: "It is with a feeling sad almost as that of a father whose daughter's beauty has been marred by some miserable accident, that we are forced, despite our wishes, to note even in this, her most perfect work, . . . strange flaws" (*Studies*, 437). In its natural—which is to say ideal—state, the body of E. B. B.'s verse would apparently have been flawless, a fit heir not merely to Milton or Shakespeare but to the critic himself. As it is, however, the "miserable accident" of Barrett Browning's own style has rendered the body of her work that of a disfigured daughter.

"You simply cannot beat in their own way—a way a trifle overluscious perhaps; but so are peaches and pine-apples—the best of the *Sonnets from the Portuguese*," the *Saturday Review* had acknowledged only the year before ("Elizabeth Barrett Browning," 467). Juicy and decadent, these last poetic fruits offer a powerful and suggestive contrast to the *Sonnets'* associations with chaste purity, and a reminder that no canonization is ever uncontested. If one looks beyond the ethereal monuments to womanhood that have served as a central focus of this chapter—and, indeed, of Barrett Browning's reception—one finds other more fleshly figures, who are not only heirs to the Pythia evoked by E. B. B.'s contemporaries but predecessors of the neurotic heroine who is to become Andromeda in Wimpole Street.[37]

That heroine was not long in coming. Whatever the love letters' publication may have done for the Brownings' status as romantic ideals, it did little to enhance the reputation of Edward Barrett Moulton-Barrett, as a surviving son angrily pointed out ("Literary Week," 488). With its fairy-tale associations, the word *ogre* quickly became a favorite descriptor for the poet's father ("Letters," *Saturday Review*, 243; Porter, "Browning Love Letters," 308; "Browning Love-Letters," 736). Other characterizations ranged from "odious old gentleman" to a modern-day, unconscious Agamemnon ("Letters," *Saturday Review*, 243; Preston, "Robert and Elizabeth Browning," 813). The resulting transformation of courtship narratives helped catalyze a crucial and damaging shift in Barrett

Browning's reputation. It had been one thing for Robert Browning to have "snatched his gifted bride from the arms of Death," and quite possibly the death of a saint (Crosse 30). It was another, however, for him to rescue her from the clutches of an increasingly vicious, "degenerate" patriarch (Preston, "Robert and Elizabeth Browning," 814).[38] Barrett Browning's canonization as a romantic heroine had already ceased to require that its subject be a great poet; now it began to dispense even with the need to present her as a great woman.

As Moulton-Barrett assumed the guise of a villain, his daughter began to be transformed into a maiden in distress—and the more distress the better. Barrett Browning's literary significance had already been proclaimed to be "a moral, and an emotional excellence, rather than a poetical excellence." Now, perhaps fueled by continuing conservative skepticism about the propriety of the Brownings' elopement as well as by fin-de-siècle fascination with accounts of abnormal feminine psychology, an emerging narrative retained the glory of the Brownings' literary romance while implicitly denying Barrett Browning even personal claims to glory. In the words of one 1899 reviewer, critics began to consider the possibility that E. B. B. had been "made hysterical by her long seclusion" (Gwynn 434).

In some cases, such an assertion could partially exonerate the father; in all, it could heighten the daughter's romantic plight. Once suspected of having "snatched" his wife, Robert could now save her—not merely from death, from membership in the "mournful sisterhood" of single women (Stedman, "Elizabeth Barrett Browning," 107), or even from her nasty father, but from incipient mental illness. E. B. B, who had once served as the "representative of her sex during the Victorian era," as a lost apotheosis of womanhood, was becoming a true fin-de-siècle heroine, an enchanting neurotic: "In short, this rather plain, thin, faded, hysterical woman was loved for herself as perhaps none of all the world's famous beauties has ever been" (Gwynn 436).

Such evocations of Barrett Browning as hysterical heroine set forth a romantic story whose outlines were to satisfy both adherents of Freud and lovers of damsels in distress. In the twentieth century, of course, Elizabeth Barrett would emerge as Andromeda in Wimpole Street—and as a clear descendent of "Peau d'Ane," the fairy-tale heroine forced to flee her father's lust in Andrew Lang's late-nineteenth-century edition of Charles Perrault's stories (77–105). Where E. B. B.'s "supreme" strength had once testified to the limits of feminine poetry or the glories of companionate marriage, her supreme weakness could now testify to the sweet, faintly ridiculous innocence of pre-Freudian romance. By 1903, an *Athenaeum* review of a translation of the *Sonnets* would assert that these works give expression to "what may be supposed to be the emotions of the celestially average good woman in love" ("'Les Sonnets,'" 183).

Ultimately, this account would bring E. B. B. to Broadway. If she thrived as a romantic heroine, however, she was in trouble as a poet. For if Barrett Browning's verses were inferior to the poet herself, E. B. B.'s fall from Victorian grace into hysteria scarcely boded well for her critical reputation. There is no more famous evidence of how the legend's fascination with her frailty had come to override interest in her work than the fate of the following passage from G. K. Chesterton: "On the day on which it was necessary for her finally to accept or reject Browning's proposal, [Elizabeth Barrett] called her sister to her, and to the amazement and mystification of that lady asked for a carriage. In this she drove into Regent's Park, alighted, walked on to the grass, and stood leaning against a tree for some moments, looking round her at the leaves and the sky. She then entered the cab again, drove home, and agreed to the elopement. This was possibly the best poem that she ever produced" (21). The truth is, of course, that E. B. B. never "produced" such a poem. Chesterton did. Such are the ironies of canonization, moreover, that his description of it may be the most famous single paragraph he ever wrote. Ironically, Chesterton's account thus offers a double testimony to the overwhelming power of literary legend making. For like Stedman, Gosse, and many others, Chesterton had recorded a number of vivid, specific responses to Barrett Browning's verse (9–10). None has been widely reprinted.

As the secular saint's life broke down and the hysterical heroine's romance gained power, critics increasingly (and retroactively) ascribed Barrett Browning's former cultural power, both as a poet and as a heroine, to the innocent enthusiasm (or gullibility) of a feminized, sentimentalized Victorian public. Barrett Browning's early success came to stand for the worst in poet worship. Not incidentally, it was also metaphorically associated with the "nerves," "gushing," and defiance of an influential nineteenth-century female readership. As contempt or condescension toward women readers began to go hand in hand with disdain toward the Victorian public as a whole, such narratives paradoxically accorded literary historians free rein for their own sentimentality. Although Barrett Browning the poet might be made to display all the worst aspects of a culture from which fin-de-siècle criticism sought to break free, Barrett Browning the sentimental heroine still offered romantic or comic relief from analysis of the "real" development of literary tradition.

Certain biographical sketches of the poet's life thus evoke all the quaint, comfortable charm of a Victorianism toward which one might still feel a kind of rueful affection. By 1906, for example, a *London Times* article (reprinted in the *Living Age*) already presents a clear paradigm for the operation of such nostalgia within the shift from canonization to decanonization. "It is the person, not the poet, who lives most," its judgment begins, conventionally enough.

"Her poetry as poetry is imperfect. She is an incomplete artist, but a complete woman; and it is as a complete woman that she will stand and endure. When we use the word 'poet' we mean, of course, a professional poet. Every woman is a poet, and she, who was more intensely woman than other women, was, in this way, a past-mistress of poetry." Not surprisingly, the "Sonnets from the Portuguese" "remain her masterpiece— . . . because they are the fullest expression of the woman in her; and, better than these, the best poem that she created, was her own life with her husband." What follows, however, is new and disquieting: "This is perhaps the reason why she is comparatively little read by the present generation; the woman of one age seldom speaks to the 'business and bosoms' of her followers fifty years later" ("Elizabeth Barrett Browning," *Living Age*, 174).

Thus, having rendered her poetry a secondary concern, E. B. B.'s individual perfection itself falls prey to a form of planned obsolescence. As faith in the Victorian poet-heroine begins to falter, references to the flawed textual bodies of E. B. B.'s works start to merge with expressions of doubt as to the perfection of their author. Writing on the "Browning-Barrett Love-Letters and the Psychology of Love," Hiram M. Stanley notes that although the "sensuous side" of love, "as might be expected, is chiefly revealed in the letters of Robert Browning," Barrett Browning's sensuous expressions were "vivid" in the sonnets (735, 736). From him, this assertion is a compliment. From Sanders, however, similar comments on the *Sonnets* take on a different tone: "Never was there a more unmistakable, nor a more intimate personal utterance" than these verses. "Never did a woman make a more entire and outspoken confession of the faith that was in her. Here, if ever, would the discoverer of indiscretions find a secret to be kept inviolate, a rapture for the eyes of the husband alone . . . a confession sacred, holy, incommunicable" (119). Once bared by the *Sonnets,* the "shrine" of E. B. B.'s love was no longer inviolate. On an explicit level, Sanders's sexual and sacred metaphors work to absolve readers of the love letters of guilt. Implicitly, however, they question the morality, or at least the modesty, of having published the *Sonnets* in the first place.

Of all such denigrations of the *Sonnets,* none is more striking than that of Browning researcher Elizabeth Porter Gould. Defending the Browning love letters' publication Gould asserts, in *Education,* that they have "been given to the world and have blessed it." "Very little, if any, of our fiction *remains* on such heights. . . . Even poetry, which perhaps is the most genuine expression of the high truth, is not free from the trail of the serpent. But here in this revelation life is *lived*" (215). Deliberately created in the awareness of stylistic good and evil, the *Sonnets* can never be free of the "trail of the serpent." Only letters, presumably written without thought of publication, can express the prelapsarian unselfconsciousness of lived revelation. Thus, in the most extreme instances, the composition of poetry itself becomes a sign of neurosis or sin. The *Sonnets* may still be their author's "supreme" works, but now they embody hysteria or the artistic trail of the serpent.[39]

The Pythia's Return:
Fin-de-Siècle Evocations
of Hysterical Victorianism

Even the most modest heroine might write love letters, the underlying argument of certain criticisms of the *Sonnets* runs; but there is something wrong with a woman who puts her love into the public form of poetry. Thus, ironically, certain turn-of-the-century criticism both reconfirms mid-Victorian unease over the *Sonnets'* revelations and extends it to far more dangerous ground. For what is immodest now is not so much the exposure of the writer's personal life as that of her artistic labors. Such ironies multiply toward the century's end, as accounts of Barrett Browning's life and works disassociate themselves both from the midcentury criticism that rendered her a poet-heroine and from the later nostalgic canonization that transformed her into an embodiment of the lost Victorian apotheosis of womanhood.

In the *Nation* in 1889, for example, Eugene Schuyler already terms the success of Barrett Browning's early poems "almost inexplicable." E. B. B. benefited from her era's dearth of good poetry, he suggests; and "then, too, she was a woman—a reason which, in her inner soul, she detested. . . . And then she was admired by women, and placed, as Miss Mitford says, 'in the situation of Wordsworth forty years ago—the foundress of a school of enthusiastic worshippers, laughed at by those who do not feel high poetry'" (7). The hysterical heroine is thus issued a mutually reinforcing hysterical audience. Never mind that there were no "Barrett Browning Clubs": with this cut at "enthusiastic worshippers," Schuyler manages to link outmoded reverence for poets with feminine "enthusiasm." His tone of knowing humor would soon become a staple in treatments of the poet's reception.

Aurora Leigh is often central to such revisions. Though it is Barrett Browning's most "important and most characteristic work," A. C. Benson writes, length alone "would prevent" the "undramatic . . . digressive" work from "ever being popular." Why, then, had it sold so many editions? His answer: the poem's autobiographical nature, along with "the comparative mystery in which the authoress was shrouded and the romance belonging to a marriage of poets— these elements are enough to account for the great enthusiasm with which the poem was received. Landor said that it made him drunk with poetry,—that was the kind of expression that admirers allowed themselves to make use of with respect to it. And yet . . . the fact remains that it is a difficult volume to work through" ("Mrs. Browning," 144). By thus retroactively (and inaccurately) establishing romance at the center of Barrett Browning's popularity, Benson could reinforce his own period's revisionist sentimentality even as he denigrated his critical predecessors, the poem's current admirers, and *Aurora Leigh* itself.

When Gosse characterizes Barrett Browning's readers in *A Short History of Modern English Literature,* he does not exempt even the author from the enthusiastic delusions evoked: "Their nerves were pleasurely excited by the choral tumult of Miss Barrett's verse, by her generous and humane enthusiasm, and by the spontaneous impulsiveness of her emotion. They easily forgave the slipshod execution, the hysterical violence, the Pythian vagueness and the Pythian shriek" (338).

Once, Barrett Browning's critics had charged her with metaphorically violating the virtues of Victorian femininity by subjecting herself to the irrational, disturbingly somatic transports of the Pythia; they had proclaimed the results of such inspiration to be out of character. Now, her character has become that of the Pythia, and the mid-Victorian public, whose enthusiasm Gosse so confidently traces to "nerves," is proclaimed to have "easily forgiven" the stylistic wildness that once rendered it so uneasy. Thus the mid-Victorian Pythia returns in a new guise. Still terrifyingly somatic in her inspiration, she is no longer divinely inspired, and no longer separated from E. B. B. herself, as a representative of Victorian womanhood.

As ever, the *Saturday Review's* representations of literary sexual politics are among the most explicit. As early as 1888, after condemning Barrett Browning's "extravagant and glaring" poetic "defects," a reviewer goes on to cite "the endless gush and the sickening sentimentality, the nauseous chatter about 'womanhood' and 'woman's heart,' and all the rest of it, which she almost invented, but of which the secret by no means died with her" ("Elizabeth Barrett Browning," 466). This is strong language from a journal so recently given to panegyrics of old-fashioned femininity. It is clear what kind of readers this reviewer would have us believe welcomed Barrett Browning's verse—and what kind of visceral revulsion the work still evokes.

Earlier critics had defended their poet-heroine by metaphorically dispossessing her of any works that did not seem to speak of "womanhood" or "woman's heart." Now, gallantry moves in the opposite direction, as the *Saturday Review* critic attempts to exonerate a new (potential) poet-heroine from responsibility for E. B. B.'s "endless gush and . . . sickening sentimentality." "Had Mrs. Browning been at all conscious of the horrible faults of her verse," this author assures readers, "it is probable that she would have been so disgusted as to produce nothing at all, and that would have been a loss indeed" (466). If she could not have helped being a Victorian woman, it seems, a fully conscious E. B. B. would at least have been heroic enough to keep silent.[40]

Like canonization, such decanonization does not go uncontested. In a fine reversal of the *Saturday Review* position, for example, Meynell attempts to separate the true E. B. B. from Victorian womanhood by deploring "that in" Barrett Browning's poetry which "always had more semblance of life than force of life—the faults that came of a too conscious and too emphatic a revolt against her time, a too resolute originality. In another age Elizabeth Barrett Browning would not have needed, or have thought she needed, to spend her strength upon a strained attitude." Just as the *Saturday Review* author's alleged condemnation of sentimentality paradoxically echoes earlier critics' anxieties over fleshly, gushing style, however, Meynell's attempt to accord *Aurora Leigh* only the "semblance of life" actually amplifies initial reviewers' unease at the poem's vitality. Indeed, the poem's greatest flaw turns out to be its "turn of assertion and menace" (Meynell, "Elizabeth Barrett Browning," 163).

In any case, the "Pythian shriek" is now Barrett Browning's: the poet herself is reassimilated to her already decanonized later works—and wished away, as they were. The once sacred embodiment of Victorian womanhood has lost her sanctity. Her final years, which once marked her preparation for an ascent into heaven, now mark her ineluctable descent into personal and poetic decay. Once, the poet-heroine was exorcised; now she herself is the figure who must be driven out if literary history is to remain sane and healthy. We have seen what happened when FitzGerald's letters expressed his relief at Barrett Browning's death. Only a few years later, however, Gosse himself asserted that after 1850 Barrett Browning's "art . . . declined, and much of her late work was formless, spasmodic, singularly tuneless and harsh, nor is it probable that what seemed her premature death, in 1861, was a real deprivation to English literature" (*Short History,* 338). Given her production of works such as *Aurora Leigh* and *Poems before Congress,* it seems, the poet's death at age fifty-five only "seemed" premature.

Gosse's magisterial tone is more offensive, because more calculated, than FitzGerald's confessional mode. Its elegiac emphasis on Barrett Browning's personal and poetic decline, however, sounds almost mild in comparison to Harriet Waters Preston's *Atlantic Monthly* essay of 1899. Terming *Aurora Leigh* "socialistic," "sensational," and "ineffective," Preston writes, "Involuntarily, we recall the profane ejaculation of Edward FitzGerald when he heard of Mrs. Browning's death, 'Thank Heaven there will be no more Aurora Leighs!' And while we love the aged Browning all the better for the furious defense he made of his wife's genius against the shade of her incorrigible censor, we know that FitzGerald was right. More Aurora Leighs would have been a heavy misfortune to letters" ("Robert and Elizabeth Browning," 824).

Though Preston seems to have read FitzGerald's comment and Browning's reply rather carelessly, hers is a considered opinion. Returning to Stedman's jangled bells metaphor, Preston goes on to imply that *Aurora Leigh* evinces nothing less than progressive mental illness on the part of its author. When the ailing poet went to Italy, "the physical taint remained, congenital and incurable; and . . . the mental taint which inevitably accompanied it was to become increasingly conspicuous in all her published utterances. . . . The woman's voice, ever soft, sympathetic, and musical by the fireside, sounded thin and shrill when uplifted in high argument upon . . . political and social questions. . . . The hysterical note . . . [is not] at any time quite absent from Mrs. Browning's longest, and in some respects most considerable poem. . . . The bells were in truth jangled beyond repair" (823–24). E. B. B., it seemed, had not died a moment too soon: her "physical taint" might otherwise have further infected literary history, creating a "heavy misfortune to letters" (825). Harriet Waters Preston, it must be noted, was to edit the first Cambridge edition of Barrett Browning's work: the current "living monument" still includes her notes.

Thus, to buy the most accessible *Complete Works* of Barrett Browning is still to buy a monument to legend—complete with keep-off signs in the introduction and prettified Field Talfourd portrait on the front cover. Still, the texts are there for those who choose to go against advice. Loss is a relative term; Barrett Browning has fared better than many. Just as canonical revision and editing ultimately failed to transform Barrett Browning, the dead sinner, into a stable saint, so romantic reverence and literary decanonization ultimately failed to fix E. B. B. as a decorous Andromeda in Wimpole Street. It seems suitable that in 1931, as Barrett Browning languished on Broadway in Rudolf Besier's *The Barretts of Wimpole Street,* she also appeared, in very different guise, in an essay by Virginia Woolf. The architectural canon that houses Woolf's vision of poets is a "mansion of literature." In it, she tracks E. B. B. to her current position, locating her in the downstairs "servants' quarters, where, in company with Mrs. Hemans, Eliza Cook, Jean Ingelow, Alexander Smith, Edwin Arnold, and Robert Montgomery she bangs the crockery about and eats vast handfuls of peas on the point of her knife" (678). Vitality, noise, fearless "vulgarity": though these attributes fit neither the "supreme woman" nor her genteelly neurotic successor, they had been ascribed to the "headlong" poet during her own lifetime. They would emerge once more, later in this century, as sources of a rising literary fame.

V

Competing Sainthoods, Competing Saints: *The Canonization of Christina Rossetti*

Now, as on former Festivals, responding to the high-pitched note of promise we catch the deep thunder of warning: the jubilant saint is balanced by the miserable sin-chooser. "Let us also fear:" yet while we fear take courage; and thank God, who instructing us in mysteries of grace through subtilties of nature, has made it perceptible by human observation that even discords of music die out in harmony.

Christina
Rossetti

"SWEET LADY, AND POET, AND SAINT" (Watts-Dunton, "Reminiscences," 355). Linked as if they were mutually reinforcing, the tripartite terms of this praise open up both the promises and the ultimate untenability of Christina Rossetti's canonization as shaped toward the end of the last century and the beginning of this one. Rossetti, whose 1894 death roughly coincides with Richard D. Altick's date for the metaphoric demise of the Victorian poet worship, was born too late to become a full-fledged sacred poet-heroine (*Lives,* 141–42). As a devout Anglo-Catholic, however, she was not too late to hope for sainthood of a different sort. Both her works and her life confronted contemporaries with aspirations toward a religious sainthood whose sources were deeply, disturbingly rooted in medieval religion as well as in nineteenth-century culture.

Christina Rossetti presented her admirers with a serious canonical challenge. For the bonds that create the apparently harmonious if hackneyed figure of "sweet lady, and poet, and saint" come to look strained, if not strangling, at close range. "Sweet lady" and "poet" stand in problematic relation, of course: claims to the silent, sacred modesty of the Acting Angel tend to sit uneasily upon the figures of historical women whose fame derives from literary composition. Even more, however, tensions between "saint" and this secular trinity's other two figures are inevitably explosive. Though a would-be saint may be a poet as well, the capacity to represent the redemptive force of literature must surely be altered, if not altogether threatened, by primary commitment to an older and potentially competitive form of redemption.

Taken seriously, after all, the struggle for a place in heaven is an unflattering foil to the glory of winning space in anthologies, be they ever so influential. What is more, on a fundamental level, the saint is no lady. In eternity there are only two separate spheres, heaven and hell. To secure herself a place in the former, the saint must be prepared not only to violate the feminine proprieties of her class but to disobey all earthly laws and authorities and to break all earthly ties. She must stand, at least potentially, as a radically autonomous rather than a relative creature. If called upon to do so, she must ignore injunctions to feminine silence, openly naming and combatting forces upon which no sweet lady should dwell—including the seductions and terrors of hell itself. In the terms set by Rossetti herself in *Called to Be Saints* as quoted above, she must be prepared to evoke both "the high-pitched note of promise" and "the deep thunder of warning" ("All Saints," 502).

Rossetti's canonizers thus faced a peculiar dilemma. On the one hand, they needed to mediate between idealizations of their subject as woman and as poet; on the other, they needed to acknowledge her commitment to a sanctity whose relations both to femininity and to literary glory might be problematic or even antagonistic. Elizabeth Barrett Browning's canonization may be read as a series of displacements, at several points partially catalyzed by biographical revelations. Increasingly shoved aside to make room for heroines, the "body" of E. B. B.'s verse is either exorcised from the pastiche of the poet's papier-mâché collapsing monument or gushes, throbs, and shrieks on the legend's margins. In Rossetti's case, canonical revision and editing works less through metaphoric displacement than through dissolution: the poetic power of her most influential works tends to be dispersed primarily through praise that more or less explicitly denies that power's sources.

Where Barrett Browning's verse was reified, Rossetti's has often been domesticated. Canonized as the modest work of a "sweet lady," the "high-pitched note" of her most joyous calls to spiritual battle has been muted, while the "deep thunder" of her "warning" has been downplayed. In retrospect, the task looks extraordinarily difficult, even if one limits consideration to those of Rossetti's verses that were most celebrated by nineteenth-century criticism. The eerie playfulness and lush, eucharistic lesbian eroticism of "Goblin Market"; the desperate, visceral fear of corruption conveyed by "The World," whose power might now call to mind Gerard Manley Hopkins's "terrible" sonnets; the technical skill and rich, ambitious intertextuality of "Monna Innominata," Rossetti's "sonnet of sonnets," with its epigraphs from Dante and Petrarch—these qualities alone suggest not only the range but the audacity of Rossetti's poetic achievement.[1]

In assimilating such works and others to the harmonious, redemptive figure of a "sweet lady, and poet, and saint," Rossetti's critics employ a range of metaphoric strategies. They extract the "saint" from the historical period in which she lived; they muffle her verse and her person in a cheery domesticity that impedes heroic courage even as it blocks out the thunder of warning; they exonerate the "poet" from responsibility for the bleakness or eroticism of her verse as well as from the suspicion of having committed deliberate artistry (to paper). Such accounts never fully succeed, of course; but taken together, they suggest how canonization can undercut the literary reputation of the very subject it seeks to glorify.

Rossetti's first major volume of verse, *Goblin Market and Other Poems,* appeared in 1862, the year after Barrett Browning's death. As a result, the younger poet's reputation took shape in the wake of hagiographic accounts of E. B. B.'s feminine glory. Given the exclusionary form of such accounts, Rossetti's critics were forced either to subordinate their heroine or to attempt to break the hold of her predecessor's claims to sanctity.

Competition thus formed the groundwork of Rossetti's canonization. Indeed, although it has not yet played any major role in this book, competition is often central to the Victorians' development of the canonization process itself. After all, if "existing [artistic] monuments form an ideal order among themselves, which is modified by the new (the really new) work of art among them," then the resulting Hall of Literary Fame seems to admit only so many monuments at any given time (T. S. Eliot 3). Nor do limiting conventions end with the walls of imaginary palaces of art. Can it be accidental, for example, that nineteenth-century poets, like mythic heroes, seem to come in threes? Most famously, there is the male Romantic Big Six, with its neat division into generational triads (Blake-Coleridge-Wordsworth; Byron-Keats-Shelley; see Mellor 7–8). Next, there is that triumvirate of the textbooks, Tennyson, Browning, and Arnold. In 1986, moreover, Romanticism gained a female Big Three, at least in the *Norton Anthology of English Literature:* Mary Wollstonecraft, Dorothy Wordsworth, and Mary Shelley entered "that most canonical of indicators" (Lindenberger 41). Victorians follow suit: though Emily Brontë, Elizabeth Barrett Browning, and Christina Rossetti may not be included among such Great Victorian Poets, they have still formed their own triad in the *Norton Anthology* since that volume's first edition.

No doubt such symmetry offers mythic satisfactions. It inevitably entails anxiety as well, however. If each new cultural "monument" shifts the imaginary "ideal order," might not one poet serve to overshadow or even exclude another? Might not the tripartite pedestals of popular teaching anthologies unfairly exclude a Robert Burns or a Felicia Hemans, a Gerard Manley Hopkins or an Alice Meynell? In this context, nothing may signal the "opening up" of the canon more distinctly than the slowly increasing numerical raggedness of the *Norton,* in whose sixth edition, for example, four women poets now represent Romanticism (Anna Laetitia Barbauld, Charlotte Smith, Joanna Baillie, and Felicia Hemans). Nonetheless, given literary historiography's long tradition of competitive rankings, any nineteenth-century writer's reputation should probably still be considered in relative terms. Unfortunately, moreover, the sexual politics of literary historiography may render such concerns particularly appropriate for students of women writers.

Victorian literary historiography is filled with heroines who appear in feminine triptychs. By the mid-1880s, two frames of such sanctifying historiography were clearly filled by Elizabeth Barrett Browning and Christina Rossetti. Charlotte and Emily Brontë, Felicia Hemans, Jean Ingelow, Alice Meynell, and Sappho herself were all suggested to make up a third. It was not until 1962, when the first *Norton Anthology of English Literature* appeared, that Emily Brontë took her place as the last of the Big Three.[2]

Unstable to begin with, the literary triptychs of Victorian women poets have often folded in on themselves as well. Like judges in a beauty pageant, conventional literary historiographers may select a three-woman court; but they accord real victory only to one "queen." From the nineteenth century, deployment of such collapsible triads comes as no surprise: after all, England's lyric throne could be expected to accommodate only one "Queen of Song" at a time.[3] Unfortunately, however, the legendary figures of Barrett Browning and Rossetti are still too often metaphorically trapped in a critical game of musical chairs, still too often driven around a threadbare sacred throne or pedestal designed for the sole "great" Victorian woman poet. Women writers' presence in standard teaching anthologies in the United States may have dramatically increased, for example, but under the weight of "major authors" status, the multiplicity of the *Norton's* feminine triads still collapses. Female writers did not even break into the *Norton Anthology of English Literature: The Major Authors* until 1987; they still appear at the rate of only one per century. For the nineteenth century, that "major author" is Barrett Browning.[4] Nor is the *Norton* alone in choosing a sole woman poet: in Houghton and Stange's *Victorian Poetry and Poetics,* which has served for decades as the single most influential teaching anthology of Victorian poetry in the United States, Christina Rossetti reigns alone.

From the beginning, then, the project of canonizing Rossetti has required refutation of Barrett Browning's exclusionary status as the single great (or at least representative) woman poet. No wonder so many of Rossetti's admirers have been Barrett Browning's detractors. If one believes that there is a single supreme womanly Victorian niche in the architectural canon—an assumption supported by some hundred years of criticism—there is only one way to make room for Rossetti. One must topple E. B. B. from what Marge Piercy has called the "Square of the Immaculate Exception": one must ensure, again in the words of Piercy's "Token Woman," that Rossetti can "replace her" predecessor "so as to become her" (71, 72).

Powerful though it was—and in some cases remains—however, the drive to elevate Rossetti by dethroning her rival was not logically and perhaps not even historically inevitable. Indeed, Rossetti herself asserted as much; and in the process, she created a key textual moment within both poets' canonization. By 1882, when Rossetti published her own ambitious sonnet sequences, "Monna Innominata" and "Later Life," canonization of the *Sonnets from the Portuguese* was well under way, and with it the potential marginalization of all other women's poetry. For the *Sonnets'* celebration as definitive or "supreme" works established them as symbols of the limits as well as the range of women's poetry. If, as Stedman claimed, chaste, joyous heterosexual love stood as the highest source of feminine poetry, and if the *Sonnets* represented such love's apotheosis, then all women's verse on other subjects was inferior, as was all previous love poetry by women. As the "*final* expression of a woman's pure, ideal, passionate love," the *Sonnets* might mark the boundaries of women's poetry of the past, the present, and even the future (Isabel Clarke 792; emphasis added).[5] Under the circumstances, Rossetti evoked E. B. B.'s fame by the mere act of publishing a sonnet sequence. In the preface to "Monna Innominata," however, she did more than acknowledge that fame: she confronted it head-on. For more than a hundred years, critics have speculated as to whether Rossetti's notoriously elliptical preface challenges Barrett Browning's right to a lyric throne. They might better have asked whether it left the throne standing at all. For whatever the younger poet's attitude toward Barrett Browning's sonnets per se, the preface to "Monna Innominata" is a direct attack on the critical assumptions underlying those works' claims to supreme status. Preempting critical deployments of the *Sonnets* as a standard of measurement, Rossetti's text glorifies a very different Barrett Browning, a figure designed to undercut the premises of E. B. B.'s exclusionary canonization itself.

Rossetti begins by invoking the figures of Beatrice, of Laura, and of those "unnamed ladies" who inspired the troubadours. She asks her readers to return to the troubadours' time, imagining "many a lady as sharing her lover's poetic aptitude, while the barrier between them might be one held sacred by both, yet not such as to render mutual love incompatible with mutual honor. Had such a lady spoken for herself, the portrait left us might have appeared more tender, if less dignified, than any drawn even by a devoted friend. Or had the Great Poetess of our own day and nation only been unhappy instead of happy, her circumstances would have invited her to bequeath to us, in lieu of the 'Portuguese Sonnets,' an inimitable 'donna innominata' drawn not from fancy but from feeling, and worthy to occupy a niche beside Beatrice and Laura" (2:86). On the surface, Rossetti's preface seems to position its speaker as a generic Woman, a figure who might fill the silences left not only for muses such as Beatrice or Laura, or for female troubadours, but for Barrett Browning herself. "Monna Innominata" would thus be an exercise in literary ventriloquism, and a peculiar one at that. Even if one accepts that the poem's speaker is shadow of a shadow, why offer so many alternatives? How can the single voice of "Monna Innominata" speak for or through so many different figures?

In fact, however, Rossetti never actually claims that the speaker of "Monna Innominata" is the figure she asks her readers to imagine; she never asserts that her poem fills the silences its preface evokes. Rather, her preface offers a guided literary fantasy whose basis is an insistence that "circumstances" alone form the dividing lines, not only between actual and potential poems, but between the literary history we know from another, shadowy history of unwritten or lost texts (2:86).

Conceived in exile, under the shadow of the *Sonnets'* fame, "Monna Innominata" speaks to (if not entirely from within) this shadow tradition of women's writing. The speaker of "Monna Innominata" does not speak for, or as, Laura, Beatrice, a troubadour, or an unhappy Barrett Browning; rather, she speaks as an heir to their silences. For as she makes clear, the silence of even the greatest female inspirational figures leaves a gap that only speech could have filled; even Laura and Beatrice "came down to us resplendent with charms, but (at least, to my apprehension), scant of attractiveness" (2:86).

When Rossetti's preface speculates as to what might have happened "had the Great Poetess of our own day and nation only been unhappy instead of happy," she neither praises nor attacks the famous, near-celestial figure whom many critics were already presenting as having chanted the apotheosis of womanhood. Instead, she anchors E. B. B. to a specific "day and nation" rather than to womanhood itself, stressing the extent to which that writer's subject matter responds to the "invitation" of mere historical "circumstances." Rossetti's E. B. B. is still a Great Poetess: indeed, far from being a How-Do-I-Love-Thee Lady whose life may be her greatest poem, this figure would have written "inimitable" verse even had she written in sorrow. For though historical circumstances rather than divine revelation determined which works she would compose, they did not determine her greatness. Indeed, as a (mere) historical circumstance, Barrett's marriage may thus represent not only the world's poetic gain but its poetic loss. "Surely not only what I meant to say but what I do say is, not that the Lady" of the *Sonnets* "is surpassable," Rossetti wrote to her brother William Michael, "but that a 'Donna innominata' by the same hand might well have been unsurpassable. . . . I rather wonder that no one (so far as I know) ever hit on my semi-historical argument before for such treatment,— it seems to me so full of poetic suggestiveness" (quoted in Harrison 139; see 139–43).

Elizabeth Barrett's premarital love "invited" the composition of one poem, one must think; but who knows whether it repelled that of another? And who knows whether the unwritten poem might not have been the better one? Although Rossetti denied intending such an implication, readers have frequently found it nonetheless. In gaining Mrs. Browning, literature lost Miss Barrett, and with her, perhaps, an "inimitable" poem (Rossetti, "Monna Innominata," 2:86; Whitla 91).

Hence, Rossetti's preface clearly implies, the author of the *Sonnets from the Portuguese* cannot have written the definitive work of women's love poetry. For the circumstances of her life did not—could not—invite her to exhaust even her own possibilities as a love poet. Far from defining or exhausting the potential of women's love poetry, then, the *Sonnets* do not even necessarily define such poetry even by E. B. B. herself.

Thus, Rossetti turns Barrett Browning's canonization on its head. As she does so, moreover, she challenges many of the assumptions that underlie the canonization of vanishing monuments—including, ironically, certain canonization strategies employed by her own admirers. By using not only Barrett Browning but Petrarch's Laura and Dante's Beatrice as bait, she creates a dazzling trap. Given the supreme roles of Beatrice and Laura in the literature of love, if one once accepts their equation with an imaginary "donna innominata" (be she female troubadour or disappointed E. B. B.), one has accorded the rank of ideal woman to a figure who, in Rossetti's own words, "shares" and not merely inspires her male lover's "poetic aptitude." What is more, Rossetti's preface suggests that such a figure may write great verse not merely to confess her love but to satisfy her fancy—or perhaps even to assuage her dissatisfaction with known literary history.

In the preface to "Monna Innominata," Rossetti envisions female poets whose writing is shaped not by eternal womanhood but by the "invitation" of historical circumstance and the conscious deployment of artistry. She evokes muses who improve literary history by speaking. Through both processes she reveals the futility of competing canonizations of poet-heroines. There is no ultimate woman poet, she makes clear; the prize cannot be awarded.

Few of Rossetti's critics even came close to following her lead. Granted, there are writers who consider Barrett Browning and Rossetti as limited, if potentially great, poets of a "day and nation" rather than as potentially supreme representatives of a transcendent and unitary (if endangered) feminine authenticity.[6] Generally, however, Rossetti's would-be canonizers seek a shift in emphasis rather than a radical reconstruction of evaluative paradigms. They still require the highest women's poetry to be love poetry; they still judge such poetry as confessional; and they still seek "the greatest English poet of the sex which is made to inspire poetry, rather than to create it" (Lang, "Month," 112). In E. C. Stedman's terms, they still wait to see a woman reveal the secrets of a "burning heart" whose purity will enrich their dreams. This time, however, the purity in question is that of another "body" of work.

Rossetti's most ambitious admirers attempted to defend both the revelation process and the burning heart of their subject, claiming for these a feminine power comparable to if not greater than that embodied by E. B. B. Such a project involved complex interplays between textual and biographical readings as well as between challenges to and acceptance of Barrett Browning's claims to supremacy. Two intertwined, though at points incompatible, strategies emerge most vividly. The first, whose watchwords are *artless art,* awards E. B. B. the palm in terms of the intrinsic value of her love while insisting that Rossetti's unveiling was more complete. Naturalized by references to birdsong and metaphorically linked to watchwords such as *chaste* or *pure,* Rossetti's art is often canonized here as a form of naive stylistic virginity, free from the artistic trail of the serpent. The second strategy, whose watchword is *modesty,* grants Barrett Browning honor and sometimes precedence as an epic (or would-be epic) poet; but it asserts that in her willingness to be "content to be merely a woman," Rossetti alone succeeds at revealing the true heart of her sex. Celebrating Rossetti as a quintessentially domestic figure, it renders her a childlike singing saint whose most painful expressions often seem no more anguished or frightening than the harmonious melancholy of the nightingales she resembles.[7]

In the course of both processes, Rossetti is to some extent lost. Visions of a sacred poet-heroine cannot survive once their subject has been denied claims to conscious artistry; visions of an aspirant to traditional sainthood cannot survive once she has been denied claims to heroic—because dangerous—spiritual struggle. Too often, the "sweet lady, and poet, and saint" would subside into merely a sweet and increasingly quaint lady.

The development of Rossetti's canonization is often more a question of strains than of stages: patterns crystallize across several decades. By 1866, for example, reviewers of *The Prince's Progress and Other Poems* offer at least three suggestive, sharply defined images of the poet-heroine behind Rossetti's text. "Minor poet" is the most flattering label these reviewers accord her; yet two of their characterizations are destined to resonate in the praise of Rossetti's most enthusiastic critics.

"There is in some of [Rossetti's] best pictures," an *Athenaeum* reviewer writes, "the air of the cathedral rather than that of the world without. Her saints and heroes have not the stir and dust of life about them; but they smile to us in a repose almost mournful, like effigies from a stained window or the sculptured forms of knight and dame in the coloured light of the aisle." Though "subtle and mature," Rossetti's verse appears as minor here, in terms both of key and stature. Her work may evoke cathedrals; it may reveal "beauty" and "pathos"; but by right of the author's very reticence, it lacks life: "She does not unveil to us the face of humanity until the flush of human impulse has died away" ("Prince's Progress," 825).

At this point, the underlying uncanniness of such images seems not far from the surface. Are Rossetti's "saints and heroes" effigies or corpses? Given Rossetti's famous evocations of goblins and ghosts, the muted gothicism here makes sense; indeed, one cannot help wondering whether a turn in critical emphasis might not have rendered the poet as much witch as saint. Certainly an *Athenaeum* reviewer of *Sing-Song* worried that "the weird spirit of 'Goblin Market' would haunt the cradles" about which Rossetti sang ("Sing-Song," 11).

At first glance, a *Saturday Review* response to the verses in the same volume could not differ more dramatically: "They are like the piping of a bird on a spray in the sunshine, or the quaint singing with which a child amuses itself when it forgets that anybody is listening. There is not much thinking in them, not much high or deep feeling, no passion, and no sense of the vast blank space which a great poet always finds encompassing the ideas of life and nature and human circumstance" ("Miss Rossetti's Poems," 761). It is a long way from the colored cathedral light to the sunny spray, from the veiled though subtle and mature creator of stained glass and effigies to the piping child or bird. In both cases, however, the route leads back, through innocence, out of this point in history and out of struggle, be it with the "stir and dust of life" or the Pascalian "vast blank space." In both cases, too, while the innocent body behind the text—whether effigy or bird—may be feminine, it is not human. The implications of such figuration are clearly negative. "It is not for thought or passion that one goes to the minor poets," a *Nation* review of the same volume notes, for example, "and Miss Rossetti's merit, though unique, will never be of the supreme order" ("Miss Rossetti's Poems," 47). With time, however, that evaluation was to change. Indeed, as a whole critical approach came to equate *minor* with *feminine,* the cathedral figure and the bird would come to evoke glory, even if they did not cease to signal weakness.[8]

So resonant have such diminishing figures become that they may seem natural or at least inevitable. An 1867 piece from the *Catholic World,* however, descries a more passionate, intransigent body behind works such as "Cousin Kate," "Sister Maude," or "Goblin Market." Terming Rossetti's verse "fairly chargeable with utterances—and reticences—of morally dangerous tendency," the author evokes "a young lady of intelligence and education, constantly in contact with real literary society and . . . well read in our best poets." The woman writer in question reveals "a strong, sensuous, impulsive, earnest, inconsiderate nature, that sympathizes well, feels finely, keeps true to itself at bottom, but does not pause to make sure that others must, as well as may, enter into the spirit that underlies her utterances" ("Christina G. Rossetti," 845–46). Most modern readers would be loathe to praise this article for open-mindedness or perception, particularly given its possible role in encouraging Rossetti to suppress certain poems in later editions. In its allegations of Rossetti's dangerous sympathy with sexual immorality, however, the *Catholic World* speaks of a woman who is too often absent from other criticism, a poet of strength, "overweening ambition," and sexual passion (842).[9]

Cathedrals and tree boughs were thus neither natural nor inevitable frames for conceiving the body of Rossetti's verse. If vivid fictionalizations of her life and works had been all that was at stake, drawing rooms filled with painters and poets—or homes for fallen women—might have provided settings that were more accurate and equally evocative.

What was at stake went far deeper. In succeeding years, critics evoke a series of revealingly constituted bodies in Rossetti's texts. Although their texts do not always treat the potential sacred heroine and the would-be saint in the same ways, they constantly renegotiate spiritual and poetic ambition as dangers to feminine literary canonization. The cathedral (or cloister) and the sunny bough are not the only frames such accounts evoke, but they rarely disappear entirely.

By the late 1870s, for example, a *Catholic World* reviewer who terms Rossetti "Queen of the Preraphaelite school" criticizes "Goblin Market" for evoking the heroism of a "Joan of Arc" to describe "a little girl struggling" against "little goblins" ("Christina Rossetti's Poems," 122, 125) "The statue is far too large for the pedestal," the author complains (125). Revealingly, however, this reviewer sees Rossetti's religious poetry as "a little devotional shrine . . . where we find her on her knees. . . . Here she is another woman. As she sinks her poetry rises, and gushes up out of her heart to heaven in strains sad, sweet, tender, and musical that a saint might envy" (126–27). Not one but two bodies lie behind this text: for Rossetti is a different writer in "her religious and in her worldly mood" (129). The secular writer—the deliberate sculptor of Lizzie's "statue"—may "warble or sing," but she is guilty of "affectation." Her notes turn "flat and discordant" (129). The religious poet, whose apparently unmediated verse "gushes up out of her heart," is "an inspired prophetess or priestess." Whether she is "chanting a sublime chant or giving voice to a world's sorrow and lament," she sings like a saint (129). (Saints, it seems, do not consider their songs; like birds, they simply pour them out.)

In the *Catholic World* the word *saint* has precise religious meaning, although that meaning scarcely leads to approval of Rossetti's own religious convictions. This reviewer, at least, acknowledges the fierce, sometimes frightening passion of Rossetti's religious verse, if only to turn the power of that verse against the poet's faith. Citing "The Three Enemies," "Good Friday," and "The World," the author warns Rossetti that only a return to Catholicism and "the one true fold" can save Rossetti from the emptiness of failed sanctity—from the "sad satire" of a life like that of George Eliot's Dorothea Brooke (127–28).

Where E. B. B. the poet-heroine tended to be protected from her poetry, different embodiments of Rossetti may be protected from one another as well as from potentially disturbing aspects of her work. The 1881 *Athenaeum* review of Rossetti's *A Pageant and Other Poems,* for example, acknowledges the poet's fondness for allegorical writing, of both the "graceful and bewitching" and the "terrible kind." Yet when the reviewer evokes the furniture of the poet's mind, praising her "fancy (not cold like most people's fancy, but warm as the snug cottage room in which the dramatic action takes place)," her playfulness, and her music, which is "apparently lawless as a bird's song, yet, like the bird's song, obeying a law too subtle to be recognized," the internal world of the "terrible" poems is nowhere to be seen. Nor, apparently, is that of intellectual labor. As the reviewer is at some pains to explain, a gift for allegory is something "quite apart from intellectual strength." "Even the uneducated peasantry of Italy systematically keep to a recognized" metrical "form." With the vast blank spaces of her own verses' religious terror and the technical efforts of composition thus shut out, the imagined body of the poet-heroine's verse remains snugly cradled by the warm fancy of one "in whom the gift of pure song is far more noticeable than any other quality" ("A Pageant," 328).

Glorifications of feminine stylistic "artlessness" begin to carry a new charge toward the century's end. There may be no more explicit expression of that shift's central assumptions than "Poetry in Petticoats," an 1890 review printed in the *Scots Observer* (later the *National Observer*). Like Victorian "songbirds," the fin-de-siècle women of "Poetry in Petticoats" "feel, therefore they sing." Now, however, because "they are women" they must be "therefore lyric poets." The weight of sexual decorum may be lifting, but that of generic decorum is descending. Women may be passionately conscious of many things, it seems, but their own poetic language is not among them. For to exercise deliberate art is to lose woman's only poetic gift, "that magic of sincerity which is in itself a sort of style." Indeed, so powerful are women's "innate incapacity of style" and "instinct of insincerity" that any efforts to control their language seem to doom female poets to "mimicry." "Sappho and George Sand notwithstanding," the "common fate" of women who "would be creative artists" is to create "not art, but 'a document'" (438–39).

As these evocations of the scandalous, bisexual George Sand and of the newly problematized Sappho suggest (DeJean, *Fictions*, 245–46), connections between such aesthetic rigidity and fears of sexual chaos are not hard to find. "Poetry in Petticoats" explicitly warns women poets that stylistic and intellectual ambitions endanger not only their femininity but their adherence to the heterosexual contract: "The Greeks once figured the Muses as women; and—for the Greeks were wise—they may well have meant to signify thereby that the Muses would endure the caresses of none but men. Certain it seems that Poetry in petticoats is only poetry on sufferance; only woman essaying to do the man's part, and . . . failing relatively if not absolutely" (439). Decades earlier, when Barrett Browning was accused of literary transvestism, the charge had far more to do with decorum than with sexuality. By now, however, the implications of female poets attempting to embrace female muses may well go much further. By 1896, when Lionel Johnson speculated that Rossetti's future reputation might suffer from the "intensely personal limitations, the wonderfully individual intentions of her Uranian muse" (59), the word *uranian* had already come to mean *homosexual* as well as *heavenly* ("Uranian"; Showalter, *Sexual Anarchy*, 23). Given the period's increasing anxieties over single women, an erotic reading of poems such as "Goblin Market" or "Amor Mundi" might not have even been necessary to cast (unspoken/ unspeakable) doubt upon Rossetti's (hetero)-sexual orthodoxy: symbolically, the mere fact of her being a female poet, and a single one at that, might have been enough.

If a woman insists upon writing, "Poetry in Petticoats" advises, "Let her fail. Now and then she sings you a song; now and then she utters a *cri de coeur;* her innate lyrism sometimes finds adequate expression" (439). Primitivistic fin-de-siècle woman may "cry," evoking the "natural music, of . . . the duet of wave and shore, the song of the wind in the leaves" (438). She may not, however, cold-bloodedly create (Dijkstra 166–74). Thus, women's poetic endeavors are countenanced only at the cost of rigid containment—and, of course, of preordained failure on the highest artistic levels.[10]

Working within such an aesthetic, much of this period's criticism seeks to establish Rossetti as a kind of sacred counterheroine, by reading her works as spontaneous, primitive, transcendent, or transparent expressions of fin-de-siècle "eternal" womanhood—as the creations of a definitive "natural" woman poet.[11] Such a figure could not represent her own time: the feminine cry of the heart is by definition instinctive and nonhistorical. She might, however, succeed in marginalizing such female representative figures altogether.

As indicated, such constructions of unhistorical, "natural" women's poetry could be easily compatible with earlier notions of unselfish women's spontaneous verse. Here, for example, is the 1877 *Athenaeum:* "The reason why no woman has ever, except in lyric, yet produced a work of art even approximately perfect is, that owing to the ethical basis of her nature her imagination is stifled before it can reach the *selfish* domain of pure art. . . . Art is too supremely selfish, perhaps, for the spirit of self-abnegation which informs the soul of a woman" ("Earlier Poems," 766). The *cri de coeur* may thus express not only "natural, primitive," femininity, but the "ethical basis" of feminine self-abnegation. Such "natural" transcendence of history had powerful and specific historical uses. "Empirical evidence to the contrary," Ann Ardis writes, "the common perception in the 1890s was that women were taking over the literary world" (43). Threatened, perhaps, by many women writers' unabashed professionalism as well as by the sexual and political audacity of poets such as Augusta Webster or Amy Levy (whose work inspired "Poetry in Petticoats"), a number of critics constructed Rossetti's reputation as a stay against sexual anarchy within literature itself. Edmund Gosse, who was one of Rossetti's most articulate and influential admirers, is quite explicit on this score in an 1893 *Century Magazine* article: Rossetti is "the type of the woman-poet who exists not by reason of the variety or volume of her work, but by virtue of its intensity, its individuality, its artistic perfection" ("Christina Rossetti," 211). As such a "type," she provides a needed corrective to the contemporary literary scene: "At no time was it more necessary to insist on this truth than it is to-day. . . . The women who write, in particular, pursued by that commercial fervor which is so curious a feature of our new literary life, and which sits so inelegantly on a female figure, are in a ceaseless hurry to work off and hurry away into oblivion those qualities of their style which might, if seriously and coyly guarded, attract a permanent attention" (211–12). Thus the poetically promiscuous, clad in the inelegant garb of those who write for a living, seem to walk (or to work) New Grub Street, squandering those charms that might, "if seriously and coyly guarded," have earned them the permanent esteem of a good male critic and a place in the household of literature.

Integrated into *Critical Kit-kats,* Gosse's essay achieved six reprintings between 1894 and 1903. Moreover, Gosse was not alone. In 1896, two years after Rossetti's death, for example, Theodore Watts-Dunton wrote that she "had more of what is called the unconsciousness of poetic inspiration than any other poet of her time. . . . The writing of poetry was not by any means the chief business of her life. . . . No one felt so deeply as she that poetic art is only the imperfect body in which dwells the poetic soul" ("Literature," 208). "She never posed as a 'literary person'—reading her productions at four o'clocks and winning high praise from the unbonneted, and the discerning society editor," Elbert Hubbard assured readers of his 1897 *Little Journeys* (167).

No New Grub Street professional, no member of the "third sex," with its "feverish hunger for work" (Green-Armytage, "Introductory," xvi), Christina Rossetti thus came to embody a new form of literary chastity. In some accounts, such sexual and stylistic innocence protected her not only from making poetry the chief "business of her life" but even from the "pretentiousness" of making stylistic revisions (Hugh Walker, "Turn of the Century," 506).[12]

By constructing Rossetti as the woman poet who knew her stylistic place, critics ensured that her "timeless" feminine heart's cry could serve as evidence of the vanishing "natural" relationship of a modest woman to poetic practice. Much as Barrett Browning had become a retroactive Angel in the House, then, Rossetti became an exemplar of that other great, vanishing Victorian woman, the songbird poet who "sings," spontaneously and exquisitely, only because it is her nature to do so. "Of Miss Rossetti," Alice Law summarized, "it must be said that she has *sung* everything" (453).[13]

Not surprisingly, the "sweet lady and poet" of such accounts also appeared as a saint—a sweetened saint, to be sure. To find sainthood in its "natural" form, however, critics often needed to reach further afield than late-Victorian England. As a literary heroine, Rossetti was "more English than any Englishwoman" (Symons, "Christina Rossetti," *Saturday Review,* 5); she was "as English as English maids and meadows" (Le Gallienne 131). Despite her "essentially English character," however, her Italian blood could be made to explain a great deal (Benson, "Christina Rossetti," 620). Gosse, for example, asserts that the body within the works of that "thorough Englishwoman," Rossetti, reveals "a sort of Tuscan candor, as of a sacred picture in which each saint or angel is robed in a dress of one unbroken color. These two qualities combined, in spite of their apparent incompatibility,—an austere sweetness coupled with a luscious and sensuous brightness,—to form one side of Miss Rossetti's curious poetic originality" ("Christina Rossetti," *Century,* 213). Gosse's image of a luscious "saint or angel" sanctifies sensuousness even as it beautifully underplays the more threatening aspects of Rossetti's faith. Elsewhere in the same piece, he may acknowledge that Rossetti's poetry is "not merely Christian and Protestant" but "Anglican" (214); here, he lends it a charmingly naive "Tuscan" exoticism. The pattern is a prominent one: where Rossetti is joyous, she is a contemporary; where harsh, she is safely assigned to some other era. Thus, for example, while her love of "physical beauty and the richer parts of nature . . . allies her with her brother and their younger friends," she leaps back into the seventeenth century when she writes religious verse, becoming instead the "sister of George Herbert" and a member "of the family of Crashaw, of Vaughan, and of Wither" (214, 217). Through such metaphoric escape hatches, the question of what it meant to be writing such devotional poetry in the late nineteenth century need never be addressed.

Striking, too, is another pattern already noted: that of acknowledging Rossetti's "terrible" verses in asides while describing—or quoting—the more playful poems in the most vivid possible terms. In absolving Rossetti from the "literary hypocrisy" that might "shrink from strong delineation of the pleasures of life," for example, Gosse offers striking citations; in acknowledging her verses' renunciation of such pleasure, he does no such thing (214). Too sincere an admirer of Rossetti's religious verse—as of her art—to be consistent in his own canonization, Gosse acknowledges the "firm touch" and "weighty intelligence" even of a grim sonnet such as "The World." Still, even in praising that work—or "Amor Mundi," for that matter—he offers no quotation, and certainly no evocation of a terrified, ascetic, or struggling body behind the text (216–17).

Theodore Watts-Dunton's 1895 "Reminiscences of Christina Rossetti" is a key text for such accounts of the "natural" saint of domestic nostalgia, and not merely because it is the source of "sweet lady, and poet, and saint."[14] From its opening, Watts-Dunton's essay strives to attain iconicity. The "time will come—it *must* come—when every authoritative word about one so beloved, every scrap of testimony from every witness, howsoever unworthy, will be accounted sacred by those to whom poetry is almost a religion" (355). It is not clear whether Watts-Dunton worships poetry, but he certainly glorifies poet-heroines: "Imagine, then, what must be the feeling of him who sits down to write about the most adored personality among the poets of our time!" (355). Shades of Stedman: what Watts-Dunton ultimately reveres in Rossetti is less her verse or even her specific, historical "personality" than her symbolic power of awakening his own ideal visions. "It was not her inspiration which overawed me at the idea of meeting her. It was the feeling that her inspiration was not of the artist at all, . . . but the inspiration of the religious devotee. It answered a chord within me, but a chord that no poet had theretofore touched. It seemed to me to come from a power which my soul remembered in some ante-natal existence, and had not even yet wholly forgotten. As to meeting Christina as an earthly woman, that had never . . . occurred to me. . . . I said, . . . 'But

Christina is a saint, you know'" (357). As it turns out, the Rossetti Watts-Dunton meets is a "very saint, no doubt; but a playful one" (358). As he puts it, "while she seemed to breathe a sainthood that must needs express itself in poetry, all the charm of the mere woman remained in her—remained, and coloured her life with those riches of earth, without which woman may be worshipped, but never loved as Christina Rossetti was loved by us all" (355). The saint is thoroughly domesticated. Rossetti does not strive for sainthood; she breathes it like air. And the poet is thoroughly spontaneous: she writes not because she chooses but because she "must needs" do so.

Though Alice Law's "Poetry of Christina G. Rossetti," published in the 1895 *Westminster Review,* reads the body of the text rather than the life of the poet, its ends are analogous. Here, Rossetti's potentially disturbing religious verse, with its calls to traditional sanctity, is distanced rather than domesticated. Law's account of the "monument" of Rossetti's "finished work," (which still omits the likes of "Amor Mundi" or "The World"), evokes a heroine who struggles "with the fears and fightings of her own bursting heart" (453, 449). She does so, however, from the safety of the Middle Ages. "There is nothing modern" about this "singing," Law assures her readers, "unless it be its hopelessness, its troubled emotion and despair" (449).

Readers moved by modern hopelessness, troubled emotion, or despair need not engage with this poet-heroine's religious renunciations or warnings; like Rossetti herself, such expressions of faith appear anachronistic. For Law, as for Gosse and others before them, the body of Rossetti's texts is as vibrantly colored, as exotic, and as flat as medieval art: "In all Miss Rossetti's pages we seem to see the mediaeval heroine herself looking out at us, from an almost cloistered seclusion, with sad patient eyes. . . . Consciously or unconsciously, [Rossetti] is her own medieval heroine. . . . Like her medieval prototype, [she] sought and found consolation for the unsatisfied yearnings of the heart in devout prostration of spirit, and the uplifting of the soul to God. . . . The unabated suffering and chastened beauty of [her] life induced [her] unconsciously to wear the uplifted adoring attitude of some mediaeval saint upon an old stained church-window" (449–50). There is no need to build nineteenth-century monuments to a woman poet who fears hell: quaint monuments of an earlier age will serve just as well, if not better.

Not surprisingly, celebrations of Rossetti's "cloistral" muse and of her "pure and perfect spirit"—her "disembodied soul of song"—emerge most dramatically just after her death (Sharp 737, 749). They continue to appear, however, in one form or another, well past the turn of the century. In such accounts, Rossetti's poetic career tends to drop off, along with her more secular verses, about 1881. Even her early works are metaphorically revised and edited to elim-

inate or curtail discussion of "terrible poems" and to stress childish or saintly
simplicity. (The erotic longings and frenzy of "Goblin Market" become child-
like; the formal intricacies of "Monna Innominata" are not acknowledged; the
terror of "The World" might never have existed.)[15]

In such contexts, even the unmarried Rossetti can assume a sacred maternal or romantic role. Not only can she sing "at her work, as the womanly
woman ever does," writing poems only because she has no babies (Hubbard
167),[16] but the "pensive, clinging, *passive*" attitude of her songs can embody
the lost or endangered womanliness of "long-tried Griseldas, . . . or the olive-
wreathed, flame-robed virgins of the *Divine Comedy*" (Law 449, 446). Whether
the terms are those of the Middle Ages, the Renaissance, or the early nineteenth
century, the body in the text of Rossetti's poems is that of a sweet, old-fashioned
woman: "Her best poems have a tender and dependent appeal—cleave to
you. . . . She is above all things womanly, as our mothers understood womanliness; with the womanliness which is parasitic and takes no shame in the fact.
The teaching of her poetry, if one may call anything so modest by the name of
teaching, accords with this spirit" (Thompson, "Christina Rossetti," 144).[17] The
key to such womanliness is modesty. This quality, which is both natural and
moral, combines several of Rossetti's potential values for late-century nostalgia:
it not only evokes sexual purity but may be assumed to spring from a radical
absence of self-consciousness and to be inseparable from Rossetti's nonprofes-
sional status.

Thus constructed by fin-de-siècle criticism, Rossetti could serve as a quintessentially domestic "poet and saint" (Meynell, "Christina Rossetti," 572), a
definitively modest "woman of genius" whose achievement reproached a "rebelliousness and self-seeking . . . not unknown among women-writers of a little
talent"—and perhaps not unassociated with Barrett Browning herself (Meynell,
Introduction to *Poems by Christina Rossetti,* vii). Where stylistic chastity was concerned, after all, Barrett Browning was well equipped to figure as an agent of
sexual chaos. Both as a vehement feminist preacher of the mid-Victorian gospel
of work and as an audacious technical innovator, she clearly betrayed an intellect
"not untinged with literary ambition" (Green 966). In such accounts, then,
whether the *Sonnets* and their author appear as too self-assured, self-aware, ambitious, sexual, or self-revelatory, one "taint" characterizes them: immodesty.

Arthur Symons's 1895 *Saturday Review* article, which asserts Rossetti's exclusive claim to feminine poetic greatness, is perhaps the most influential work in
this mode. Barrett Browning appears here not merely as a contemporary but as,
"one might almost say, a companion" of George Sand. Moreover, she is linked
to the doubly discredited figure of L. E. L., in whose reputation sentimentality

and scandalousness had been damningly (if at points incongruously) merged ("Christina Rossetti," 5). E. B. B. is thus a perfect foil for Rossetti, who appears in an expanded version of this essay as a poet whose style "seems to be innocently unaware of its own beauty" (Symons, "Christina Rossetti," *Studies,* 140).[18]

Implicit in Symons, dissatisfaction with Barrett Browning's open stylistic self-awareness is overt in an 1881 *Literary World* review. "Even Mrs. Browning's sonnets, disguised as translations from the Portuguese, are less beautiful in form, less self-forgetful in spirit" than the sonnets of "Monna Innominata" ("The Rossettis," 396). An 1892 *Spectator* review echoes and augments that mild comment: "There is an air of self-consciousness, a suggestion of 'attitude'" about the *Sonnets.* Such qualities "impair their charm. Mrs. Browning seems all the while to be watching the spectacle of her own emotions, with scarcely disguised interest in so beautiful and impressive an exhibition" ("Books," 259). This last image of E. B. B. engaged in narcissistic (if not downright erotic) posturing in front of a mirror is worth noting; such characterizations have had lasting resonance. As late as 1981, for example, nearly a hundred years after the *Spectator* article, Joan Rees's competitive criticism still describes the *Sonnets'* effect as that "of somebody declaiming aloud and gesticulating melodramatically all by herself in a small retired room where, to our embarrassment, we have strayed" (151). Moreover, it still elevates Rossetti's verse in terms of stylistic virginity. The *Sonnets,* Rees writes, "yielded too much, too quickly" (147). To turn to "Monna Innominata" after these earlier works is to move from an "adventurous vocabulary and rash images" to a diction that is "chaste" (152).

Where Rossetti the modest nightingale is set against Barrett Browning the histrionic poseur, Rossetti's competitive canonization attains its most dramatic and dangerous form. The very terms that shape her temporary victory transform her into a vanishing monument, and a "minor" one at that. Double-edged though the canonization of Barrett Browning was, that of Rossetti was even more so.

Two biographical problems faced Rossetti's canonizers: the poet's refusal to marry and her dying fear of damnation. As long as Rossetti could be metaphorically removed to the Middle Ages, her marital status was no problem: medieval saints should be chaste, after all. In a late-nineteenth-century culture torn by conflicts between the (sometimes radical and feminist) "spinster and her enemies," however (Jeffreys), suspicion of celibacy rendered claims to the exemplary role of a poet-heroine deeply problematic—particularly, perhaps, when the poet in question wrote so frequently and so passionately from the perspectives of single and fallen women (McGann, "Christina Rossetti's Poems," 244–46). And despite some critics' endeavors, Rossetti could not be entirely removed from such a culture. On both textual and biographical grounds, then, her reception was often colored by suspicion that she had engaged in what feminist theorist Janice Raymond calls "marriage resistance" (117).

One could, of course, cast the poet as having been disappointed in love. Certain accounts do align her with earlier feminine figures of whom this might be said, whether "nightingale poets" or nuns. One could also assert, as Hubbard did, that the "burdens" of managing the Rossetti "household" had fallen on the poet; she had given up "society, refused the thought of marriage and joined that unorganized sisterhood of mercy—the women who toil that others may live" (167). Ultimately, however, such accounts were doomed. By 1896, the *Literary World* was already reporting on William Michael Rossetti's unequivocal identification of religious scruples as the grounds for his sister's refusal of not one but two offers of marriage ("Major and Minor Poetry"). Religious celibacy might be more respectable than sex radicalism, but it was still far from being an attractive attribute in a would-be exemplary poet-heroine.

Criticism in Stedman's vein was sure to rate Rossetti as at best merely an inferior embodiment of womanhood: if one sought to assert the "true," imperative "relation" of marriage to women's art, the lessons of a career such as Rossetti's could only be bitter or melancholy. To be sure, such criticism had no monolithic hold. Barrett Browning was far from universally admired as a model of womanhood ("Reviews," 466); Robert Browning was not always credited with having been a positive influence on his wife (Thompson, "Mrs. Browning," 163). Identifications of marital and artistic fulfillment were somewhat common nonetheless; and in such writing, Rossetti's status tended to be dubious at best.[19]

Toward the century's end, moreover, as accounts of the hysterical heroine emerged from characterizations of Barrett Browning, visions of the repressed religious fanatic began to enter into portrayals of Rossetti. Hattie Tyng Griswold's 1898 *Personal Sketches of Recent Authors* offers a particularly explicit instance. Blending stylistic and sexual perversions, Griswold aligns Rossetti's chastity with her poetry's flaws. Here, virginal style is bad style. Capable of loving a man as well as of writing as "naturally as a bird sings," Griswold's doomed poet-heroine falls prey both to celibacy and to "far-fetched imagery and artificial and morbid phases of thought" instead (288). The misguided Rossetti, who turns her "high heroic soul" against herself on religious grounds, thus does "violence to her own nature": "The pity of it all was infinite. A warped womanhood resulted, a narrow life, the life of a zealot and recluse, where gracious motherhood and sweet marital companionship, might have widened the nature and deepened the insight of this true, though limited poet, in some senses one of the finest of her day" (290–91). By 1897, the *Dictionary of National Biography* was characterizing most of Rossetti's verse as "melancholy and even morbid," imbued with the "taint of disease" (Garnett 283). Thus, in the context of rising anxieties over sexual anarchy, glorification of virginal style was double-edged. Celibacy could be nearly as problematic for domestic sainthood as marriage could be for religious sainthood.

Nor, as noted, was marriage the only biographical stumbling block to Rossetti's transformation into a comfortably domestic saint. While Rossetti's life brought her too close to traditional sainthood to render her an easy candidate for domestic sainthood's glories, her death rendered references to the rewards of religious sanctity difficult as well. Saints—of all sorts—should die well; yet Christina Rossetti died hard, worn out by battling terror for her eternal soul as well as physical pain. Though it was scarcely quoted with the enthusiasm accorded his description of Rossetti's allegedly spontaneous composition techniques, William Michael Rossetti's biographical writing provided an account: "She took finally to her bed, in a calm and resigned mood, but, as the time advanced, with troublous agitation, both of spirit and of the bodily frame. Not that she was abashed by pain, or craven-hearted—far indeed from that; but the terrors of her religion compassed her about, to the overclouding of its radiances. At the close of a week of collapse and semi-consciousness, she died without a struggle, in the act of inarticulate prayer" ("Memoir," lix).

Rossetti's friend William Sharp wrote that "she gained, by prayer and renunciation, and long control, a sunlit serenity which made her mind, *for others,* a delectable Eden, and her soul a paradise of fragrance and song" (748; emphasis added). Less delicately, many of the poet's chroniclers discounted the labor or the limited success of such endeavors. Hubbard's heroine, for example, is too blessed to endure physical suffering, much less spiritual torments: "She felt that her work was done, and feeling so, the end soon came. . . . Glad to go, rejoicing that the end was nigh, and soothed by the thought that beyond lay a Future, she fell asleep" (172). In contrast, Griswold writes, "So gloomy were her religious views, and so melancholy her nature, that one almost fears that even in her chamber beneath the moss, she will continue to hear 'the nightingale sing on as if in pain.' But a more robust and cheerful faith rebukes the morbid fancy" (297).

Such decanonization of the simple nightingale saint may have been inevitable. Within fin-de-siècle paradigms of domestic or religious sainthood, Rossetti's canonization as a harmonious, "natural" holy virgin was already beginning to crumble. There had been little place for a historical woman—or even a saint—who went down fighting. Without such a place, Rossetti's would-be canonizers could only gloss over her very death as a failure.[20] Cruelly, moreover, Barrett Browning took the palm even here: for like the most sacredly conventional of Victorian fictional heroines, she was known to have died quietly in her husband's arms. What is more, her last speech, so the story went, had been "Beautiful."

Though Rossetti's candidacy for sweet, domestic sainthood often involved dramatic (and ultimately futile) biographical evasions or elisions, its literary costs may have been even higher. Rossetti feared going to hell. Devout as she was, if she feared for herself, what would she have thought of the most of her readers' eternal prospects? One might well believe William Sharp that the historical woman was "reticent" as well as "scrupulous . . . in any matter where conscience impelled her to protest," and that such protests as she did issue were "gentle, or at least courteous" (744). Yet the "thunder of warning," be it ever so courteous, was bound to be unnerving coming from any woman; and coming from a prospective embodiment of natural femininity, it could well have seemed unbearable. Marian figures do not threaten damnation, after all; they intercede for salvation. "Natural" women and nightingales do not conjure up the horrors of hell. And thus, as we have seen, many of Rossetti's greatest admirers sought, ingeniously and energetically, for metaphors capable of modulating or even drowning out the thunder both of her verses and of her faith. By thus trying to cut their heroine off from hell, they also attempted to deprive her of the prerequisite for her spiritual heroism and for much of her most powerful— and terrible—verse.

Turning from attempts to canonize the Rossetti as "sweet lady and saint" to attempts to canonize her as "sweet lady and poet," one finds analogous problems. Consider, for example, the 1892 *Spectator* article that sets Rossetti's stylistic modesty against Barrett Browning's poetic posturing. Praising Rossetti's "sequestered and cloistral spirit," the author credits her verse with "the attainment of *almost* the highest ends by a wonderful restraint and husbandry of means" ("Books," 259; emphasis added).[21] The "almost" is crucial here: it goes to the heart of critics' paradoxical insistence on Rossetti's role as supreme exemplar of the stylistic virtues of the second sex.

Rossetti's verse might well be definitively feminine. As "Poetry in Petticoats" stresses, however, "at its best her work [was] almost art" (438). Cited as authoritative by no less a critic than Meynell, the phrase "almost art" is the deadly corollary of praise for the poet's "artless art" ("Christina Rossetti," 571). It would figure largely in Rossetti's reception. Put bluntly: praise in petticoats remains second-rate praise. Consider, for example, one of the most influential instances of such double-edged admiration: "Content to be merely a woman, wise in limiting herself within somewhat narrow bonds, [Rossetti] possessed, in union with a profoundly emotional nature, a power of artistic self-restraint. . . . It is through this mastery over her own nature, this economy of her own resources, that she takes rank among poets rather than among poetesses" (Symons, "Christina Rossetti," *Saturday Review,* 5). This passage from Symons's essay, which appears in his *Studies* (135–36), still introduces Rossetti in the most recent edition of *Nineteenth-Century Literature Criticism* (Laurie Lanzen Harris 554–55). No other critic's work is thus honored.

In some sense, Arthur Symons does read Rossetti as a deliberate artist. By accepting the narrow bonds of womanhood, he asserts, she "masters" her own nature and thus paradoxically transcends the limits of her sex. This is high praise; yet witness his judgment of "Monna Innominata." Rossetti's sequence represents "delicate art, perfect within its limits." Still, limited as "Monna Innominata" is "within a certain range," its "right of admission among the stronger and more varied sequences of Dante and Petrarch, of Mrs. Browning and Rossetti," is uncertain ("Christina Rossetti," *Studies,* 145–46).

Such ambivalence is not unique. Gosse, for example, asserts that "artlessness nowadays must be the result of the most exquisitely finished art" (Introduction, xxxii). Yet even his praise of Rossetti's art trips up on petticoats. "In order to succeed in poetry," he writes, women "must be brief, personal, and concentrated" ("Christina Rossetti," *Century,* 211). Only their "lyric gift, their cry from the heights or the depths of feeling, . . . has won them" a "place upon Parnassus" ("Mr. Gosse," 38).[22] By abstaining from the "great solid branches of poetry," such as epic, tragedy, and "didactic and philosophical verse,"("Mr. Gosse," 37), Gosse asserts, Rossetti has thus become "one of the most perfect poets of the age—not one of the most powerful, *of course,* nor one of the most epoch-making, but . . . one of the most perfect" ("Christina Rossetti," *Century,* 212; emphasis added).

Under the circumstances, it seems no wonder that glorification of Rossetti's transcendent modesty failed to dislodge the *Sonnets'* primacy, even among many of Rossetti's most ardent admirers. After all, the claims of "the happier lover" rested upon a love that was presumably unmatched, and if Barrett Browning had attempted too much, there was some glory in that as well. "The better poet," on the other hand, had attained only the secondary values of the second sex. Critics praise her, faintly, for a feminine inability to "grapple with . . . metrical structure—to seize the form by the throat, as it were," as well as for a lack of "self-criticism" (Watts-Dunton, "Christina Georgina Rossetti," 18), a relative readiness "to look with complacency on her failures" (Gosse, Introduction, xxxii). Such assessments were still being damningly echoed as late as 1971: "Her aims were small and her gifts were small" (Curran 299). Like a female Andrea del Sarto, then, this version of Rossetti may achieve perfection, but only because her poetic reach does not exceed her feminine grasp.[23]

Such an outcome of Rossetti's competitive canonization was bad enough:

it locked Rossetti into a competition that she could never win. Even worse, however, was the effect of such nostalgically glorified artlessness and modesty upon more general conceptions of Rossetti's significance as a poet. The office of domestic angel might have rendered E. B. B.'s poetic and political ambitions more or less beside the point; Rossetti's role as embodiment of transcendent feminine silence renders those aspects of her work beyond the pale.

As noted, critics often associated Rossetti's verse with birdsong. Within such writing, Rossetti's "songs" are not deliberate, like those of the female troubadours she cites in "Monna Innominata"; they are, rather, instinctive, or nearly so. The metaphors of the nightingale tradition are rarely far from such writing, and as always, they link women's poetry to pain (Cheryl Walker 21–22, 36). Late-century praise of Rossetti's old-fashioned modesty often emphasizes a new aspect of the nightingale myth, however; it insists upon reading her verses not only as unpremeditated but as unwilling. "It is as if the writer were forced, in spite of her utmost endeavour, to give voice to certain deep emotions," Symons writes. "The words seem as if wrung out of her" ("Christina Rossetti," *Saturday Review,* 6). This claim reverberates in ambitious critical readings such as Meynell's, which unfavorably compares Barrett Browning to Rossetti in the expression of passion, "abundant as was the earlier poet, and few and reluctant as are here [in "The Convent Threshold"] the words of the later" (Introduction to *Poems by Christina Rossetti,* ix). It is rarely far from serious discussions of the "unpremeditated" natural style of Rossetti's poetry (Meynell, "Christina Rossetti," 572). It rings, too, in cruder statements such as the *Bookman's* claim that she was "essentially a singer, because her soul could not keep absolute silence" (William Michael Rossetti, "Extracts," xviii).

Such praise does more than absolve Rossetti from the onus of having deliberately shaped her work: it frees her from any suspicion of having deliberately violated injunctions to feminine silence altogether. Like Philomela, it would seem, she has been driven into song. For some critics, however, even this absolution was not enough. Watts-Dunton, for example, writes, "No one felt so deeply as [Christina Rossetti] that as the notes of the nightingale are but the involuntary expression of the bird's emotion. . . . so it is and must be with the song of the very poet." In the end, however, he reserves his highest praise not for Christina Rossetti but for her mother, "the sweetness of whose nature was never disturbed by that exercise of the egoism of the artist in which Christina indulged." Apparently, just as the violated Philomela ceased to be a virgin, her metaphoric successor, once driven into song, could no longer represent the silence of the "ideal Christian woman" ("Literature," 208).

In its most extreme forms, praise of Rossetti's definitive natural feminine modesty eventually meets even such challenges. A 1904 *Atlantic Monthly* article by Paul Elmer More, later reprinted in his *Shelburne Essays,* brings such praise to its culmination and simultaneous vanishing point. Rossetti composed, More asserts, "without any guiding and restraining artistic impulse; she never drew to the shutters of her soul, but lay open to every wandering breath of heaven. In comparison with the works of the more creative poets her song is like the continuous lisping of an aeolian harp beside the music elicited by cunning fingers" ("Christina Rossetti," *Atlantic Monthly,* 815). The harp metaphor, More notes, expresses "the purely feminine spirit of her inspiration. There is in her a passive surrender to the powers of life" (816).

Rendered absolutely innocent of the "egoism" of art, More's poet is metaphorically deprived of sentience as well. Utterly modest, utterly free of artifice, she lies "open to every wandering breath of heaven," in passive surrender to a poetry created by nature itself (815). And thus, ironically, the attempt to cast Rossetti as representative of natural womanly modesty reaches full circle, ending in the erotic image of an artificial instrument open to every wind.

At its climax, More's glorification of Rossetti as the "flower of strictly feminine genius" reveals what "the feminine heart speaks with a simplicity and consummate purity": silence (816, 820). (Such a silence, to be sure, is "more musical than any song." It is "such as I quite fail to hear in the *Portuguese Sonnets,*" [820].)[24] "Into that region of rapt stillness," More writes, "it seems almost a sacrilege to penetrate with inquisitive, critical mind; it is like tearing away the veil of modesty" (820). And thus, having fully positioned its subject where at least one modern critic still places her—"beyond worldly vanities" in a "sphere of female silence" (Antony H. Harrison 140), More's criticism must ultimately become silent itself.[25] (As Hélène Cixous puts it, "What is the 'Other'? If it is truly the 'other,' there is nothing to say; it cannot be theorized" [Cixous and Clément 71]).

Certainly, as Walter Raleigh testifies, such admiration for Rossetti's natural stylistic transparency could indeed endow Rossetti with great symbolic power. It could even serve to dethrone E. B. B.: "I have been reading Christina Rossetti—three or four of her poems . . . leave E. B. B. barely human. I think she is the best poet alive. . . . The worst of it is you cannot lecture on really pure poetry any more than you can talk about the ingredients of pure water—it is adulterated, methylated, sanded poetry that makes the best lectures" (164). Yet at what cost? Rossetti's "really pure" poetry succeeds as a poetic antidote: it knocks the poet's rival out of the running, leaving her "barely human" in the process. There is no question whose work will win out on the lecture circuit, however: "The only thing that Christina makes me want to do is cry, not lecture" (164).[26] Like pure water, such poetry has become so transparent as to be virtually invisible.

Such criticism could scarcely attend to the passionate spiritual agonies and ambitions of a poet whose religious tracts vehemently exhorted fellow believers to crouch low so as to spring high; nor was it likely to do justice to "Monna Innominata." Unlike Rossetti, naive, natural poets presumably do not explicitly challenge or counterpoint the works of their immediate rivals for canonization, nor do they propose to amend Dante and Petrarch in the process. Moreover, even if one can imagine the "lyric cry" as emerging accompanied by a series of Italian epigraphs, spontaneous, unwilling feminine *cris de coeur* are unlikely to form a "sonnet of sonnets."

In seeking to celebrate in Rossetti a transcendent feminine modesty enamored of "the lowest place," turn-of-the-century criticism attempted to do more than revise a dead sinner into a secular saint. It attempted to exonerate an artist of the onus of having created art. What is more, it attempted to domesticate a would-be religious saint into a secular one, by detaching this nineteenth-century aspirant to sanctity from both the specific cultural and religious struggles of her own time and the ambitious, uncompromising passions of the long-standing religious tradition to which she belonged. By naturalizing Rossetti's texts and by denying the extent to which those texts as well as the poet's life were shaped by a specifically Victorian rejection of the "world," such criticism paradoxically deprived Rossetti's verse of the worldliness necessary to make it live—that is, of its "circumstantiality," its "status as an event having sensuous particularity as well as historical contingency" (Said 39; see McGann, "Religious Poetry," 141–42). Fin-de-siècle criticism thus did more than subject Rossetti to a canonical disappearing act: it constructed its own vanishing point as well.

Afterword

And we go prating that the age of saints is
over. . . . Fool! Go and be a saint, go and   Mrs. Humphry Ward
give yourself to ideas.

ONE OF THE "SHADOW SELVES" of this book is a volume entitled *Speaking Saints*. It begins with the quotation above, in which Mrs. Humphry Ward tells women to become saints and defines the beginning of that process as giving oneself to ideas; it ends with readings of female sainthood's role as an authorizing and inspirational model for both the first and second waves of feminism. A deeply personal book about the powers and dangers of the "call to sainthood," this imaginary work is no less focused upon connections between medieval and Victorian conceptions of feminine virtue than is *Lost Saints* itself.

I would like to draw toward the close of *Lost Saints*, however, by pointing into the margins of the book as it actually exists, and perhaps just barely beyond its framework—to Victorian women writers' mobilization of the subversive aspects of female sainthood. As I have already suggested, Elizabeth Barrett Browning and Christina Rossetti, along with many other Victorian women writers and activists, appropriated the models of female religious saints in imagining and authorizing themselves as intellectual and cultural agents. Such women's evocations of speaking, struggling sainthood draw upon medieval precedents every bit as clearly as do more conventional glorifications of feminine silence. It is no wonder that the first wave of feminist organizing, toward the end of the nineteenth century, should have called upon metaphors of sainthood and martyrdom as central sources of symbolic power (Showalter, *Sexual Anarchy*, 28–31).

As we have seen, Barrett Browning's career dramatically demonstrates how evocations of medieval ascetic models could authorize speech and action as well as enjoin silent submission. Presenting her father as her confessor and the crucifixion as her model, E. B. B. begins by constructing a feminine canonicity that merges the sufferings of the Christian with those of the Romantic genius, the invalid and the dutiful daughter. By the end of her life, however, she has radically shifted positions. Openly courting critical martyrdom, she takes the Sermon on the Mount as her model and God as her only confessor.

By refusing secularization, Rossetti presents another form of resistance to the domestication of female sainthood. Even at her most submissive, she writes not as an Acting Angel but as an aspirant to traditional religious sanctity. As such, she hearkens back to a long tradition of powerful, visionary saints. The spiritual ambition expressed by much of her verse is ruthless, agonized, and radically autonomous; its sensuality resonates with that of the most brilliant female contemplative writers. In Rossetti's terms, the "call to be saints" is not a call to domesticity but to the highest possible spiritual duty, a duty that may or may not be domestic, and may require not only silence but speech.

Finally, I must return *Lost Saints* to its central issues: those of reverence and of monumental canonization. The project of contesting poets' status as saints is ambitious; challenges to literary sanctity have come to look like attacks on the love of reading itself. Until we have freed ourselves from monumental sainthood, however, we will never succeed in moving beyond the metaphoric imprisonment of the architectural canon. Moreover, as a character in Max Frisch's *Stiller* insists, it is "a sign of non-love, and thus of sin, to make a graven image of . . . any human being, to say: You are this and this, and that's that" (116; author's translation). In this sense, written texts are indeed like human beings. What we stand to lose in giving up our monumental saints, we may gain in our capacity to understand different kinds of literary love.

Notes

Works Cited

Index

Notes

Introduction

1. *Aurora Leigh* first reentered the "accessible canon" (Fowler 215–16) thanks to the daring of small presses such as the British Women's Press, whose 1978 edition was introduced by Cora Kaplan, and Academy Chicago, whose 1979 "Cassandra" edition was introduced by Gardner Taplin. Since then, the poem has appeared in those most canonical of educational packages, a Norton Critical Edition and an Oxford University Press "World's Classics" paperback. (See also the recent Ohio University Press edition.)

2. Naive as such expectations were, they were not totally unfounded. For particularly notorious responses, see the letters of Edward FitzGerald (1:280–81) and the anonymous *Dublin University Magazine* review whose author regrets that Barrett Browning has "written a book which is almost a closed volume for her own sex" ("Aurora Leigh," 470).

3. Later, I found Michel Foucault's suggestive description of such connections: "Silence itself . . . is less the absolute limit of discourse, the other side from which it is separated by a strict boundary, than an element that functions alongside the things said, with them and in relation to them within over-all strategies. . . . There is not one but many silences, and they are an integral part of the strategies that underlie and permeate discourses" (*History*, 27). See also Baldick 8–9.

4. In so doing, I seek to provide what Toni Morrison calls an "instructive parallel" to analysis of the relationship of African-American literature to the canon (14). For a discussion of this "ornamental vacuum in literary discourse," see Morrison's *Playing in the Dark*, with its emphasis on connections between influential critics' refusals to read African-American literature and their creation of a "lavish exploration of literature" that "manages *not* to see meaning in the thunderous, theatrical presence of black surrogacy—an informing, stabilizing, and disturbing element—in the literature they do study" (11, 13).

5. Such reverence was not exclusively literary; consider, for example, popular characterizations of Florence Nightingale.

6. See, for example, the conflicts over F. W. Faber's series of the lives of the saints, as summarized in J. H. Newman's *Letters,* 12:278, n.2, and by Ker 341–42. For a sample attack on faith in religious sanctity, see Thomas Wright. For defenses, see Renouf; "Veneration of the Saints."

7. Nemoianu asserts that the term's current literary uses essentially go back only some "ten or fifteen years" (216), for example. Clausen also refers to "what has recently come to be known as the canon" (199).

8. Nemoianu implies, for example, that if one cannot find "*full* substitution" of litera-

ture for religion—"of actual sacralization or sanctification, or of a fully prescriptive canon"—then affinities between religious and literary canonizations are insignificant (216–17). See Pierre A. Walker's general discussion of religious rhetoric in current criticism.

9. Henry Louis Gates, Jr., for example, dates the "first use of the word 'canon' in relation to the Afro-American literary tradition" to 1846, when Theodore Parker asserted that American literature was "rising, but is not yet national, still *less canonized*" (172). Just as "the lives of the early martyrs and confessors are purely Christian," Parker wrote, so the "Lives of Fugitive Slaves" are purely American (173). See, too, James Russell Lowell, "Dryden," 96.

10. The same is actually true for the modern *canon*, Gorak acknowledges (9).

11. By A.D. 426, Curtius finds reference to "the canon of jurists to whom 'authority' is conceded" (256).

12. Even as Eliot rejects personality as a central focus for literary study, thus challenging central aspects of dominant Victorian literary faith, his metaphor of text as body (or statue) echoes earlier canonic criticism. For Eliot's role in conceptualizing canon formation, see Guillory.

Chapter 1: Saint Shakespeare and the "Body" of the Text

1. Concepts of religious sanctity are limited neither to Catholicism nor to Christianity, of course. (See, for example, Hawley.) Like their highly structured institutional counterpart, however, informal "religions of humanity" tended to draw on Catholic sainthood as their model.

2. In 1891, the London Positivist Society could claim ninety-three official members; in 1898, Richard Congreve's sacerdotal fund numbered 137 subscribers. This was the "high-water mark of Positivist adhesion" (T. R. Wright 5).

3. Indeed, this book seeks to problematize insistence upon "representative passages" altogether. See Foucault, "Author," 114.

4. Significantly, Johnson's *Lives of the Poets* has been cited as marking "the real beginning of the canon of English literature" (Kaplan and Rose 15).

5. T. S. Eliot echoes the connection between canonic "rule" and amputation—though not castration per se—in "Tradition and the Individual Talent" when he states that writers must be "judged, not amputated," by "the standards of the past"—"and certainly not judged by the canons of dead critics" (5).

6. Not all uses evoked such acceptable processes, of course: Dobson cites an anonymous author from 1691 who charges adaptor Thomas Durfey with the grisly crime of having laid "violent hands on Shakespeare," "killing [Shakespeare's] living beauties by joining them" to his own "dead lameless deformities" (103). Botanical metaphors for literary study—and expurgation—provide interesting counterpoints to evocations of textual bodies throughout the century. See, for example, Hunt, "Answer," 300; Moulton, in Graff and Warner 62; and Raleigh, in Baldick 78. Writers with fewer scientific pretensions were more likely to cast themselves as weeding or culling bouquets from the garden of literature.

7. Scott later wavered: "I fear that without absolutely gelding the bard, it will be indis-

pensable to circumcise him a little, by leaving out some of the most obnoxious lines." In the end, however, the lines remained in, and the poet intact (Perrin 58–59; on actual expurgations, see 60–114).

8. Such a grandiloquent vision may be particularly difficult to retain. In 1913, some sixteen years after publishing this vision of the critic as agent of resurrection, Raleigh wrote, "I can't read Shakespeare any more, so I have to remember the old tags. . . . I suppose I've got to go on and be an old mechanical hack on rusty wires, working up a stock enthusiasm for the boyish lingo of effusive gentlemen long since dead" (quoted in Baldick 77).

9. As it is, "Today the two enter the canon of eighteenth-century literature by the back door" (McCrea 11).

10. Clark's approach differs, it seems, by being based not on faith in church doctrine but on the conviction that "every one knows more than any one" (viii).

11. Indeed, so active was this master canonizer that Perrin has named an emendatory law after him: Palgrave's First Rule of Expurgation is "Do it, but don't talk about it much" (200).

12. Perrin suggests that discreet and perhaps misleading euphemisms such as "select edition" or "family edition" allowed expurgators the freedom of "not merely tampering with one's author, but lying to one's readers" (112). See also his comments on the relationship between class and expurgations or decisions not to translate certain material (22–24, 194, 240–41, 251–52, 258–62).

13. Schoenbaum offers an extensive discussion of nineteenth-century biographies of Shakespeare, many of which are shaped by such idealizations (181–451).

14. I use the masculine poet-hero advisedly: poet-heroines' relation to generic glory is more complex.

15. Bristol, Dobson, Granqvist, Loomba, and Viswanathan offer more detailed and differentiated treatments of how "Shakespeare" has served in the construction of national identities.

16. Shakespeare also unifies the "Greater England" of present and former colonies ("Shakespeare and Greater England"). Verses appropriating the Bard for the New World seem to have constituted a subgenre of nineteenth-century American poetry. See, for example, Holmes, Sheppard, and Bayard Taylor, "Shakespeare's Statue." Bostoner Charles Sprague's 1823 ode became a "Shakespearian manifest" long before the appearance of Carlyle's "On Heroes, Hero-Worship, and the Heroic in History" (Granqvist 38):

> Our Roman-hearted fathers broke
> Thy parent empire's galling yoke;
> But thou, harmonious master of the mind,
> Around their sons a gentler chain shalt bind;   (120)
> Once more in thee shall Albion's sceptre wave,
> And what her monarch lost, her monarch Bard shall save.

17. Shakespeare's power to connect military and moral authority continued into this century, of course. See, for example, Israel Zangwill's 1916 "The Two Empires,"

where England's "twin" sons, St. George and Shakespeare, join in holding "all faiths and races 'neath her sway."

18. While arguing that "we can no longer afford to regard the uses to which literary works were put in the service of British imperialism as extraneous to the way these texts are to be read," Viswanathan also opposes "conceptions of the British literary curriculum as unmediated assertion of cultural power" (169).

19. For a medievalist's reading of nineteenth-century empiricism's "legacy of misreading sacred biography," see Heffernan 38–71.

20. Newman distinguishes authors, like fictional characters and fictional works, by their unified, ideal "moral centres." "Walter Scott's centre," for example, is "chivalrous honor" (211).

21. Given the focus of this book, I emphasize legend as saint's life (in German, *Legende*). There are, of course, other forms of legend. I strongly suspect that uncanny or demonic representations of writers draw their power from those nonreligious legends that German terms *Sagen* (see Bausinger 170–99).

22. Saints' lives and saints' legends are very different things, too. For the purposes of this argument, however, what matters are their shared functions in the canonization process.

23. There is a long tradition of division between academics' theoretical positions and their teaching practices. See Graff and Warner 7; see also Kaplan and Rose 21–22 on the *New York Times Magazine*'s presentation of Frank Lentricchia's pedagogy as a consoling counterpoint to his political stances.

24. Indeed, prestigious editors may actually be more willing to consider innovations than are the teachers polled (114).

25. Originality of a sort is necessary, of course. To borrow Kermode's phrase, however, it must be "an originality that remains close to the consensual norms" (82).

26. Certain phrases may be repeated "almost ritually," Rodden notes (83). "Watchwords" are key elements of reputation formation (86–87, 110, 117–18); even in the twentieth century, "*pre-inflated* watchwords" such as *saint* seem "to be ready-made cornerstones for laying a 'monumental reputation'" (330).

27. Heffernan explicitly distinguishes medieval sacred lives from later biographies, whose authority rests on pretensions of unequalled expertise and whose audiences are specific, highly restricted communities of the cognoscenti (19).

28. Such iconicity survives into this century. The phrase *the crystal spirit,* for example, was George Orwell's poetic description of an "illiterate Italian militia man." Once used as the title of George Woodcock's study of Orwell, however, it became an unattributed watchword used to describe Orwell himself (Rodden 160–62; see also 423, n.11).

29. As Heffernan notes, the achievement of Boswell's life of Johnson is inconceivable in terms of medieval sacred biography (21). Although that work lacks the authority of communal authorship, however, it exerts the power of iconicity: no initiate to the cult of Johnson studies could escape familiarity with the "inspired" work of Johnson's most famous biographer.

30. Profiteering from dubious relics—or even dubious saints—may have sparked centralization and formalization of the religious canonization process (Kemp 105–6).

Thomas Wise and John Payne Collier, those great founders of literary societies and forgers of literary masterpieces, stand as powerful nineteenth-century examples. On Wise, see Altick, "Case"; Barker and Collins; Carter and Pollard. On Collier, see Stavisky 26–39; Halliday 136–46; Schoenbaum 245–66. See also Widdowson's account of establishing and maintaining canonicity as an industry (*Hardy*, 28).

31. Nemoianu, for example, cites "offensive or attractive peculiarities of writers' biographies" as explanations for the inclusion of certain texts in the curriculum—although he terms such causes for canonization "purely random" (218).

32. On Shakespeare, see Sinfield, "Give an Account" and "Heritage and the Market." See also Widdowson, *Hardy*, 16, 77, 79, 80–82; and Rodden's discussion of the "puzzling mix of elevations and exclusions" that characterizes Orwell's curricular status (383; 382–98).

33. Foucault suggests many of these points when he asserts that modern criticism comes strikingly close to St. Jerome's *De Viris Illustribus* in its "strategies for defining the author" ("Author," 127–28). Such definition establishes the author as "a standard level of quality," "a certain field of conceptual or theoretical coherence," "a stylistic uniformity," and "a definite historical figure in which a series of events converge" (128).

Chapter 2: Poet Worship Meets "Woman" Worship

1. Houghton offers a classic account of mid-Victorian "woman worship" (348–53).

2. Theologically termed the "marriage debt," such duty was theoretically imposed upon both partners (Weinstein and Bell 56). For a dramatic nineteenth-century instance of such rebellion, see the case of Cornelia Connelly as presented by Paz (13–14) and by the Sacred Congregation for the Causes of Saints.

3. George Eliot's "O May I Join the Choir Invisible" was actually integrated into the Positivist liturgy (T. R. Wright 176).

4. Bynum also addresses this issue in *Holy Feast* (28; 318–19, n.68).

5. "In the case of female saints," Petroff continues, "what constitutes [the necessary] exceptionality [of sainthood] is in opposition to what constitutes female goodness" (3). Bynum offers exceptions to this situation (*Holy Feast*, 84–86). See also Weinstein and Bell 46.

6. As Heffernan notes, such conjectures cannot be proven (294–95). Similar attitudes often seem to inform present-day approaches to feminist activism: I cannot count the number of times I have heard praise for a feminist political activist countered by, "Well, if you ask me, she's no saint."

7. In contrast to Bynum, Weinstein and Bell identify "a male type of saint and a second type that we shall call androgynous rather than female" (216, 237). See also Bynum, *Holy Feast*, 316–17, n.47.

8. See, for example, Weinstein and Bell 94, 298 n. 15; Bynum, *Holy Feast*, 23, 316 n.45.

9. To be fair, Landon contributed heavily to such views of female creativity. Her own account of Felicia Hemans's life is a case in point.

10. Sappho thus became the "founding archetype" for "fictions of women's writing as the narrative of female abandonment" (*Fictions*, 77; see 75–78). DeJean's work pro-

vides an indispensable context and counterpoint for the processes described in this study.

11. Inspirational as well as monitory, Sappho serves a wide range of purposes for female poets. See, for example, Leighton, *Poets;* Gubar, "Sapphistries"; Linley 47–96; Lipking; and McGann, "Mary Robinson."

12. By 1888, Mrs. Humphry Ward's *Robert Elsmere* asserted that "every good Comtist" believes that "the husband is the wife's pope" (quoted in T. R. Wright 231). Ward echoes George Eliot's description of Dorothea Brooke's devotion to Casaubon in *Middlemarch* (138).

13. Mary's emergence as a domestic model was a long-standing, complex process, of course (Marina Warner 130–31).

14. Weinstein and Bell also note the "growth of bourgeois life" during this period. Their data "strongly suggest that the affective family," far from being the eighteenth-century creation that it is sometimes termed, "began to come into its own in the thirteenth century" only to decline from the mid-sixteenth century through the late seventeenth century (246).

15. Olsen offers an early and invaluable discussion of the role of class privilege in constructing the Angel in the House as a model (34–37, 42–43, 213–17).

16. The Greek and Russian Orthodox Churches still refuse to accept the Immaculate Conception as dogma. On the doctrine's popular and doctrinal history, see Marina Warner 236–54; Perry and Echeverría, esp. 22–23.

17. Perry and Echeverría (115–31), and Marina Warner (237–38) discuss the bull's wider political implications.

18. More general discussion of hostility toward Catholicism appears in Klaus, esp. 211–301. See also Paz.

19. Interestingly, *The Angel in the House* attained popular success only when reissued among the "Home Books of the English People" in 1887, more than thirty years after its initial publication (Anstruther 97–100).

20. Jameson's influence on nineteenth-century literary criticism and art history is only now coming to be recognized. See Beer 123–24; Hilary Fraser. Homans's emphasis on the "interdict on Mary's own manipulation of language" and on women writers' construction as sacred vessels (*Bearing the Word,* 158) illuminates the reviewing practices I have found, which also present female poets as vessels of divine feminine silence rather than of a masculine Word.

21. The Immaculate Conception does not deny Mary the exercise of free will, but it does protect her from innate temptation to abuse such freedom (Marina Warner 236–37).

22. On a larger level as well, reverence for Mary does not necessarily imply respect for historical women. See Marina Warner 77–78; Mecklin 98; Shahar 31–32.

23. Under the Carolingians, strict cloistering and "shrinking economic resources" may also have made monastic life less attractive to religious women (Wemple 171).

24. Such an increase has been variously interpreted. See Weinstein and Bell 211, 224; Renna 287; Bynum, *Holy Feast,* 13–23.

25. Bynum offers a revealing discussion of Francis's and Clare's differing social standings and relationships to fasting (*Holy Feast*, 95–102). See also Rudolph Bell's analysis of differences between Franciscan and Dominican models of feminine asceticism (130–33).

26. Gilbert and Gubar discuss food and eating throughout *The Madwoman in the Attic*. Victorian constructions of feminine fasting, as characterized in Michie's discussion of "ladylike anorexia," bear suggestive resemblances to medieval understandings of asceticism (12–29).

27. In a larger sense as well, Bynum argues, food was a "female concern" (*Holy Feast*, 73–112). The eucharistic miracle, for example, is "almost entirely a female genre" (76, 81). See also Bynum, *Fragmentation*, 44–46, 48, 61–62, 119–50.

28. The life of Honoria's mother in Patmore's *The Angel in the House*, for example, "observed, with awe / Which cross experience could not mar, / The fiction of the Christian Law / That all men honourable are" (29–30). By playing her role, the mother inspires men to play theirs: "And so her smile seem'd to confer / At once high flattery and reproof, / And self-regard, inspired by her, / Grew courtly in its own behoof" (30).

29. To be sure, Rosamond's is an unsanctified (if not downright demonic) form of feminine influence. Ellis herself warned readers that they should not allow "light reading" to mislead them into seeking marriage as an escape from the restraints of home or hope to "imitate the heroines they read of" by continuing to develop their accomplishments after marriage (*Wives*, 6; *Women*, 65).

30. If a woman is able to "look at her domestic trials as her haircloth, her ashes, her scourges—accept them—rejoice in them," writes Harriet Beecher Stowe, "smile and be quiet, silent, patient and loving under them . . . [she] is a victorious saint" (quoted in Ann Douglas 129).

31. Douglas's discussion of the sacred role claimed for feminine influence in nineteenth-century American texts complements many of my readings. See esp. 44–48 and 128–29.

32. A woman intent upon retaining such poetry must attempt to "maintain the calm dignity of a pure and elevated character, earthly in nothing but its suffering and weakness; refined almost to sublimity in the seraphic ardour of its love, its faith, and its devotion" (Ellis, "Poetry," 114).

33. Discussions of such connections appear in Alexander Welsh 182–95; Gilbert and Gubar 24–27; Ann Douglas 200–226.

34. Women's true text is "the pure, unsullied page of childhood." Here, "time will prove to them that they *have* written, if not by any direct instrumentality, by their example, their conversation, and the natural influence of mind on mind." Moreover, the "transcript of *what* they have written, will be treasured up, either for or against them, among the awful records of eternity" (Ellis, *Women*, 17). See also Mermin, "Damsel."

35. "The feminine factor in the mind of the great poet is, indeed," Patmore continues, "a greater thing than woman—it is goddess." Suggestively, the two poets who do succeed at being "wholly feminine" in this sense are men: Percy Bysshe Shelley and John Keats ("Mrs. Meynell," 762).

36. So, too, of course is Samuel Johnson's dancing dog.

37. Gubar's "Blank Page" addresses the extension of such gendered compliments into this century (245).

38. Papier-mâché may even be too innocent a metaphor. In analyzing the "paradoxes of heroine description," Michie posits the existence of not merely dead but "murderous" metaphors (88–89). Constituting "all women" as "alike, all replaceable," such metaphors "deny the concept of individual or non-normative bodily experience," purging "the deviant woman from representability" and restricting "sexual and intellectual arousal" (89). As M. Sidney Watson's "Murder by Anthology?" documents in the case of Anna Letitia Barbauld, many nineteenth-century texts tended to canonize—and ultimately decanonize—women writers as precisely such heroines. For discussion of the need for metaphoric dress reform, see Michie 71–78, 88–89, 145–50.

39. DeJean attributes a similar stance to Ovid. "By placing Sappho on the border between life and art," she argues, "Ovid assured that the *Heroides* would make him Sappho's heir. Whenever the creation of a discourse of female desire would become a literary issue, Sappho's name and her literary authority would be bound up with Ovid's" (*Fictions*, 75).

40. More is writing in 1904. As Leigh Hunt's much earlier "Blue-Stocking Revels" makes clear, however, this approach is scarcely new.

41. Ross addresses how the "contours of masculine desire" helped to shape conceptions of the generation of female poets directly preceding the Victorians. See also Gubar, "Blank Page," 243–44. The "classic Pygmalion and Galatea pattern," as Susan Morgan calls it, helps shape openly fictional eighteenth- and nineteenth-century heroines as well (12).

42. Such practices are scarcely limited to Englishwomen or to poets, of course. Prettifications of Emily Dickinson are notorious, and as Margaret Kirkham notes, even Jane Austen's standard portrait has been subtly sentimentalized (frontispiece; 59). A colleague reports that the portrait of George Eliot on the cover of a recent popular edition of *Middlemarch* is so conventionally lovely that at first he took it to be a rendering of Dorothea Brooke.

43. Witness Patmore's comment, for example: "It is a great consolation to reflect that, among all the bewildering changes to which the world is subject, the character of woman cannot be altered; and that, so long as she abstains from absolute outrages against nature—such as divided skirts, free-thinking, tricycles, and Radicalism—neither Greek, nor conic sections, nor political economy, nor cigarettes, nor athletics can even really do other than enhance the charm of that sweet unreasonableness" (*Religio Poetae*, 155).

44. Rossetti's assessment stands in strong contrast to Jameson's frequently cited 1834 celebration of Hemans as authentically, "essentially feminine" (*Visits and Sketches*, 1:220). Still, like other decanonizations, Hemans's intensifies strains already present in her reception: her monumental stature crumbles along already established fault lines. See, for example, *Short Sketch*, 13–15.

45. To be fair, the author of the prefatory memoir holds out hope that once "the vexed pulse of this feverish age" is dead, Hemans's womanhood—and verse—will return to favor (xv).

46. Hemans has recently begun to claim more critical attention. It is interesting to note, however, that the most recent *Norton* anthology still presents those of her poems that are most closely associated with her Victorian reputation for patriotism and decorum.

Chapter 3: Developing Character(s)

1. As late as 1886, for example, "the first American Shakespearean of any consequence," Richard Grant White, wrote that most women disliked Shakespeare, "with the exception of a few who are not always the most lovable or happiest of the sex" (Gary Taylor 19, 205). See also Thom, "Shakespeare Study," 98–99.

2. Consider, for example, Mary Lamb's contributions to the *Tales from Shakespear* and Henrietta Bowdler's (unacknowledged) role in the editorship of her brother's notorious *Family Shakespeare*. Both first published in 1807, these works peaked in popularity during the Victorian period (Gary Taylor 206–8).

3. Such study groups involved women in a larger, sometimes politicized "culture of reading" (Theodora Penny Martin 36–37; Sicherman 201).

4. This nineteenth-century critical usage lays new stress upon a much older metaphoric treatment of the playwright's characters as his progeny. Interestingly, although Shakespeare's "daughters" are everywhere, no one mentions his "sons."

5. Shakespeare sometimes won the palm in such competition: see "Ingersoll," 289–90. See also Loomba on "imperialism, patriarchy, and post-colonial English studies" (10–37) and Loeffelholz on gender's role in midcentury U.S. transformations of "Shakespeare as an ideological property" (58).

6. Novy offers a related distinction ("Introduction," 7).

7. In 1807, William Duff anticipates Coleridge's application of Pope's dictum to Shakespearean figures. "The severest punishment which a woman of spirit" could have wished upon Pope, Duff suggests, is "the coupling him with a termagant" who, while dooming him to "ineffectual attempts in 'the Taming of the Shrew,' . . . would probably have convinced her loving consort, in language not quite so harmonious indeed as his own poetry, that there was *some little variety* in the character of women" (23–24).

8. In an 1889 edition of *King John*, for example, he terms the consequences of "showy" feminine "intellectualism" "too appalling to be so much as hinted here: I can but speak the word *motherhood*,—a word even more laden with sacred and tender meaning than *womanhood*" (xxiv). His editorializing still appears in an edition of *Romeo and Juliet* as late as 1912 (xxxii–xxxiv).

9. This is from an 1813 lecture. To be fair, a revised 1818 version glorifies a "*sane* equipoise during which the feelings are representative of all past experience, not of the individual *only*, but of all those by whom she has been educated, and their predecessors even up to the first mother that lived" (*Collected Works*, 2:269–70; emphasis added).

10. The fair Theodora, who would have been guarded by a "halo of [her] own innocence," would also have sung "like St. Cecilia" (268–69).

11. An admirer of Jameson ("Shakspeare," 74), De Quincey was not always consistent. See, for example, his contrasting of classical Greek and Shakespearean women, along

with his claim that Shakespeare presents in "woman, the sister and coequal of man" (70–75; 72).

12. Interestingly, the phrase "innate, unconscious," which is Hudson's own, was originally applied to Shakespeare himself ("Female Characters," 199).

13. To be fair, the nineteenth century produced a wide variety of images from Shakespeare, many of which deal with female characters in more complex ways (Altick, *Paintings*, 256–331).

14. As one might expect from volumes whose commentators ranged from Heinrich Heine to W. E. Henley, "galleries" or "galaxies" of heroines varied greatly. In Henley's volume, for example, keepsake portraits mix with depictions of scenes from the plays; in Heine's, relatively conventional drawings ground serious Shakespearean criticism, including moving analyses and condemnations of anti-Semitism (139–62).

15. References to Shakespeare's plays as mirrors abound, of course, from Coleridge to Woolf and beyond. See, for example, Desmet 42; Froula, "Virginia Woolf," 123; and Howard and O'Connor 11.

16. At one point, in a clear reference to Shakespeare, Ellis compares practitioners of such protean femininity to "the great enchantress of the Nile" ("Poetry," 116–17). Novy argues that when applied to creating fictional characters, the model of Shakespeare's "feminine" protean selflessness could be deeply inspiring for a woman writer such as George Eliot ("*Daniel Deronda*," 93–94, 104).

17. Green echoes this citation in concluding a disturbing fin-de-siècle vision of femininity's approaching "great emancipation" (307).

18. Thom's plan is explicitly fueled by anxieties about immigration in general—a common concern. See, for example, Charles F. Johnson's claim that "the moral standards of alien races should not be held up before our young men. . . . Shakespeare is closely akin to us, and, as the creator of Imogen and Miranda, is one of our moral teachers" (497). See also Bristol 79–80.

19. Some editors apparently saw the problem: not all collections included Lady Macbeth (Altick, *Paintings*, 318).

20. Ironically, Hudson takes such criticism as an occasion for setting off what his admirer Whipple terms "epigrammatic torpedoes in the faces of the champions of woman's rights" (248). Attributing disapproval of Ophelia's "loving, self-sacrificing obedience" "especially" to "lady critics," Hudson warns that there "must, yes, *must* be domestic obedience somewhere" (*Shakespeare*, 2:307, 304).

21. Though Thom was far from tracing out the implications of his research, he was also linguist enough to note how closely African-American speech paralleled the sacred language of Shakespeare ("Some Parallelisms").

22. To be sure, there is a less joyous side of Shakespeare's position in Angelou's writing. See Froula, "The Daughter's Seduction," 634.

23. Even critics who disagreed with many of Jameson's basic premises praised her work. See, for example, Whipple 223; Hudson, *Shakespeare*, 1:369. Desmet (40, n. 54) and Ross (259–66) address the reception of *Characteristics*.

24. References to *Characteristics of Women* are drawn from *Shakspeare's Heroines: Characteristics of Women: Moral, Poetical, and Historical*, as cited in the bibliography.

25. Two other key works are *Legends of the Madonna* and *Sacred and Legendary Art*. The latter served George Eliot in writing *Middlemarch, Romola*, and perhaps *The Mill on the Floss* (Eliot, *Notebook*, 58–68, 183–88).

26. This reading resonates as late as the 1880s. See Latham 424, 430.

27. Later critics would echo her. See, for example, Green 300; Elliott 70.

28. Mary Cowden Clarke puts it more bluntly: "Shakespeare has read all gentle-charactered women a lesson on the danger of allowing gentleness to merge into timidity, and timidity into untruthfulness, by the picture he has drawn of Desdemona and of her ill-fated career" ("Shakespeare as the Girl's Friend," 360).

29. Jameson's analysis of Lady Macbeth was "almost entirely rewritten" for the second edition of *Characteristics* (*Characteristics*, viii). See Auerbach, *Ellen Terry*, 252–66; Charlemont; and Heine 117–18 for other (at least potentially) sympathetic nineteenth-century readings.

30. Jameson does hedge here: Alda asserts that analyzing wax figures "is the safer and the better way—for us, at least" (*Characteristics*, 14). (Does Alda refer to women or to critics?) When Alda attempts to substitute a less graphic metaphor, however, Medon responds, "Your illustration is the most poetical . . . but not the most just" (15).

31. Desmet suggests a possible autobiographical impulse behind this passage (45).

32. Such claims form part of larger celebrations of Shakespearean characters. See Auerbach, *Woman*, 200–217.

33. Here as elsewhere, nineteenth-century women critics anticipate twentieth-century feminist criticism. See, for example, Jeanne Addison Roberts; Gary Taylor 340–41.

34. "The perfect independence of women—its effects—is it to be desired?" Such was the discussion topic recorded by one nineteenth-century American women's Shakespearean reading group (Theodora Penny Martin 107–8).

35. "Few more fitly than women can study his writing," Clarke insists. After all, "we have been told that 'the proper study of mankind is Man.'" Thus "the properest study of Woman may be herself"—as represented by Shakespeare ("Shakspeare-Studies," 25).

36. Indeed, Dowden wryly anticipates Woolf: Women "are seldom courageous enough to tell us what they know, and we are pleased by this timidity, choosing to live on in our fool's paradise" (*Transcripts*, 340).

37. Charlemont suggests, for example, that Duncan may have resembled his grandfather, who had slaughtered members of Lady Macbeth's family (194–95). Emery refuses "to dissect" Lady Macbeth "with the instruments of our own times," given that "Lady Macbeth lived in the midst of an age hard, cruel, and ignorant" (221). See also Cavazza.

38. Though Clarke is the great example here, many others followed her lead. See, for example, Latham. The heroines' imagined childhoods also shaped Shakespearean performance (Ziegler 96, 107; Helena Faucit Martin 7).

39. "The character of Anne, as Shakespeare has drawn it," writes Tucker, "casts a slur upon feminine nature which I am glad to believe the true historic Anne does not deserve. . . . If Shakespeare was ever visited by ghosts, he must have seen in his

dreams the pale countenance of Anne, reproaching him for having made her infamous to posterity and sacrificed her womanly dignity to dramatic effect" (305–6).

40. Terry herself wrote that "in [Sargent's] picture is all that I meant to do" (Auerbach, *Ellen Terry*, 263). See also Altick, *Paintings*, 318, as well as Pearce's discussion of a range of pictorial literary heroines. On portraits of Ophelia, see esp. Altick, *Paintings*, 299–302; Dijkstra 42–50; Melchiori 124–28; and Showalter, "Representing Ophelia."

41. Such accounts correspond to more general Victorian conceptions of acting as "mediumistic" possession (Auerbach, *Woman*, 209–10).

42. For related discussions, see Novy, "*Daniel Deronda*"; Wolfson 16–17.

43. "Cordelia Pronounced a Vixen" offers one lively instance of such iconoclasm; Spearman is another (252–53). See also Jackson 15; and Novy, "Introduction," 8.

Chapter 4: Canonization through Dispossession

1. Unless otherwise noted, all references to Barrett Browning's work are to *Complete Works*.

2. This situation has been changing for some time, of course. Early indications of reviving interest in the *Sonnets* include Mermin, "The Female Poet"; Leighton, "Stirring a Dust"; and Sullivan. Stephenson's and Dow's works also represent critical landmarks.

3. Further reading will benefit a "sympathetic" reader, Adams writes, though "the reward is rather in separate coins than in a golden shower" (xiii–xiv). E. B. B. is, among other things, "too feverishly intense for twentieth-century taste" (xiii).

4. Such a reading seems to underlie Alethea Hayter's disparagement of the *Sonnets* as "personal, even idiosyncratic . . . not enough removed from personal relationship" (105). See Cooper, *Elizabeth Barrett Browning*, 101; Leighton, *Elizabeth Barrett Browning*, 98; Stephenson 69–73.

5. The gesture may also be Greek. It derives, editors Porter and Clarke suggest, from the *Iliad*, where Athena seizes Achilles' hair (Barrett Browning, *Complete Works*, 3:393).

6. See, for example, the 1883 Thomas Y. Crowell edition of Barrett Browning's *Complete Poetical Works*. Close to sixty years later, *The Best Known Poems of Elizabeth and Robert Browning* still opens with the 1844 dedication.

7. Barrett was also compared to other figures, of course, including Prometheus and Milton (Grant 324). Sandra Donaldson's *Elizabeth Barrett Browning* has been an invaluable resource in identifying authors of periodical literature on Barrett Browning.

8. Though Hayter had noted the *Sonnets'* undemonstrative reception by the 1960s (118; see also Cooper 99), faith in fin-de-siècle revisionist accounts of the *Sonnets'* reception has not yet died. See, for example, Spender 62. As late as 1990, Antony Harrison asserts that the *Sonnets* "generated a paradigm of the sentimental and patriarchal amatory ideology of mid-Victorian England" (141).

9. See, too, Mermin's assertion that the *Sonnets* "inaugurated a new Victorian convention" of long, autobiographical poems "that play specifically 'modern' experience against some of the traditions of amatory poetry" ("Female Poet," 359).

10. "Essentially English" ("Poems, by Elizabeth Barrett Browning," 303), she is a "genuine and natural poetess" who possesses the "character and learning of a noble-minded Englishwoman" ("Poems. By Elizabeth Barrett Browning," 552). See also Chorley, "Poems. By Elizabeth Barrett Browning," 1243.

11. In the early 1840s, R. H. Horne's *New Spirit of the Age* already offered a comic account of E. B. B.'s insubstantiality, suggesting that historians might come to deny Barrett's existence as they did that of Ossian (266).

12. To Nathaniel Hawthorne, in contrast, E. B. B. appears not as a saint but as a member "of the elfin race" (10).

13. The development of Barrett Browning's conception of speaking sanctity is long and complex. Two key works in this vein, which space prevents me from addressing here, are "The Runaway Slave at Pilgrim's Point" and *Aurora Leigh*.

14. E. B. B. was not exaggerating. See Howitt 293–95; "Elizabeth Barrett and Mr. Howitt." Others had suggested that Louis Napoleon had won her political support through "private attentions and flatteries," she reported. "Now, of the two imputations, I much prefer 'the inspiration from hell.' There's something grandiose about that, to say nothing of the superior honesty of the position" (*Letters of Elizabeth Barrett Browning*, 2:406–7).

15. Hayter, who quotes Gosse's condemnation of E. B. B.'s "hysterical violence, the Pythian vagueness and the Pythian shriek," adopts the phrase as title for a chapter dealing with *Poems before Congress* (193–203). Even Helen Cooper's useful *Elizabeth Barrett Browning, Woman and Artist* cuts off discussion of Barrett Browning's career after *Aurora Leigh*. See, however, Schuyler 7; Cooper, "Working into Light," 72, 80–81; and Cora Kaplan.

16. In William Henry Smith's *British Quarterly Review* obituary, for example, the *Sonnets* and the *Seraphim* rate about a page apiece (365–66, 359–60). *Poems before Congress* receives two pages; roughly eleven pages are devoted to *Aurora Leigh* (378–80, 366–78).

17. See, for example, the *Saturday Review* author's assertion that "it would be improper to refer to Mrs. Browning's personal history, except as reflected in her writings" and omission of any mention of the *Sonnets* ("Mrs. Browning," 41). In the twenty pages that Stigand's 1861 *Edinburgh Review* essay devotes to the poet's career, no space is given to the *Sonnets*. See also "Obituary"; Chorley, "Elizabeth Barrett Browning"; "Our Foreign Bureau"; "Elizabeth Barrett Browning," *Eclectic Review;* and "Elizabeth Barrett Browning," *National Magazine*.

18. For private praise of *Aurora Leigh*'s usefulness in underscoring the limits of feminine poetry, see the letters of Sydney Dobell. After reading *Aurora Leigh* as the work of the female Terminus, and, moreover, as a work devoted to the inculcation of feminine silence, Dobell writes, "'I suffer not a woman to speak in the Church' is of far wider application than to the 'assembly of saints,' and applicable for *reasons not derogatory, but in the highest and divinest degree honorable, to womanhood*" (67).

19. Avis's gesture parallels and perhaps draws upon a literary legend: through an anecdote that quickly achieved iconicity, the young Felicia Hemans was famed for having perched in an apple tree to read Shakespeare. See, for example, William M. Rossetti, "Prefatory Notice," xiii. See also Linley's analysis (115–21).

20. As Field put it later, in an article for the *Christian Examiner,* "No one could possess more simplicity and unaffectedness of character than did Mrs. Browning, *and be human*" ("Mrs. Browning's Essays," 34).

21. Among the more explicitly reverent accounts are Trollope; Field, "English Authors," 660; and Kinney 186–87.

22. As late as 1896, for example, one American textbook supplements quotations from Barrett Browning's verses with depictions of the sacred poet-heroine as she filled Stedman's critical dreams (Irish 224–27).

23. By 1898, *Victorian Poets* was already in its twenty-sixth edition. Although Stedman revised other essays in the book, he left the Barrett Browning piece essentially intact, thus stabilizing the text upon which later accounts of the poet's life as secular saint's legend were to draw (*Victorian Poets,* vii).

24. In this, Stedman and his successors follow what Robert Petsch sees as a traditional pattern whereby saints' legends marginalize narratives of childhood (Rosenfeld 13).

25. "'I hate a disputacious woman,' he once snapped out . . . and said [of single women], 'If I were a King, I'd marry every one'; and it is reported that he jokingly said, 'A woman would better marry and be beaten than not to marry.' 'Where draw the line?' he was asked by a lady: 'The clothes-line,' was flashed back" (Stedman and Gould, 2:518).

26. In this respect, Hugh Walker's *The Greater Victorian Poets,* which treats Barrett Browning almost exclusively as an inspiration for Robert Browning's poetry—with her own poetry appearing only as an example of the "spirit" of the nineteenth century in a negative sense—stands out primarily for being ahead of its time (99, 195). See Leighton, *Elizabeth Barrett Browning,* 96–98.

27. Ritchie underscores this emphasis elsewhere, asserting that although "Mrs. Browning was a great writer, . . . I think she was even more a wife and mother than a writer" ("Robert and Elizabeth Barrett Browning," 845).

28. The comparison of Pen and *Aurora Leigh* was first made public in 1862; see Hunt, *Correspondence,* 2:264–68. See Dennis, "Elizabeth Barrett Browning," 89; "With the Elect"; "Reminiscences."

29. Even in the 1870s, assertions of E. B. B.'s chastity are often fairly explicit. Of the *Sonnets'* composition, for example, Couthouy writes, "This pure, delicate, virgin soul had hitherto dwelt apart in seclusion. . . . All this new soul-fire flashed from her pen. . . . Was she not a true woman? . . . She hastens to fling her very life upon the altar of holy love—love to both God and man" (751–52). In 1882, Molloy writes of the *Sonnets* as expressing "the first ecstasy of virgin love" (372).

30. "Perfect" marriages come in many forms, of course. It is revealing to note that sexual radicals such as Havelock Ellis, as well as conservatives, turned to the Brownings' marriage as a model (395, 630–31).

31. Stedman elevates E. B. B.'s sonnets over Shakespeare's as more "mature," just as he ranks them above *In Memoriam* as expressions of the "most ecstatic of human emotions" rather than of "philosophic Grief" ("Elizabeth Barrett Browning," 110). Such choices of contrasting texts are noteworthy, however, particularly in light of his later "determinedly hostile" attitude toward Oscar Wilde (Ellmann 177; 161).

32. Anxiety about Shakespeare's sonnets clearly predates this period (Pequigney 1, 2–3, 30–32, 64).

33. The lock that Barrett actually gave her future husband rests next to the hair of John Milton in a "silver shell-shaped reliquary, with centre doubled-glazed case" (Kelley and Colley 509–10).

34. "Do not bring me in as if *parenthetically,* illustrative of her and her poems," he warned F. J. Furnivall in response to such a process, as early as 1881. "These, I rejoice with all my heart to know and say, are in no need of any assistance" (*Letters,* 205).

35. In private, Browning directed his anger primarily against the letters' editor, William Aldis Wright. Wright's apology appeared in the *Athenaeum* in the same month as Browning's poem.

36. Browning refused to assist John Ingram, the author of Barrett Browning's first full-scale biography, for example. Although Browning granted R. H. Horne permission to print some of E. B. B.'s earlier letters, he did so only because Horne, "poor, old and pitiable, saw a golden resource in the publication" of a "correspondence which began, and, in the main, ended before I knew the writer" (Browning and Barrett Browning, 1:xxxv). In defending Browning's objection to publication of a volume of E. B. B.'s early verse, the *Athenaeum* essentially accused that volume's editor, Richard Herne Shepherd, of being a thief ("Literary Gossip"). Shepherd responded with some heat (722).

37. Not all corporeal representations of E. B. B. are negative. For a vivid and highly unusual positive evocation of the poet as fleshly figure, see Massey, "Last Poems," 527–31. "Warm with passion and welling with poetry," this E. B. B. produces a non-Marian maternal body of verse, whose bursting, gushing spontaneity suggests an almost literal birth of art (531). See also Couthouy 749–50, 753.

38. Reviewers frequently commented that Moulton-Barrett must have been unbalanced. See "Memoirs," 490; Gwynn 428; "Browning Love-Letters," 736; "The Letters of Elizabeth Barrett Browning." *Church Quarterly Review,* 378. At one point the *Academy* even hinted that more "sordid details" of Moulton-Barrett's behavior were still being withheld ("Memoirs," 490).

39. For a modern reading that privileges the letters over the *Sonnets,* as possessing more "true dramatic quality," see Rees 148–52.

40. R. H. Shepherd had anticipated such tactics when he defended his publication of E. B. B.'s juvenilia by asserting that "had Mrs. Browning been still among us now, it would probably be rather her laudatory odes to Napoleon the Third than these early poems of hers that she would desire to withhold or withdraw from the world's knowledge" (722).

Chapter 5: Competing Sainthoods, Competing Saints

1. Jerome McGann offers an analysis of the difference between early-twentieth-century receptions of Hopkins and Rossetti as well as a crucial reading of Rossetti's verse within the context of specific nineteenth-century Christian beliefs ("Religious Poetry," 129–33).

2. Representative pairings of Rossetti and Barrett Browning include "Christina Georgina Rossetti," 33; "Christina Rossetti," *Literature,* 66–68; Garnett 283; "Elizabeth

Barrett Browning," *Living Age,* 176; Payne 4; William Michael Rossetti, "Extracts,"
xvii, xviii–ix; Law 444, 452–53; Saintsbury, "Second Poetical Period," 277, 293;
Thompson, "Christina Rossetti," 143; Mountstuart Duff 95; Wilde, "English Poetesses," 101; "Books," 259. For suggestions of a third female poet, see "Poetesses,"
678–79; Hugh Walker, "Minor Poets," 362; Warre-Cornish 69; Saintsbury, "European Literature," 30; William Watson 2:107. R. W. Crump's *Christina Rossetti: A
Reference Guide* has been an invaluable bibiliographic resource.

3. As early as 1841, a review of Caroline Norton's poetry cast her as "unquestionably—
since the death of Mrs. Hemans, the queen of English song" ("'The Dream,'" 93).
For later references to queens of song or of literature, see Herridge 621; "Letters of
Elizabeth Barrett Browning," *Book Reviews,* 176; Watts-Dunton, "Literature," 208.

4. Virginia Woolf is the only "major" twentieth-century woman author. See Homans,
Women Writers for another interesting example of the collapsibility of female triads.
(Dorothy Wordsworth and Emily Brontë serve as the warm-up and backdrop for
the single "major author," Emily Dickinson.) Wendy Martin's "triptych" of Anne
Hutchinson, Emily Dickinson, and Adrienne Rich also suggests connections be-
tween such triads and the survival of poetic secular sanctity.

5. This is a worst-case scenario, of course. Nonetheless, even Rossetti herself expressed
doubts as to "whether the woman is born, or for many a long day, if ever, will be
born, who will balance, not to say outweigh Mrs. Browning" (Mackenzie Bell 103).

6. Benson (620, 625) and Bell (357–62) provide two such basically noncompetitive
comparisons. After an initial judgment against E. B. B., Andrew Lang eventually
asserted that "to institute comparisons between [Rossetti] and Mrs. Browning is apt
to cause injustice to either or to both" ("Month," 112; "Late Victorian Poets," 598).
"Some Women Poets," which focuses primarily upon competition, nevertheless
stresses both authors' expression of a "joy in love, which is concerned, not with the
fulfillment of its cravings, but with the realization of its finest capacities" (32).

7. McGann documents twentieth-century echoes of such approaches ("Religious Poetry," 130–31).

8. An 1894 *Academy* article, for example, links Rossetti to Dante and the Pre-
Raphaelites in her "intimate sense of spiritual beauty and . . . desire to embody this
beauty in a concrete symbol. Some of her verses are almost archaic in this respect;
they are one in spirit with those groups of heavenly figures drawn rather stiffly with
trumpets and uplifted faces on a gold background" (Chambers 163).

9. "Miss Rossetti's Poems," in the *Nation,* also charges that Rossetti prefers "that aspect
of love in which the passion is little more than the instinctive attraction between the
sexes," citing "The Blessed Damozel" and "A Triad" as evidence (48). The former
poem was composed, of course, by Dante Gabriel Rossetti; the latter, Christina
Rossetti removed from later printings of her work. (Amid some controversy, her
brother William Michael Rossetti restored it after her death.) In 1876, the *Literary
World* praises Rossetti's "grace and strength" ("Minor Book Notices," 182); that
same year, Sarah Josepha Hale refers to her "sweetness and strength" (902).

10. Such a gendered primitivist aesthetics could serve—and irritate—opposing interests.
Blackburn suggests, for example, that if critics succeeded in fully gendering language, "the male words (having less than human brains) would deny the very life of

the female, and with no children born to them, the tongues of Nations should presently fail" (513). In contrast, Green celebrates primitivistic womanhood as a millenarian social force (966), while Stutfield ruefully ascribes the New Woman's role as "an enigma in flounces" to faith in feminine primitivism (106).

11. Praise of Rossetti's artlessness began early, with her brothers. It is most intense among later critics, however.

12. William Michael Rossetti's suggestion that his sister did not revise her work was scarcely borne out by his own 1903 *Rossetti Papers* (82, 88, 97–99). Indeed, as McGann notes, Crump's *Complete Poems* reveals "prunings" that are "unusual and very important" ("Christina Rossetti's Poems," 239). Mackenzie Bell's biography tends to be (somewhat misleadingly) cited as evidence of the poet's spontaneous composition methods (14; Cary 251–54; "Some Women Poets," 30–31, 33; Green-Armytage, "Christina Rossetti," 292–94). For (sometimes ambiguous) suggestions that Rossetti's art is more deliberate and controlled, see Lionel Johnson 59; Chambers 163; Stedman, *Victorian Poets,* 280–81; Thompson, "Christina Rossetti," 143; and "Christina Georgina Rossetti," 33.

13. Other references to Rossetti as a songbird include Le Gallienne 130; "Miss Rossetti's Poems," *Saturday Review,* 761; Sharp 745; "A Pageant," 328; and Cary 252.

14. Not all his glorifications of Rossetti succeeded, of course. It seems no wonder, for example, that Watts-Dunton's successors failed to quote his characterization of the poet's conversation as a "spiritual tonic" that "braced up" one's moral nature ("Reminiscences," 355).

15. Lionel Johnson is a notable exception. Though the more lighthearted of his characterizations of Rossetti's verse ("the nursery songs of Heaven," "the national hymns of Heaven") are the most frequently quoted, he characterizes Rossetti as an "artist through and through, mistress of her craft." Moreover, he addresses a full range of her religious verse, including poems that "are the very dirges and burdens of earth." Her "most characteristic greatness," he writes, "lies in her most intimate, most severe, most passionate and sacred poems" (59).

16. Such assertions found support in scholarship as well as popular accounts. See Chamberlain.

17. Thompson's editor, Terence Connolly, suggests that this essay should still provide "food for thought" to "emancipated women whose voices are raised in 'poetic' effusions of free verse" (144).

18. Charles repeatedly stresses how Rossetti's admirers use E. B. B. as an "unfeminine" foil (13–14, 39, 45, 99–101).

19. Instances of such criticism include Charlotte Porter, "Review of *New Poems,*" 149–50; "Christina Rossetti," *Nation,* 272–73; Cary 263; and Hugh Walker, *Age of Tennyson,* 234, 245.

20. As always, there are exceptions. Watts-Dunton's *Athenaeum* obituary, for example, speaks of Rossetti's life as "the most notable example that our time has produced of a masterful power of man's spiritual nature when at its highest to conquer in its warfare with earthly conditions. . . . There was no martyrdom she would not have undertaken" ("Christina Georgina Rossetti," 16–17).

21. At points, ambivalence concerning Rossetti's "artlessness" was more explicit. See Le Gallienne 131; Warre-Cornish 66.

22. Other writers made similar claims: see "Some Women Poets," 123; Charles 44. In a *Scots Observer* piece, a woman writer ingenuously asks male critics to explain why gender bars her access to the "grand style." "She cannot have it, she cannot, and she cannot," they reply. "And so they shake their heads and fasten tight their mouths and close their eyes and shut up their ears with their fingertips" (Blackburn 512).

23. In contrast, consider Thompson, in 1901, on "Mrs. Browning as Prophetess": "No other woman has reached her hand to such things; and Elizabeth Browning could not keep her grasp on them, but clutched desperately for them, capturing them only at moments. She was best when she contented herself with a lesser scope. But, that she could seize such images at times, all honour to her fervid, ultra-feminine soul in a frame too weak!" (163).

24. Ironically, in the same essay, More asserts that "Monna Innominata" holds "a lower rank in every way than that passionate self-revelation of Mrs. Browning's," despite the latter's "annoying confusion of masculine and feminine passion" ("Christina Rossetti," *Atlantic Monthly,* 819).

25. With its nuanced readings, carefully framed historical analysis, and unproblematized reliance upon century-old watchwords, Harrison's work represents both the great strengths and the weaknesses of certain current Rossetti criticism. As it helps set the groundwork for more serious reading of Rossetti's works, it ironically continues the old internecine competition between Rossetti and E. B. B., with the prize, this time, being the exclusionary position of Queen of Feminist Song.

26. Raleigh's criticism, as well as the approach represented by "Poetry in Petticoats," inspired Virginia Woolf to pointed parody ("I Am Christina Rossetti," 324).

Works Cited

Abbott, Lyman. "The Love Letters of Two Poets." *Outlook* 62 (1899): 485–90.

Abrams, M. H., et al., eds. *The Norton Anthology of English Literature,* 1st ed. Vol. 2. New York: Norton, 1962.

———. *The Norton Anthology of English Literature,* 6th ed. Vol. 2. New York: Norton, 1986.

———. *The Norton Anthology of English Literature: The Major Authors,* 5th ed. New York: Norton, 1987.

Adams, Ruth M. Introduction to *The Poetical Works of Elizabeth Barrett Browning.* Cambridge Edition. Boston: Houghton Mifflin, 1974.

Aldrich, Thomas Bailey. "Guilielmus Rex." In Silsby, ed., 232–33.

Altick, Richard D. "The Case of the Curious Bibliographers." In *The Scholar Adventurers,* 37–64. Columbus: Ohio State Univ. Press, 1987.

———. *Lives and Letters: A History of Literary Biography in England and America.* New York: Knopf, 1966.

———. *Paintings from Books.* Columbus: Ohio State Univ. Press, 1985.

———. *The Scholar Adventurers.* Columbus: Ohio State Univ. Press, 1987.

———. "Victorians on the Move; Or, 'Tis Forty Years Since." In *Writers, Readers, and Occasions: Selected Essays on Victorian Literature and Life.* 309–29. Columbus: Ohio State Univ. Press, 1989.

Altieri, Charles. "An Idea and Ideal of a Literary Canon." In Von Hallberg, ed., 41–61.

Angelou, Maya. Talk at the University of Georgia, 1990.

Anstruther, Ian. *Coventry Patmore's Angel.* London: Haggerston Press, 1992.

Ardis, Ann L. *New Women, New Novels: Feminism and Early Modernism.* New Brunswick, N.J.: Rutgers Univ. Press, 1990.

Armstrong, Isobel. "Thatcher's Shakespeare?" *Textual Practice* 3 (Spring 1989): 1–14.

Arnold, Matthew. "The Study of Poetry." In *English Literature and Irish Politics.* Vol. 9, *The Complete Prose Works of Matthew Arnold,* ed. R. H. Super, 161–88. Ann Arbor: Univ. of Michigan Press, 1973.

———. "Wordsworth." In *English Literature and Irish Politics.* Vol. 9, *The Complete Prose Works of Matthew Arnold,* ed. R. H. Super, 36–55. Ann Arbor: Univ. of Michigan Press, 1973.

Arnold, William T. "Elizabeth Barrett Browning." In *The English Poets,* ed. Thomas Humphry Ward, 4:563–67. New York: Macmillan, 1885.

Ashe, Geoffrey. *The Virgin.* London: Routledge, 1976.

Atwood, Margaret. "The Curse of Eve—Or, What I Learned in School." In *Second Words: Selected Critical Prose,* 215–28. Boston: Beacon Press, 1984.

Auerbach, Nina. *Ellen Terry: Player in Her Time.* New York: Norton, 1987.

——. *Woman and the Demon: The Life of a Victorian Myth.* Cambridge: Harvard Univ. Press, 1982.

"Aurora Leigh" (review). *Dublin University Magazine* 49 (1857): 460–70.

[Aytoun, W. E.] "Poetic Abberrations." *Blackwood's* 87 (1860): 490–94.

Babcock, Robert. *The Genesis of Shakespeare Idolatry.* Chapel Hill: Univ. of North Carolina Press, 1931.

Bagehot, Walter. "Shakespeare: The Man." In *Literary Studies,* 1:112–53. London: J. M. Dent [1911].

Baldick, Chris. *The Social Mission of English Criticism 1848–1932.* Oxford: Clarendon Press, 1983.

Barker, Nicolas, and John Collins. *A Sequel to an Enquiry into the Nature of Certain Nineteenth Century Pamphlets by John Carter and Graham Pollard.* Berkeley, Calif.: Scolar Press, 1983.

Barrett, Dorothea. *Vocation and Desire: George Eliot's Heroines.* New York: Routledge, 1989.

Bausinger, Hermann. *Formen der "Volkspoesie."* Berlin: E. Schmidt, 1968.

Becher, Tony. *Academic Tribes and Territories: Intellectual Enquiry and the Cultures of Disciplines.* Milton Keynes, England: Open Univ. Press, 1989.

Beer, Gillian. *George Eliot.* Bloomington: Indiana Univ. Press, [1986].

Bell, Mackenzie. *Christina Rossetti: A Biographical and Critical Study.* Boston: Roberts Brothers, 1898.

Bell, Rudolph. *Holy Anorexia.* Chicago: Univ. of Chicago Press, 1985.

Benjamin, Walter. "Literaturgeschichte und Literaturwissenschaft." In *Gesammelte Schriften,* ed. Rolf Tiedemann and Hermann Schweppenhaueser, 3:283–90. Frankfurt: Suhrkamp, 1972.

——. "The Work of Art in the Age of Mechanical Reproduction." In *Illuminations,* 217–51. New York: Schocken, 1978.

Benson, Arthur Christopher. "Christina Rossetti." *Living Age* 204 (March 1895): 629.

[——.] "Mrs. Browning." *Macmillan's* 59 (1888): 138–45.

Berger, John, Sven Blomberg, Chris Fox, Michael Dibb, and Richard Hollis. *Ways of Seeing.* London: British Broadcasting Corporation and Penguin Books, 1972.

Besier, Rudolf. *The Barretts of Wimpole Street: A Comedy in Five Acts.* London: Victor Gollancz, 1933.

Bierce, Ambrose. "Saint." In *The Devil's Dictionary,* 306. Cleveland: World Publishing, 1944.

Blackburn, Vernon. "'Twixt Man and Woman." *Scots Observer* (4 October 1890): 512–13.

Bloom, Allan. *The Closing of the American Mind.* New York: Simon and Schuster, 1987.

"Books. *The Poetesses of the Century.*" *Spectator* (20 August 1892): 258–60.

Brantlinger, Patrick. *Rule of Darkness: British Literature and Imperialism, 1830–1914.* Ithaca: Cornell Univ. Press, 1988.

Bristol, Michael D. *Shakespeare's America, America's Shakespeare.* New York: Routledge, 1990.

Brontë, Charlotte. *Jane Eyre.* Ed. Margaret Smith. New York: Oxford Univ. Press, 1991.

Brooks, Sarah Warner. *English Poetry and Poets.* Freeport, N.Y.: Books for Libraries Press, 1972.

Browning, Elizabeth Barrett. *Aurora Leigh.* In *Complete Works,* 4:1–159; 5:1–197. New York: AMS Press, 1973.

——. *Aurora Leigh.* Introduced by Gardner Taplin. Chicago: Academy Chicago Press, 1979.

——. *Aurora Leigh.* Introduction by Cora Kaplan. London: Women's Press, 1978.

——. *Aurora Leigh.* Ed. Kerry McSweeney. New York: Oxford Univ. Press, 1993.

——. *Aurora Leigh.* Ed. Margaret Reynolds. New York: Norton, 1994.

——. *Aurora Leigh.* Ed. Margaret Reynolds. Athens: Ohio Univ. Press, 1992.

——. *Casa Guidi Windows.* In *Complete Works,* 3: 249–313.

——. *Complete Works.* Ed. Charlotte Porter and Helen A. Clarke. 6 vols. New York: AMS Press, 1973.

——. "A Curse for a Nation." In *Complete Works,* 3:354–58.

——. "Fragment of an 'Essay on Woman.'" *Studies in Browning and His Circle* 12 (1984): 10–12.

——. *Mrs. E. B. Browning's Letters and Essays.* Ed. Richard Henry Stoddard. 2 vols. New York: James Miller, 1877.

——. *The Letters of Elizabeth Barrett Browning.* Ed. Frederic Kenyon. 2 vols. London: Smith, Elder, 1898.

——. *Poems before Congress.* In *Complete Works,* 3:314–58.

——. *The Poetical Works of Elizabeth Barrett Browning.* Cambridge Edition. Boston: Houghton Mifflin, 1974.

——. "The Runaway Slave at Pilgrim's Point." In *Complete Works,* 3:160–70.

——. *Sonnets from the Portuguese.* In *Complete Works,* 3:227–48.

——. *Sonnets from the Portuguese.* Ed. William S. Peterson. Barre, Mass.: Imprint Society, 1977.

——. *A Varorium Edition of Elizabeth Barrett Browning's Sonnets from the Portuguese.* Ed. Miroslava Wein Dow. New York: Whitston, 1980.

——. "A Vision of Poets." In *Complete Works,* 2: 310–85.

Browning, Elizabeth Barrett, and Robert Browning. *The Best Known Poems of Elizabeth and Robert Browning.* New York: Book League of America, 1942.

Browning, Robert. "The Bishop Orders His Tomb at St. Praxed's." In *The Complete Works of Robert Browning,* ed. Roma King, et al., 4:189–93. Athens: Ohio Univ. Press, 1973.

——. *Letters of Robert Browning, Collected by Thomas J. Wise.* Ed. Thurman L. Hood. New Haven: Yale University Press, 1933.

——. *Robert Browning and Julia Wedgwood*. Ed. Richard Curle. New York: Frederick A. Stokes, 1937.

——. "To Edward FitzGerald." *Athenaeum* (1889): 64.

——. "Transcendentalism: A Poem in Twelve Books." In *Robert Browning: The Poems*, ed. John Pettigrew, 1:735–36. New Haven: Yale Univ. Press, 1981.

Browning, Robert, and Elizabeth Barrett Browning. *The Brownings' Correspondence*. Ed. Philip Kelley and Ronald Hudson. Winfield, Kans.: Wedgestone Press, [1984].

"The Browning Letters." *Academy* (1899): 235–37.

"Browning Love-Letters." *Eclectic Magazine* 132 (1899): 736–40.

Butler, Judith. *Gender Trouble: Feminism and the Subversion of Identity*. New York: Routledge, 1990.

Butler, William Archer. "Poetesses of Our Day." *Dublin University Magazine* 10 (August 1837): 123–41.

Bynum, Caroline Walker. *Fragmentation and Redemption: Essays on Gender and the Human Body in Medieval Religion*. New York: Zone Books, 1991.

——. *Holy Feast and Holy Fast: The Religious Significance of Food to Medieval Women*. Berkeley: Univ. of California Press, 1987.

[Cameron, William.] "Mrs. Browning." *Good Words* 39 (1898): 43–46.

Canton, William. "From an Idler's Day-Book." *Good Words* 40 (1899): 285–88.

Capps, Jack L. *Emily Dickinson's Reading, 1836–1886*. Cambridge: Harvard Univ. Press, 1966.

Carlyle, Thomas. *On Heroes, Hero-Worship, and the Heroic in History*. New York: AMS Press, 1969.

Carter, John, and Graham Pollard. *An Enquiry into the Nature of Certain Nineteenth Century Pamphlets,* ed. Nicolas Barker and John Collins. 2d ed. London: Scolar Press, 1983.

Cary, Elisabeth Luther. *The Rossettis: Dante Gabriel and Christina*. New York: Knickerbocker Press, 1900.

Cavazza, E. "The Sisters of Portia." *Shakespeariana* 3 (1886): 495–500.

Chamberlain, Alexander F. "Primitive Woman as Poet." *Journal of American Folklore* (October–December 1903): 205–21.

Chambers, Edmund K. Review of *Verses*. *Academy* 45 (24 February 1894): 162–64.

Chandler, James. "The Pope Controversy: Romantic Poetics and the English Canon." In Von Hallberg, ed., 197–225.

"*Chapters on Wives*. By Mrs. Ellis" (review). *Athenaeum* (14 July 1860): 52–53.

"Characteristics of Women. No. II. Characters of the Affections." *Blackwood's* 33 (1833): 107–27.

Charlemont, Countess of. "Gruach (Lady Macbeth)." *New Shakespeare Society Transactions* 1 (1875–76): 194–98.

Charles, Edna Kotin. *Christina Rossetti: Critical Perspectives, 1862–1982*. Selinsgrove, Pa.: Susquehanna Univ. Press, 1985.

Chesterton, G. K. "Browning and His Marriage." In *The Bodley Head G. K. Chesterton*, 8–22. London: Bodley Head, 1985.

[Chorley, Henry.] "Elizabeth Barrett Browning" (obituary). *Athenaeum* (1861): 19–20.

[——.] "Poems before Congress." *Athenaeum* (1860): 371–72.

[——.] "Poems. By Elizabeth Barrett Browning." *Athenaeum* (1850): 1242–43.

"Christina G. Rossetti." *Catholic World* 4 (1867): 839–46.

"Christina Georgina Rossetti." *Dial* 18 (16 January 1895): 37–38.

"Christina Rossetti." *Athenaeum* (22 January 1898): 109.

"Christina Rossetti." *Literature* 2 (22 January 1898): 66–68.

"Christina Rossetti." *Nation* 66 (7 April 1898): 272–73.

"Christina Rossetti's Poems." *Catholic World* 24 (1876–77): 122–29.

Cixous, Hélène, and Catherine Clément. *The Newly Born Woman*. Trans. Betsy Wing. Minneapolis: Univ. of Minnesota Press, 1986.

Clark, J. Scott. *A Study of English and American Poets: A Laboratory Method*. New York: Scribner's, 1900.

Clarke, Isabel. "Some Women-Poets of the Present Reign." *Living Age* 249 (30 June 1906): 791–98.

Clarke, Mary Cowden. *The Girlhood of Shakespeare's Heroines*. 1850. 3 vols. New York: AMS, 1974.

——. "Shakespeare as the Girl's Friend." *Shakespeariana* 4 (1887): 355–69.

——. "Shakspeare-Studies of Women." *Ladies' Companion* 1 (1849): 25, 59, 156–57, 188, 214–15, 295, 343, 402–7.

Clausen, Christopher. "'Canon,' Theme, and Code." In Nemoianu and Royal, eds., 199–213.

Cockshut, A. O. J. *Truth to Life: The Art of Biography in the Nineteenth Century*. London: Collins, 1974.

Coleridge, H. N. "Modern English Poetesses." *Quarterly Review* 66 (1840): 347–89.

Coleridge, Mary Elizabeth. "The Making of Heroines." 1888. In *Gathered Leaves from the Prose of Mary E. Coleridge*, ed. Edith Sichel, 177–80. London: Constable, 1910.

Coleridge, Samuel Taylor. *Lectures and Notes on Shakspere and Other English Poets*. Ed. T. Ashe. Freeport, N.Y.: Books for Libraries Press, 1972.

——. *Collected Works of Samuel Taylor Coleridge*. Ed. R. A. Foakes. V: *Lectures 1808–1819 on Literature*. Princeton: Princeton Univ. Press, 1987.

[Collins, Mortimer.] "Elizabeth Barrett Browning." *Dublin University Magazine* 60 (1862): 157–62.

Comte, Auguste. *Auguste Comte and Positivism: The Essential Writings*. Ed. Gertrud Lenzer. Chicago: Univ. of Chicago Press, 1975.

——. *The Catechism of Positive Religion*. 3d ed. Trans. Richard Congreve. Clifton, N.J.: Augustus M. Kelley, 1973.

Conant, C. B. "Elizabeth Barrett Browning." *North American Review* 94 (1862): 338–57.

Conrad, Joseph. *Heart of Darkness*. Ed. Robert Kimbrough. New York: Norton, 1988.

Cooper, Helen. *Elizabeth Barrett Browning: Woman and Artist*. Chapel Hill: Univ. of North Carolina Press, 1988.

——. "Working into Light: Elizabeth Barrett Browning." In *Shakespeare's Sisters: Feminist*

Essays on Women Poets, ed. Sandra M. Gilbert and Susan Gubar, 65–81. Blooming-ton: Indiana Univ. Press, 1979.

"Cordelia Pronounced a Vixen." *Shakespeariana* 4 (1887): 527–29.

Couthouy, Marion. "Elizabeth Barrett Browning." *Lippincott's* (1878): 747–53.

Crawford, Robert. *Devolving English Literature.* Oxford: Clarendon Press, 1992.

Crosby, Christina. *The Ends of History: Victorians and "The Woman Question."* New York: Routledge, 1991.

Cross, Alan Eastman. "Sonnets from the Portuguese." *Poet Lore* (1889): 172.

Crosse, Cordelia. "The Wedded Poets." *Temple Bar* 94 (1892): 29–46.

Crump, R. W., ed. *Christina Rossetti: A Reference Guide.* Boston: G. K. Hall, 1976.

Curran, Stuart. "The Lyric Voice of Christina Rossetti." *Victorian Poetry* 9 (1971): 287–99.

Curtius, Ernst Robert. *European Literature and the Latin Middle Ages.* Trans. Willard R. Trask. New York: Pantheon, 1953.

Davenport, Fanny. "Beatrice." *Shakespeariana* 4 (1887): 273–79.

David, Deirdre. *Intellectual Women and Victorian Patriarchy: Harriet Martineau, Elizabeth Barrett Browning, George Eliot.* Ithaca: Cornell Univ. Press, 1987.

Davies, Tony. "Common Sense and Critical Practice: Teaching Literature." In Widdow-son, ed., 32–43.

DeJean, Joan. "Fictions of Sappho." *Critical Inquiry* 13 (1987): 787–805.

——. *Fictions of Sappho 1546–1937.* Chicago: Univ. of Chicago Press, 1989.

DeJean, Joan, and Nancy K. Miller. Editors' Preface to *Displacements: Women, Tradition, Literatures in French,* vii–xiii. Baltimore: Johns Hopkins Univ. Press, 1991.

Dennis, John. "Elizabeth Barrett Browning." *Leisure Hour* (1889): 86–90.

——. *Studies in English Literature.* London: Stanford, 1876.

De Quincey, Thomas. "Joan of Arc." *Biographies and Biographic Sketches.* Vol. 5, *De Quincey's Collected Writings,* ed. David Masson, 384–416. London: A. and C. Black, 1897.

——. "Shakspeare." In De Quincey, *Biographical Essays,* 1–93. Boston: Ticknor, Reed, Fields, 1850.

Desmet, Christy. "'Intercepting the Dew-Drop': Female Readers and Readings in Anna Jameson's Shakespearean Criticism." In Novy, ed., 41–57.

Dickens, Charles. *Bleak House.* Ed. Norman Page. New York: Penguin, 1985.

Dijkstra, Bram. *Idols of Perversity: Fantasies of Feminine Evil in Fin-de-Siècle Culture.* New York: Oxford Univ. Press, 1986.

Dixon, W. Macneile. "Finality in Literary Judgment." *Westminster Review* 143 (1895): 401–12.

Doane, Janice, and Devon Hodges. *Nostalgia and Sexual Difference: The Resistance to Con-temporary Feminism.* New York: Methuen, 1987.

Dobell, Sydney. *Life and Letters of Sydney Dobell.* Ed. Emily Jolly. 2 vols. London: Smith, Elder, 1878.

Dobson, Michael. *The Making of the National Poet: Shakespeare, Adaptation, and Authorship, 1660–1769.* Oxford: Clarendon Press, 1992.

Dollimore, Jonathan, and Alan Sinfield, eds. *Political Shakespeare: Essays in Cultural Materialism.* 2d ed. Ithaca: Cornell Univ. Press, 1994.

Donaldson, Sandra. *Elizabeth Barrett Browning: An Annotated Bibliography of the Commentary and Criticism 1826–1990.* New York: G. K. Hall, 1993.

Douglas, Alfred. "Two Loves." In *The Penguin Book of Homosexual Verse,* ed. Stephen Coote, 262–64. New York: Penguin Books, 1983.

Douglas, Ann. *The Feminization of American Culture.* New York: Knopf, 1977.

Dowden, Edward. *Essays Modern and Elizabethan.* New York: Dutton, 1910.

———. *New Studies in Literature.* London: Kegan Paul, Trench, Truebner, 1895.

———. *Shakspere: A Critical Study of His Mind and Art.* 3d ed. New York: Harper and Brothers, 1875.

———. *Transcripts and Studies.* 2d ed. London: Kegan Paul, 1896.

"The Drama: Modjeska." *Shakespeariana* 1 (1883–84): 176–79.

"'The Dream and Other Poems.' By the Hon. Mrs. Norton." *Graham's* 8 (1841): 93–95.

Duff, Mountstuart E. Grant. "Introductory Notes: Christina Georgina Rossetti." In *An Anthology of Victorian Poetry,* 95. London: Swan Sonnenschein, 1902.

Duff, William. *Letters on the Intellectual and Moral Character of Women.* New York: Garland, 1974.

Eagleton, Terry. *Literary Theory: An Introduction.* Minneapolis: Univ. of Minnesota Press, 1983.

"The Earlier Poems of Elizabeth Barrett Browning." *Athenaeum* (15 December 1877): 765–67.

Eliot, George. *Daniel Deronda.* Ed. Graham Handley. New York: Oxford Univ. Press, 1991.

———. *Middlemarch.* Ed. Bert G. Hornback. New York: Norton, 1977.

———. "O May I Join the Choir Invisible." In Eliot, *Collected Poems,* ed. Lucien Jenkins, 49–50. London: Scoob Books, 1989.

———. *A Writer's Notebook, 1854–1879, and Uncollected Writings.* Ed. Joseph Wiesenfarth. Charlottesville: Univ. Press of Virginia, 1981.

Eliot, T. S. "Tradition and the Individual Talent." In *Selected Essays 1917–1932,* 3–11. New York: Harcourt Brace, 1932.

"Elizabeth Barrett Browning." *Eclectic Review* 115 (1862): 189–212.

"Elizabeth Barrett Browning." *Literary World* 19 (1888): 361.

"Elizabeth Barrett Browning." *Living Age* 249 (21 April 1906): 173–79.

"Elizabeth Barrett Browning." *London Quarterly Review* 72 (1889): 22–42.

"Elizabeth Barrett Browning." *National Magazine* 10 (1861): 210–14.

"Elizabeth Barrett Browning." *Outlook* 58 (1898): 380–82.

"Elizabeth Barrett Browning." *Saturday Review* 66 (1888): 466–67.

"Elizabeth Barrett Browning and Mr. Howitt." *Spiritual Magazine* (1860): 404–6.

[Elliott, Madeline Leigh-Noel.] *Shakspere's Garden of Girls.* London: Remington, 1885.

Ellis, Havelock. *My Life.* Boston: Houghton Mifflin, 1939.

Ellis, Sarah Stickney. *The Daughters of England: Their Position in Society, Character, and Responsibilities*. New York: Edward Walker, n.d.

——. "The Poetry of Woman." In *Guide to Social Happiness*, 111–26. New York: Edward Walker, 1850.

——. *The Wives of England: Their Relative Duties, and Domestic Influence, and Social Obligations*. New York: Edward Walker, n.d.

——. *The Women of England: Their Social Duties, and Domestic Habits*. New York: Edward Walker, n.d.

Ellmann, Richard. *Oscar Wilde*. New York: Knopf, 1988.

Emerson, Ralph Waldo. "Shakspeare, or the Poet." In *The Collected Works of Ralph Waldo Emerson*, 4:107–25. Cambridge, Mass.: Belknap, 1987.

Emery, E. S. "A Study of Lady Macbeth." *Shakespeariana* 1 (1883–84): 221–25.

"English Literature in 1892." *Athenaeum* (1893): 19–25.

"Essay Writing on a Great English Author." *Girl's Own Paper* 9 (1887): 32.

Fetterley, Judith. *The Resisting Reader: A Feminist Approach to American Fiction*. Bloomington: Indiana Univ. Press, 1981.

[Field, Kate.] "Elizabeth Barrett Browning." *Atlantic Monthly* (1861): 368–76.

[——.] "English Authors in Florence." *Atlantic Monthly* (1864): 660–71.

[——.] "Mrs. Browning's Essays on the Poets." *Christian Examiner* 75 (1863): 24–43.

FitzGerald, Edward. *Letters and Literary Remains*. Ed. William Aldis Wright. 3 vols. London: Macmillan, 1889.

Foucault, Michel. *Discipline and Punish: The Birth of the Prison*. Trans. Alan Sheridan. New York: Vintage Books, 1979.

——. *The History of Sexuality*. Trans. Robert Hurley. 3 vols. New York: Vintage Books, 1990.

——. "What Is an Author?" In *Language, Counter-Memory, Practice: Selected Essays and Interviews,* ed. Donald F. Bouchard, trans. Donald F. Bouchard and Sherry Simon, 113–38. Ithaca: Cornell Univ. Press, 1992.

Fowler, Alastair. *Kinds of Literature: An Introduction to the Theory of Genres and Modes*. Cambridge: Harvard Univ. Press, 1982.

Fraser, Hilary. "St. Theresa, St. Dorothea, and Miss Brooke in *Middlemarch*." *Nineteenth-Century Fiction* (1986): 400–411.

Frisch, Max. *Stiller*. Frankfort: Suhrkamp, 1973.

Froula, Christine. "The Daughter's Seduction: Sexual Violence and Literary History." *Signs* 11 (1986): 621–44.

——. "Virginia Woolf as Shakespeare's Sister: Chapters in a Woman Writer's Autobiography." In Novy, ed., 123–42.

Gardener, H. H. "The Immoral Influence of Women in Literature." *Arena* 1 (February 1890): 322–35.

Garnett, Richard. "Rossetti, Christina Georgina." In *Dictionary of National Biography*, 49:282–84. New York: Macmillan, 1897.

Gates, Henry Louis, Jr. "The Master's Pieces: On Canon-Formation and the Afro-

American Experience." In *Reconstructing American Literary and Historical Studies,* ed. Guenter H. Lenz, Hartmut Keil, and Sabine Broeck-Sallah, 169–91. New York: St. Martin's Press, 1990.

Gerould, Gordon Hall. *Saints' Legends.* New York: Houghton Mifflin, 1916.

Gerwig, George W. Foreword to *Shakespeare's Ideals of Womanhood.* East Aurora, N.Y.: Roycroft Shops, 1929.

Gilbert, Sandra M., and Susan Gubar. *The Madwoman in the Attic: The Woman Writer and the Nineteenth-Century Literary Imagination.* New Haven: Yale Univ. Press, 1979.

Gilder, Richard Watson. "A Romance of the Nineteenth Century." *Century* 70 (October 1905): 918–27.

Gilfillan, George. "Mrs. Hemans." In *Modern Literature and Literary Men: Being a Gallery of Literary Portraits,* 229–39. New York: D. Appleton, 1850.

Goodich, Michael. *Vita Perfecta: The Ideal of Sainthood in the Thirteenth Century.* Stuttgart: Anton Hiersemann, 1982.

Gorak, Jan. *The Making of the Modern Canon: Genesis and Crisis of a Literary Idea.* Atlantic Highlands, N.J.: Athlone, 1991.

Gosse, Edmund. "Christina Rossetti." *Century Magazine* 46 (June 1893): 211–17.

——. "Christina Rossetti." In *Critical Kit-kats,* 135–62. New York: Dodd, Mead, 1896.

——. Introduction to *Victorian Songs: Lyrics of the Affections and Nature,* collected and illustrated by Edmund H. Garrett, xxiii–xli. Boston: Little, Brown, 1895.

——. "Mr. Gosse on 'The Poetry of Women.'" *The Critic* 22 (21 January 1893): 37–38.

——. *A Short History of Modern English Literature.* New York: Appleton, 1897.

——. "The Sonnets from the Portuguese." In *Critical Kit-kats,* 1–17. New York: Dodd, Mead, 1896.

Gould, C. H. "Portia and the Office of Woman." *Shakespeariana* 4 (1887): 97–106.

Gould, Elizabeth Porter. "The Browning Letters." *Education* 20 (1889): 214–20.

——. "The Supremacy of Mrs. Browning." *Unitarian Review* (1889): 43–50.

Graff, Gerald, and Michael Warner, eds. *The Origins of Literary Studies in America.* New York: Routledge, 1989.

Granqvist, Raoul. "Some Traits of Cultural Nationalism in the Reception of Shakespeare in Nineteenth Century U.S.A." *Orbis Litterarum* 43 (1988): 32–57.

[Grant, Charles.] "Miss Barrett's Poems." *Metropolitan Magazine* (1845): 322–34.

Green, Alice Stopford. "Woman's Place in the World of Letters." *The Nineteenth Century* (1897): 964–74.

Green-Armytage, A. J. "Introductory" and "Christina Rossetti." In *Maids of Honour,* xv–xxii, 273–301. London: Blackwood's, 1906.

Griswold, Hattie Tyng. "Christina Rossetti." In *Personal Sketches of Recent Authors,* 280–97. Chicago: A. C. McClurg, 1898.

Gubar, Susan. "'The Blank Page' and the Issues of Female Creativity." *Critical Inquiry* 8 (1981): 243–63.

——. "Sapphistries." *Signs* 10 (1984): 43–62.

Guild, Marion Pelton. "To Robert and Elizabeth Barrett Browning." *Atlantic Monthly* 86 (1900): 420–21.

Guillory, John. "The Ideology of Canon-Formation: T. S. Eliot and Cleanth Brooks." In Von Hallberg, ed., 337–62.

[Gwynn, Stephen.] "Discretion and Publicity." *Edinburgh Review* (1899): 420–39.

Hale, Sarah Josepha. *Biography of Distinguished Women*. New York: Harper and Brothers, 1876.

Halliday, F. E. *The Cult of Shakespeare*. London: Duckworth, 1957.

Harris, Laurie Lanzen. "Christina Georgina Rossetti: 1830–1895." In *Nineteenth-Century Literature Criticism*, 2:554–79. Detroit: Gale Research, 1981–93.

Harris, Wendell V. "Canonicity." *PMLA* 106 (1991): 110–21.

Harrison, Antony H. "In the Shadow of E. B. B.: Christina Rossetti and Ideological Estrangement." In *Victorian Poets and Romantic Poems: Intertextuality and Ideology*. 108–43. Charlottesville: Univ. Press of Virginia, 1990.

Harrison, Frederic. *The New Calendar of Great Men*. New York: Macmillan, 1892.

——. *Realities and Ideals: Social, Political, Literary, and Artistic*. London: Macmillan, 1908.

Hawkes, Terence. *That Shakespeherian Rag: Essays on a Critical Process*. New York: Methuen, 1986.

Hawley, John Stratton, ed. *Saints and Virtues*. Berkeley: Univ. of California Press, 1987.

Hawthorne, Nathaniel. *French and Italian Sketch Books*. 2 vols. Boston: Osgood, 1871.

Hawthorne, Sophia. *Notes in England and Italy*. New York: Putnam, 1869.

Hayter, Alethea. *Mrs. Browning: A Poet's Work and Its Setting*. New York: Barnes and Noble, 1963.

Hazlitt, William. *Characters of Shakespear's Plays and Lessons on the English Poets*. London: Macmillan, 1920.

Heath, Charles. *The Heroines of Shakspeare*. London: W. Kent, 1858.

Heffernan, Thomas. *Sacred Biography: Saints and Their Biographers in the Middle Ages*. New York: Oxford Univ. Press, 1988.

Heine, H. *Shakspeares Maedchen und Frauen*. Paris: Brockhaus und Avenarius, 1839.

Hemans, Felicia. Prefatory Memoir to *Poetical Works of Mrs. Hemans*. Albion Ed. London: Frederick Warne, 1900.

Henley, William Ernest. *The Graphic Gallery of Shakespeare's Heroines*. Boston: Estes and Lauriat, n.d.

"Henry Norman Hudson." *Shakespeariana* 3 (1886): 81–82.

Herridge, William T. "Elizabeth Barrett Browning." *Andover Review* 7 (1887): 607–23.

Herring, Jack W. *The Armstrong Browning Library*. Waco, Tex.: Armstrong Browning Library, n.d.

Hillard, George Stillman. *Six Months in Italy*. 2 vols. Boston: Ticknor, Reed, and Fields, 1853.

Holcombe, Samuel. "Death of Mrs. Browning." *Southern Literary Messenger* 33 (1861): 412–17.

Holmes, Oliver Wendell. "Shakespeare." 1864. In Silsby, ed., 142–46.

215   *Works Cited*

Homans, Margaret. *Bearing the Word: Language and Female Experience in Nineteenth-Century Women's Writing.* Chicago: Univ. of Chicago Press, 1986.

——. *Women Writers and Poetic Identity.* Princeton: Princeton Univ. Press, [1980.]

Horne, Richard Henry. *New Spirit of the Age.* New York: Harper, 1844.

Houghton, Walter E. *The Victorian Frame of Mind, 1830–1870.* New Haven: Yale Univ. Press, 1978.

Houghton, Walter E., and G. Robert Stange. *Victorian Poetry and Poetics.* 2d ed. Boston: Houghton Mifflin, 1968.

Howard, Jean E., and Marion F. O'Connor. Introduction to *Shakespeare Reproduced: The Text in History and Ideology,* ed. Jean E. Howard and Marion F. O'Connor, 1–17. New York: Methuen, 1987.

Howitt, William. "The Earth-Plane and the Spirit-Plane of Literature." *Spiritual Magazine* (1860): 292–95.

Hubbard, Elbert. "Christina Rossetti." In *Little Journeys to the Homes of Famous Women,* 147–72. New York: G. P. Putnam's Sons, 1897.

Hudson, Henry Norman. "Female Characters." In *Lectures on Shakspeare,* 1:192–204. New York: AMS, 1971.

——. Notes to *History of King John,* by William Shakespeare. Boston: Ginn, 1889.

——. Notes to *Romeo and Juliet,* by William Shakespeare. New York: Collier, 1912.

——. *Shakespeare: His Life, Art, and Characters.* 4th ed. 2 vols. Boston: Ginn, Heath, 1882.

Hueffer, Ford Madox. *The Critical Attitude.* London: Duckworth, 1911.

Hughes, Cecil Eldred, ed. *The Praise of Shakespeare: An English Anthology.* London: Methuen, 1904.

Hunt, Leigh. "An Answer to the Question, What is Poetry?" In *English Critical Essays: Nineteenth Century,* ed. Edmund D. Jones, 255–303. London: Oxford, 1971.

——. "Blue-Stocking Revels." *Monthly Repository* 11 (July 1837): 33–57.

——. *Correspondence of Leigh Hunt.* Ed. Thornton Hunt. 2 vols. London: Smith, Elder, 1862.

Hutcheon, Linda. *A Theory of Parody: The Teachings of Twentieth-Century Art Forms.* New York: Methuen, 1985.

"Ingersoll on Shakespeare and the Bible." *Shakespeariana* 5 (1888): 289–90.

Ingram, John H. *Elizabeth Barrett Browning.* Boston: Roberts, 1888.

Irish, Frank V. *American and British Authors: A Text-Book on Literature for High Schools, Academies, Seminaries, Normal Schools, and Colleges.* Columbus, Ohio: Irish, 1896.

Jackson, Russell. "'Perfect Types of Womanhood': Rosalind, Beatrice and Viola in Victorian Criticism and Performance." *Shakespeare Survey* 32 (1979): 15–26.

James, Henry. "George Barnett Smith's Poets and Novelists." In *Literary Reviews and Essays,* ed. Albert Mordell, 330–32. New York: Grove, 1957.

——. *The Portrait of a Lady.* Ed. Robert D. Bamberg. New York: Norton, 1975.

Jameson, Anna. *A Commonplace Book.* London: Longman, Brown, Green, and Longmans, 1855.

——. *Legends of the Madonna.* New York: Houghton Mifflin, 1897.

———. *Sacred and Legendary Art.* London: Longman, Brown, Green, 1848.

———. *Shakspeare's Heroines: Characteristics of Women: Moral, Poetical, and Historical.* 2d ed. London: George Bell, 1879. (First published as *Characteristics of Women: Moral, Poetical, and Historical.*)

———. *Studies, Stories, and Memoirs.* New York: Houghton, Mifflin, 1885.

———. *Visits and Sketches at Home and Abroad.* 2 vols. New York: Harper, 1834.

Jeffreys, Sheila. *The Spinster and her Enemies: Feminism and Sexuality 1880–1930.* Boston: Pandora, 1985.

Jewsbury, Geraldine. "Felicia Dorothea Hemans: Personal." In *Moulton's Library of Literary Criticism,* 5:254. New York: Henry Malkin, 1910.

Johnson, Charles F. "Shakespeare as a Text-Book." *Shakespeariana* 4 (1887): 487–98.

Johnson, E. D. H., ed. *The World of the Victorians.* New York: Scribner's, 1964.

Johnson, Glen M. "The Teaching Anthology and the Canon of American Literature: Some Notes on Theory in Practice." In Nemoianu and Royal, eds., 111–35.

Johnson, Lionel. "Literature: Miss Rossetti and Mrs. Alexander." *Academy* (25 July 1896): 59–60.

Johnson, Samuel. "Preface." [1765 Shakespeare.] In Beverley Warner, ed., 111–70.

Jonson, Ben. "To the Memory of My Beloved, the Author, Mr. William Shakespeare: And What He Hath Left Us." In Hughes, ed., 42–44.

Kaplan, Carey, and Ellen Cronan Rose. *The Canon and the Common Reader.* Knoxville: Univ. of Tennessee Press, 1990.

Kaplan, Cora. "Elizabeth Barrett Browning." In *Salt and Bitter and Good: Three Centuries of English and American Women Poets.* 105–7. New York: Paddington Press, 1975.

Keightley, Thomas. "Life of Shakespeare." In *The Shakespeare-Expositor: An Aid to the Perfect Understanding of Shakespeare's Plays,* 1–19. London: J. Russell Smith, 1867.

Kelley, Philip, and Betty A. Colley. *The Browning Collections: A Reconstruction with Other Memorabilia.* Winfield, Kans.: Wedgstone Press, 1984.

Kemble, Frances Anne. "To Shakespeare." In Hughes, ed., 183.

Kemp, Eric Waldram. *Canonization and Authority in the Western Church.* New York: AMS Press, 1980.

Kent, David, ed. *The Achievement of Christina Rossetti.* Ithaca: Cornell Univ. Press, 1988.

Ker, Ian. *John Henry Newman: A Biography.* Oxford: Clarendon Press, 1988.

Kermode, Frank. "Institutional Control of Interpretation." *Salmagundi* 43 (Winter 1979): 72–86.

[Kinney, Elizabeth C.] "A Day with the Brownings at Pratolino." *Scribner's* 1 (1870): 185–88.

Kirkham, Margaret. *Jane Austen, Feminism, and Fiction.* Totowa, N.J.: Barnes and Noble, 1983.

Klaus, Robert James. *The Pope, the Protestants, and the Irish: Papal Aggression and Anti-Catholicism in Mid-Nineteenth-Century England.* New York: Garland, 1987.

Landon, Letitia E. "On the Character of Mrs. Hemans's Writings." *Colburn's* 44 (1835): 425–33.

Lang, Andrew. *History of English Literature from "Beowulf" to Swinburne.* New York: Longmans, Green, and Co., 1912.

——. "The Month in England." *Cosmopolitan Magazine* (London) 19 (June 1895): 112.

Langton, Jane. *Emily Dickinson Is Dead.* New York: St. Martin's, 1984.

"Last Poems" (review). *Saturday Review* (1862): 472–74.

Latham, Grace. "O Poor Ophelia!" *New Shakespeare Society Transactions* 1 (1880–86): 401–30.

Law, Alice. "The Poetry of Christina G. Rossetti." *Westminster Review* 143 (1895): 444–53.

Lawrence, Karen R. "Introduction: The Cultural Politics of Canons." In *Decolonizing Tradition: New Views of Twentieth-Century "British" Literary Canons,* ed. Karen R. Lawrence, 1–19. Urbana: Univ. of Illinois Press, 1992.

Le Gallienne, Richard. "*Poems.* By Christina Rossetti." *Academy* 39 (7 February 1891): 130–31.

Leighton, Angela. *Elizabeth Barrett Browning.* Bloomington: Indiana Univ. Press, 1986.

——. "Stirring a Dust of Figures: Elizabeth Barrett Browning and Love." *Browning Society Notes* 17 (1987–88): 11–24.

——. *Victorian Women Poets: Writing against the Heart.* Charlottesville: Univ. Press of Virginia, 1992.

"'Les Sonnets du Portugais' d'Elizabeth Barrett Browning" (review of translation). *Athenaeum* (1903): 182–83.

"Letters of the Brownings" (review). *Saturday Review* 87 (1899): 242–43.

"Letters of Elizabeth Barrett Browning." *Book Reviews* (December 1897): 176–77.

"The Letters of Elizabeth Barrett Browning." *Church Quarterly Review* 46 (1898): 369–91.

"The Letters of Robert Browning and Elizabeth Barrett Barrett." *Church Quarterly Review* 49 (1899): 153–67.

Levine, Lawrence. *Highbrow/Lowbrow: The Emergence of Cultural Hierarchy in America.* Cambridge: Harvard Univ. Press, 1988.

Lindenberger, Herbert. *The History in Literature: On Value, Genre, Institutions.* New York: Columbia Univ. Press, 1990.

Linley, Margaret. "Truly a Poetess and a Good One: Christina Rossetti and the Cultural Category of the Poetess." Ph.D. diss., Queen's University, Kingston, Ont., 1995.

Lipking, Lawrence. "Sappho Descending: Eighteenth-Century Styles in Abandoned Women." *Eighteenth-Century Life* 12 (1988): 40–57.

"Literary Gossip." *Athenaeum* (1876): 690.

"Literary Notes" (review of Thom's *Shakespeare and Chaucer Examinations*). *Shakespeariana* 5 (1888): 188–89.

"Literary Week." *Academy* (1899): 488.

Loeffelholz, Mary. "Miranda in the New World: *The Tempest* and Charlotte Barnes's *The Forest Princess.*" In Novy, ed., 58–75.

Longhurst, Derek. "'Not for All Time, but for an Age': An Approach to Shakespeare Studies." In Widdowson, ed., 150–63.

Loomba, Ania. *Gender, Race, Renaisssance Drama.* New York: Manchester Univ. Press, 1989.

Lootens, Tricia. "Elizabeth Barrett Browning: The Poet as Heroine of Literary History." Ph.D. diss., Indiana University, Bloomington, 1988.

Lowell, James Russell. "Dryden." *Literary Essays.* Vol. 3, *Complete Works.* New York: Fireside Edition, 1910.

——. "The 'Hectic Flush' in 'Aurora Leigh.'" *Critic* 20 (1892): 344.

——. *My Study Windows.* 1871. Boston: Osgood, 1875.

McCrea, Brian. *Addison and Steele Are Dead: The English Department, Its Canon, and the Professionalization of Literary Criticism.* Newark: Univ. of Delaware Press, 1990.

McGann, Jerome. "Christina Rossetti's Poems: A New Edition and a Revaluation." *Victorian Studies* (1980): 237–54.

——. "Mary Robinson and the Myth of Sappho." *Modern Language Quarterly* 56 (March 1995): 55–76.

——. "The Religious Poetry of Christina Rossetti." *Critical Inquiry* 10 (1983): 127–44.

McNamara, Jo Ann. "The Need to Give: Suffering and Female Sanctity in the Middle Ages." In *Images of Sainthood in Medieval Europe,* ed. Renate Blumenfeld-Kosinski and Timea Szell, 199–221. Ithaca: Cornell Univ. Press, 1991.

"Major and Minor Poetry." *Literary World* (1896): 85.

"The Married Life of Elizabeth Barrett Browning." *Review of Reviews* 16 (1897): 529–30.

Martin, Helena Saville [Faucit]. *On Some of Shakespeare's Female Characters.* 3d ed. London: Blackwood, 1888.

Martin, Theodora Penny. *The Sound of Our Own Voices: Women's Study Clubs 1860–1910.* Boston: Beacon Press, 1987.

Martin, Wendy. *An American Triptych: Anne Bradstreet, Emily Dickinson, Adrienne Rich.* Chapel Hill: Univ. of North Carolina Press, 1984.

[Massey, Gerald.] "Last Poems and other Works of Mrs. Browning." *North British Review* 36 (1862): 514–34.

——. Untitled poem. In Hughes, ed., 209.

Masson, David. *Essays Biographical and Critical: Chiefly on English Poets.* Cambridge: Macmillan, 1856.

Mecklin, John. *The Passing of the Saint: A Study of a Cultural Type.* Chicago: Univ. of Chicago Press, 1941.

Melchiori, Barbara Arnett. "Undercurrents in Victorian Illustrations of Shakespeare." In *Images of Shakespeare,* ed. Werner Habicht, D. J. Palmer, and Roger Pringle, 120–28. Newark: Univ. of Delaware Press, 1988.

Mellor, Anne K. Introduction to *Romanticism and Feminism.* 3–9. Bloomington: Indiana Univ. Press, 1988.

"Memoirs of the Moment." *Academy* (1899): 489–90.

"Memories of Tennyson, Ruskin, and Browning." *Dial* 13 (1892): 339–42.

Mermin, Dorothy. "The Damsel, the Knight, and the Victorian Woman Poet." *Critical Inquiry* 13 (1986): 64–80.

——. "The Female Poet and the Embarrassed Reader: Elizabeth Barrett Browning's *Sonnets from the Portuguese*." *ELH* 48 (1981): 351–67.

Meynell, Alice. "Christina Rossetti." *Living Age* 204 (2 March 1895): 569–72.

——. "Elizabeth Barrett Browning." In *The Wares of Autolycus: Selected Literary Essays*, 160–66. London: Oxford Univ. Press, 1965.

——. Introduction to *Poems by Christina Rossetti*. London: Blackie and Son, 1910.

——. Introduction to *Prometheus Bound*, trans. Elizabeth Barrett Browning. London: Ward, Lock and Bowden, 1896.

Michie, Helena. *The Flesh Made Word: Female Figures and Women's Bodies*. New York: Oxford Univ. Press, 1987.

Mill, John Stuart. *The Subjection of Women*. In *Essays on Sex Equality*, by John Stuart Mill and Harriet Taylor Mill, ed. Alice S. Rossi, 123–242. Chicago: Univ. of Chicago Press, 1970.

"Minor Book Notices." *Literary World* 6 (1876): 178–82.

"Miss Rossetti's Poems." *Nation* 3 (1866): 47–48.

"Miss Rossetti's Poems." *Reader* 7 (30 June 1866): 613.

"Miss Rossetti's Poems." *Saturday Review* 21 (1866): 761–62.

Mitford, Mary Russell. *Recollections of a Literary Life*. New York: AMS Press, 1975.

Moers, Ellen. *Literary Women*. New York: Doubleday, 1976.

Molloy, J. Fitzgerald. "Elizabeth Barrett Browning." *Tinsley's Magazine* 30 (1882): 366–74.

More, Paul Elmer. "Christina Rossetti." *Atlantic Monthly* 94 (December 1904): 815–21.

——. "Christina Rossetti." In *Shelburne Essays, First through Eleventh Series*, 3:124–42. New York: Putnam's-Knickerbocker Press, 1909.

Morgan, Susan. *Sisters in Time: Imagining Gender in Nineteenth-Century Fiction*. New York: Oxford Univ. Press, 1989.

Morgan, Thaïs. "Sage Discourse and the Feminine." In Thaïs Morgan, ed., 11–18.

——, ed. *Victorian Sages and Cultural Discourse: Renegotiating Gender and Power*. New Brunswick, N.J.: Rutgers Univ. Press, 1990.

Morley, Henry. *A First Sketch of English Literature*. Enlarged ed. London: Cassell, 1912.

Morrison, Toni. *Playing in the Dark: Whiteness and the Literary Imagination*. Cambridge: Harvard Univ. Press, 1992.

"Mrs. Browning." *Saturday Review* 12 (1861): 41–42.

"Mrs. Browning Complete." *Literary World* 29 (1898): 13.

"Mrs. Browning's Letters." *Spectator* 79 (1897): 685–86.

[Mulock, Dinah.] "To Elizabeth Barrett Browning on her Later Sonnets." *Athenaeum* (1851): 191.

Myers, F. W. H. "George Eliot." In *Essays-Modern*, 251–75. New York: Macmillan, 1902.

Neely, Carol Thomas. "Epilogue: Remembering Shakespeare, Revising Ourselves." In Novy, ed., 242–52.

Nemoianu, Virgil. "Literary Canons and Social Value Options." In Nemoianu and Royal, eds., 215–47.

Nemoianu, Virgil, and Robert Royal, eds. *The Hospitable Canon: Essays on Literary Play, Scholarly Choice, and Popular Pressures.* Philadelphia: John Benjamins, 1991.

Newman, Caroline. "Cemeteries of Tradition: The Critique of Collection in Heine, Nietzsche, and Benjamin." *Pacific Coast Philology* 19 (1984) 12–21.

Newman, John Henry. *The Letters and Diaries of John Henry Newman.* Ed. Charles Stephen Dessain. 31 vols. New York: Thomas Nelson, 1962.

——. "Poetry with Reference to Aristotle's Poetics." In *English Critical Essays: Nineteenth Century,* ed. Edmund D. Jones, 190–215. New York: Oxford: 1971.

Norton, Caroline. "'The Angel in the House' and 'The Goblin Market.'" *Macmillan's* (August 1863): 398–404.

Novy, Marianne. "Introduction: Women's Re-Visions of Shakespeare 1644–1988" and "*Daniel Deronda* and George Eliot's Female Re-Vision of Shakespeare." In Novy, ed., 1–15; 89–107.

——, ed. *Women's Re-Visions of Shakespeare.* Chicago: Univ. of Illinois Press, 1990.

"Obituary." *Gentlemen's Miscellany* 211 (1861): 215.

Olsen, Tillie. *Silences.* New York: Delacorte Press, 1978.

"Our Foreign Bureau." *Harper's* 23 (1861): 563.

"Our Prize Competition." *Girl's Own Paper* 9 (1888): 380–81.

"A Pageant, and Other Poems." *Athenaeum* (10 September 1881): 327–28.

Patmore, Coventry. *The Angel in the House: The Betrothal.* Boston: Ticknor and Fields, 1856.

——. "Mrs. Meynell, Poet and Essayist." *Fortnightly Review* 58 (1892): 761–66.

——. *Religio Poetae, etc.* London: Bell and Sons, 1893.

Payne, William Morton. *The Greater English Poets of the Nineteenth Century.* New York: Henry Holt, 1909.

Paz, D. G. *Popular Anti-Catholicism in Mid-Victorian England.* Stanford, Calif.: Stanford Univ. Press, 1992.

Pearce, Lynne. *Woman / Image / Text: Readings in Pre-Raphaelite Art and Literature.* Toronto: Univ. of Toronto Press, 1991.

Pequigney, Joseph. *Such Is My Love: A Study of Shakespeare's Sonnets.* Chicago: Univ. of Chicago Press, 1985.

Perrault, Charles. *Perrault's Popular Tales.* Ed. Andrew Lang. New York: Arno Press, 1977.

Perrin, Noel. *Dr. Bowdler's Legacy: A History of Expurgated Books in England and America.* Boston: Godine, 1992.

Perry, Nicholas, and Loreto Echeverría. *Under the Heel of Mary.* New York: Routledge, 1988.

Peterson, William S. *Interrogating the Oracle: A History of the London Browning Society.* Athens: Ohio Univ. Press, 1969.

——. Introduction to *Sonnets from the Portuguese,* by Elizabeth Barrett Browning. Barre, Mass.: Imprint Society, 1977.

Petroff, Elizabeth. *Consolation of the Blessed.* Millerton, N.Y.: Alta Gaia Society, 1979.

Phelps, Elizabeth Stewart. *The Story of Avis.* Ed. Carol Farley Kessler. New Brunswick, N.J.: Rutgers Univ. Press, 1992.

Piercy, Marge. "The Token Woman." In *Living in the Open,* 71–72. New York: Knopf, 1976.

Piper, David. *The Image of the Poet: British Poets and Their Portraits.* Oxford: Clarendon, 1982.

"Poems, by Elizabeth Barrett Browning." *Eclectic Review* 93 (1851): 295–303.

"Poems. By Elizabeth Barrett Browning." *Littel's Living Age* 28 (1851): 552–54.

"Poems of Elizabeth Barrett Barrett." *New Quarterly Review* 4 (1844): 132.

"Poetesses." *Saturday Review* 25 (23 May 1868): 678–79.

"Poetesses—Mrs. Browning and Miss Lowe." *English Review* 14 (1850): 320–33.

"Poetry in Petticoats." *Scots Observer* (8 March 1890): 438–39.

"The Poetry of Mrs. E. B. Browning." *Westminster Review* (1882): 373–92.

Pope, Alexander. "Preface." [1728 Shakespeare.] In Beverley Warner, ed., 30–49.

P[orter, Charlotte.] "The Browning Love Letters." *Poet-lore* 11(1899): 301–9.

[———.] Review of *New Poems. Poet-lore* 8 (March 1896): 149–50.

P[reston], H[arriet] W[aters.] "Biographical Sketch." In *The Complete Poetical Works of Elizabeth Barrett Browning,* by Elizabeth Barrett Browning, xi–xviii. Cambridge Edition. St. Clair Shores, Mich.: Scholarly Press, 1972.

———. "Robert and Elizabeth Browning." *Atlantic Monthly* 83 (1899): 812–26.

"The Prince's Progress." *Athenaeum* (23 June 1866): 824–25.

Ragland, Fanny E. "Prize Examination on the Play of *Othello.*" *Shakespeariana* 1 (1883–84): 251–54.

Raleigh, Walter. *The Letters of Sir Walter Raleigh.* Ed. Lady Raleigh. 2 vols. New York: Macmillan, 1926.

Raymond, Janice. *A Passion for Friends: Toward a Philosophy of Female Affection.* Boston: Beacon Press, 1986.

Reader's supplement to *Wuthering Heights,* by Emily Brontë. New York: Pocket Books, 1976.

Rees, Joan. *The Poetry of Dante Gabriel Rossetti: Modes of Self Expression.* Cambridge: Cambridge Univ. Press, 1981.

"Reminiscences of the Brownings." *Review of Reviews* (1892): 467.

Renna, Thomas. "Hagiography and Feminine Spirituality in the Low Countries." *Citeaux* 39 (1988): 285–96.

[Renouf, Peter le Page.] "Primitive Christian Worship: Or the Evidence of Holy Scripture and the Church Concerning the Invocation of Saints and Angels, and the Blessed Virgin Mary. By the Rev. J. Endell Tyler, B.D." (review). *Dublin Review* 16 (1844): 307–45.

"Reviews: Elizabeth Barrett Browning." *Saturday Review* (20 October 1888): 466–67.

Rich, Adrienne. "Cartographies of Silence." In *The Dream of a Common Language,* 16–20. New York: Norton, 1978.

Ricks, Christopher. *New Oxford Book of Victorian Verse*. New York: Oxford Univ. Press, 1987.

Rinder, E. Wingate. Introduction to *Aurora Leigh,* by Elizabeth Barrett Browning, v–xxii. London: Walter Scott, 1899.

Ritchie, Anne Thackeray. "Browning, Elizabeth Barrett." In *The Dictionary of National Biography,* ed. Leslie Stephen, 3:78–82. London: Oxford Univ. Press, 1921.

——. *Records of Tennyson, Ruskin, and Browning*. London: Macmillan, 1892.

——. "Robert and Elizabeth Barrett Browning." *Harper's* 84 (May 1892): 832–55.

"Robert Browning." *Athenaeum* (1889): 858–60.

Roberts, Jeanne Addison. "Making a Woman and Other Institutionalized Diversions." *Shakespeare Quarterly* 37 (1986): 366–69.

Robinson, A. Mary F. "Felicia Hemans." In *English Poets,* ed. T. H. Ward, 4:334–35. New York: Macmillan, 1880.

Robinson, Lillian S. "Canon Fathers and Myth Universe." In *Decolonizing Tradition: New Views of Twentieth-Century "British" Literary Canons,* ed. Karen R. Lawrence, 23–36. Urbana: Univ. of Illinois Press, 1992.

Rodden, John. *The Politics of Literary Reputation: The Making and Claiming of "St. George" Orwell*. New York: Oxford Univ. Press, 1989.

Rosenfeld, Hellmut. *Legende*. Stuttgart: J. B. Metzler, 1961.

Ross, Marlon B. *The Contours of Masculine Desire: Romanticism and the Rise of Women's Poetry*. New York: Oxford Univ. Press, 1989.

Rossetti, Christina. "All Saints." In *Called to Be Saints: The Minor Festivals Devotionally Studied,* 502–19. London: Society for Promoting Christian Knowledge, 1902.

——. "In an Artist's Studio." In *Complete Poems,* ed. R. W. Crump, 3:264. Baton Rouge: Louisiana State Univ. Press, 1986.

——. "Monna Innominata." In Crump, ed., 2:86–93.

Rossetti, William Michael. "Extracts from Reviews." In *Poems of Christina Rossetti,* ed. William Michael Rossetti, v–xix. New York: Macmillan, 1904.

——. "Memoir." *Poetical Works of Christina Rossetti*. New York: Georg Olms Verlag, 1970.

——. "Prefatory Notice." In *The Poetical Works of Mrs. Felicia Hemans,* iii–xviii. New York: A. L. Burt, n.d.

——, ed. *Rossetti Papers, 1862–1870*. London: Sands and Co., 1903.

"The Rossettis." *Literary World* (5 November 1881): 395–96.

Rowland, K. M. "The Brownings." *Manhattan* (1884): 553–62.

Rowton, Frederic. "Felicia Hemans." In *The Female Poets of Great Britain,* 386–92. Detroit: Wayne State Univ. Press, 1981.

Ruskin, John. "Of Queens' Gardens." In *Sesame and Lilies,* 74–119. New York: John Wiley, 1865.

Sacred Congregation for the Causes of Saints. *Positio: Documentary Study for the Canonization Process of the Servant of God Cornelia Connelly (nee Peacock) 1809–1879*. 3 vols. Rome: Society of the Holy Child Jesus, 1983.

Said, Edward W. *The World, the Text, and the Critic.* Cambridge: Harvard Univ. Press, 1983.

Saintsbury, George. "European Literature—Later Nineteenth-Century English and French Poetry." In *The Later Nineteenth Century*, 30–31. London: Blackwood, 1907.

———. "The Second Poetical Period." In *A History of Nineteenth Century Literature (1780–1895)*, 276–81, 293–94. New York: Macmillan, 1896.

Sanders, H. M. "Other Indiscretions, and the Browning Letters." *Temple Bar* 120 (1900): 110–26.

Say, Elizabeth A. *Evidence on Her Own Behalf: Women's Narrative as Theological Voice.* Savage, Md.: Rowman, Littlefield, 1990.

Schoenbaum, S. *Shakespeare's Lives.* Rev. ed. Oxford: Clarendon Press, 1991.

Schork, R. J. "Victorian Hagiography: A Pattern of Allusions in 'Robert Elsmere' and 'Helbeck at Bannisdale.'" *Studies in the Novel* 21 (1980): 292–305.

Schulenburg, Jane Tibbetts. "Female Sanctity: Public and Private Roles, ca. 500–1100." In *Women and Power in the Middle Ages,* ed. Mary Erler and Maryanne Kowaleski, 102–25. Athens: Univ. of Georgia Press, 1988.

S[chuyler], E[ugene.] "Mrs. Browning: Florence, October 1888." *Nation* 48 (1889): 7–8.

Shahar, Shulamith. *The Fourth Estate: A History of Women in the Middle Ages.* London: Methuen, 1983.

"*Shakespeare and Chaucer examinations*" (review). *Shakespeariana* 5 (1888): 233.

"Shakespeare and Greater England." *Shakespeariana* 3 (1886): 377–78.

Sharp, William. "Some Reminiscences of Christina Rossetti." *Atlantic Monthly* 75 (1895): 736–49.

Shelley, Percy Bysshe. "A Defense of Poetry." In *Shelley's Prose: Or, The Trumpet of a Prophecy,* ed. David Lee Clark, 275–97. New York: New Amsterdam, 1988.

Shepherd, R. H. "Mrs. Browning's Earlier Poems." *Athenaeum* (1876): 722.

Shepherd, Simon. "Shakespeare's Private Drawer: Shakespeare and Homosexuality." In *The Shakespeare Myth,* ed. Graham Holderness, 96–110. Manchester: Manchester Univ. Press, 1988.

Sheppard, John H. "Ode on Shakespeare's Birthday." In Silsby, ed., 142–50.

Shields, Carol. *Swann.* New York: Viking, 1989.

A Short Sketch of Mrs. Hemans: With Remarks on Her Poetry and Extracts. London: James Paul, 1835.

Showalter, Elaine. "Representing Ophelia: Women, Madness, and the Responsibilities of Feminist Criticism." In *Shakespeare and the Question of Theory,* ed. Patricia Parker and Geoffrey Hartman, 77–94. New York: Methuen, 1985.

———. *Sexual Anarchy: Gender and Culture at the Fin de Siècle.* New York: Viking Press, 1990.

Sicherman, Barbara. "Sense and Sensibility: A Case Study of Reading in Late-Victorian America." In *Reading in America: Literature and Social History,* ed. Cathy N. Davidson, 201–25. Baltimore: Johns Hopkins Univ. Press, 1989.

Silsby, Mary R., ed. *Tributes to Shakespeare.* New York: Harper, 1892.

Sinfield, Alan. "Give an Account of Shakespeare and Education, Showing Why You

Think They Are Effective and What You Have Appreciated about Them. Support Your Comments with Precise References." In Dollimore and Sinfield, eds., 158–81.

——. "Heritage and the Market, Regulation and Desublimation." In Dollimore and Sinfield, eds., 255–79.

Singleton, John. "The Virgin Mary and Religious Conflict in Victorian Britain." *Journal of Ecclesiastical History* 43 (1992): 16–34.

"Sing-Song." *Athenaeum* (1872): 11.

Smith, Barbara. "Toward a Black Feminist Criticism." In *All the Women Are White, All the Blacks Are Men, But Some of Us Are Brave: Black Women's Studies,* ed. Gloria T. Hull, Patricia Bell Scott, and Barbara Smith. 157–75. Old Westbury, N.Y.: Feminist Press, 1982.

Smith, Barbara Herrnstein. *Contingencies of Value: Alternative Perspectives for Critical Theory.* Cambridge: Harvard Univ. Press, 1988.

S[mith], G[eorge] B[arnett.] "Elizabeth Barrett Browning." *Cornhill* 29 (1874): 469–90.

[Smith, William Henry.] "Elizabeth Barrett Browning." *British Quarterly Review* 34 (1861): 350–81.

"Some Recent Women Poets." *Scribner's* 10 (1875): 100–6.

"Some Women Poets, Parts I and II." *Living Age* 221 (April–June 1899): 26–34, 123–33.

Spearman, Edmund R. "Eve's Mission." *Westminster Review* 136 (1891): 245–54.

Spelman, Elizabeth V. *Inessential Woman: Problems of Exclusion in Feminist Thought.* Boston: Beacon Press, 1988.

Spender, Lynn. *Intruders on the Rights of Men: Women's Unpublished Heritage.* London: Pandora, 1983.

Sprague, Charles. "Shakespeare Ode." In Silsby, ed., 109–20.

Stanley, Hiram M. "The Browning-Barrett Love-Letters and the Psychology of Love." *Open Court* 8 (1899): 731–41.

Stavisky, Aron Y. *Shakespeare and the Victorians: Roots of Modern Criticism.* Norman: Univ. of Oklahoma Press, 1969.

Stedman, E. C. "Elizabeth Barrett Browning." *Scribner's* 7 (1873): 101–14.

——. *Elizabeth Barrett Browning.* Boston: James R. Osgood, 1877.

——. *Victorian Poets.* Rev. ed. Boston: Houghton Mifflin, 1896.

Stedman, Laura, and George M. Gould. *Life and Letters of E. C. Stedman.* 2 vols. New York: Moffat, Yard, 1910.

Stephen, Leslie. "The Browning Letters." In *Studies of a Biographer.* 2d. ser. 3:133. London: Duckworth, 1902.

Stephenson, Glennis. *Elizabeth Barrett Browning and the Poetry of Love.* Ann Arbor: UMI Research Press, 1989.

Sternburg, Janet. "The Writer Herself: An Introduction." In *The Writer on Her Work,* ed. Janet Sternburg, xi–xix. New York: Norton, 1980.

Stevenson, Mrs. Hackett. "Elizabeth Barrett Browning." *Victoria* 22 (1873): 231–38.

[Stigand, William]. "The Works of Elizabeth Barrett Browning." *Edinburgh Review* 114 (1861): 513–34.

Stutfield, Hugh E. M. "The Psychology of Feminism." *Blackwood's* 161 (Jan. 1897): 104–17.

Sullivan, Mary-Rose. "'Some Interchange of Grace': 'Saul' and *Sonnets from the Portuguese.*" *Browning Institute Studies* 15 (1987):55–68.

Super, R. H. "Critical and Explanatory Notes. Wordsworth." In *English and Irish Politics,* by Matthew Arnold, 336–45.

Swinburne, Algernon Charles. "Aurora Leigh." *Complete Works of Algernon Charles Swinburne,* ed. Edmund Gosse and Thomas James Wise, 16:3–8. New York: Russell and Russell, 1925.

———. "Sonnet.—To England." In Silsby, ed., 178.

———. *A Study of Shakespeare.* 3d ed. London: Chatto and Windus, 1895.

[Symons, Arthur.] "Christina Rossetti." *Saturday Review* (5 January 1895): 5–6.

———. "Christina Rossetti." In *Studies in Two Literatures,* 135–49. London: Leonard Smithers, 1897.

Taine, H. A. *History of English Literature.* Trans. H. Van Laun. 3 vols. New York: Henry Holt, 1877.

Taplin, Gardner B. *The Life of Elizabeth Barrett Browning.* New Haven: Yale Univ. Press, 1957.

Taylor, Bayard. "Casa Guidi Windows." *Atlantic Monthly* 21 (1868): 61–72.

———. *Critical Essays and Literary Notes.* New York: Putnam's, 1880.

———. "Shakespeare's Statue." In Silsby, ed., 162–67.

Taylor, Gary. *Reinventing Shakespeare: A Cultural History, from the Restoration to the Present.* New York: Weidenfeld and Nicolson, [1989].

Tennyson, Alfred. "St. Simeon Stylites." *The Poems of Tennyson.* Ed. Christopher Ricks. London: Longmans, 1969.

Terry, Ellen. *Four Lectures on Shakespeare.* Ed. Christopher St. John. New York: Benjamin Blom, 1969.

Thackeray, William Makepeace. *The History of Pendennis.* Ed. Peter L. Shillingsburg. New York: Garland, 1991.

———. *Vanity Fair: A Novel without a Hero.* Ed. John Sutherland. New York: Oxford Univ. Press, 1987.

Theobald, Lewis. "Preface." [*Shakespeare's Works,* 2d ed., 1740.] In Beverley Warner, ed., 51–84.

Thom, William Taylor. *Shakespeare and Chaucer Examinations: Edited, with Some Remarks on the Class-Room Study of Shakespeare.* Boston: Ginn, 1889.

———. "Shakespeare Study for American Women." *Shakespeariana* 1 (1884): 97–102.

———. "Some Parallelisms between Shakespeare's English and the Negro-English of the United States." *Shakespeariana* 1 (1884): 129–35.

Thomas, Edith M. "Elizabeth Barrett Browning." *The Critic* 37 (1900): 516–17.

Thompson, Francis. "Christina Rossetti." In *The Real Robert Louis Stevenson and Other*

Critical Essays, ed. Terence L. Connolly, 142–45. New York: University Publishers, 1959.

——. "Mrs. Browning as Prophetess." In *Literary Criticisms by Francis Thompson,* ed. Terence L. Connolly, 159–63. New York: E. P. Dutton, 1948.

[——.] "The Poetical Works of Christina Rossetti." *Athenaeum* (2 April 1904): 423–24.

Tompkins, Jane. *Sensational Designs: The Cultural Work of American Fiction, 1790–1860.* New York: Oxford Univ. Press, 1985.

Towle, Eleanor A. "Literary Courtships." *Littel's Living Age* (1899): 220–31.

[Trollope, Theodosia.] "Elizabeth Barrett Browning." *Athenaeum* (1863): 153.

Trudgill, Eric. *Madonnas and Magdalens: The Origins and Development of Victorian Sexual Attitudes.* New York: Holmes and Meier, 1976.

Tucker, Margaret Isabella. "Shakespearian Characters: II. Lady Anne." *Shakespeariana* 1 (1883–84): 305–6.

Tuckerman, H. T. "Essay." In *Poems by Felicia Hemans,* ed. Rufus W. Griswold. New York: Leavitt and Allen, n.d.

"Uranian." *Oxford English Dictionary,* 2d ed. Oxford: Clarendon Press 1989.

"The Veneration of Saints and Holy Images." *The Catholic World* 7 (1868): 721–35.

Viswanathan, Gauri. *Masks of Conquest: Literary Study and British Rule in India.* New York: Columbia Univ. Press, 1989.

Von Hallberg, Robert. *Canons.* Chicago: Univ. of Chicago Press, 1984.

Walker, Cheryl. *The Nightingale's Burden: Women Poets and American Culture before 1900.* Bloomington: Indiana Univ. Press, 1982.

Walker, Hugh. "Elizabeth Barrett Browning" and "Christina Georgina Rossetti." In *The Age of Tennyson,* 234–36, 244–246. London: George Bell, 1904.

——. *The Greater Victorian Poets.* London: Swan Sonnenschein, 1895.

——. "The Minor Poets: Earlier Period. The Poetesses" and "The Turn of the Century: New Influences." In *The Literature of the Victorian Era,* 360–73, 501–7. Cambridge: Cambridge Univ. Press, 1910.

Walker, Pierre A. "Arnold's Legacy: Religious Rhetoric of Critics on the Literary Canon." In Nemoianu and Royal, eds., 181–97.

Ward, Benedicta. *Miracles and the Medieval Mind: Theory, Record, and Event 1000–1215.* Philadelphia: Univ. of Pennsylvania Press, 1982.

Warner, Beverley, ed. *Famous Introductions to Shakespeare's Plays: By the Notable Editors of the Eighteenth Century.* New York: Burt Franklin, 1968.

Warner, Marina. *Alone of All Her Sex: The Myth and the Cult of the Virgin Mary.* New York: Knopf, 1976.

Warre-Cornish, Blanche. "A Woman Poet." *Fortnightly* 69 (1897): 66–69.

Watson, M. Sidney. "Murder by Anthology? The Silencing of Anna Laetitia Barbauld." Paper presented at the Fourth Annual Eighteenth- and Nineteenth-Century British Women Writers Conference, University of Notre Dame, South Bend, Ind., 2–4 March 1995.

Watson, William. "To Christina Rossetti." In *Poems,* 2:107. New York: John Lane, 1905.

Watts-Dunton, Theodore. "Christina Georgina Rossetti." *Athenaeum* (5 January 1895): 16–18.

———. "*New Poems*. By Christina Rossetti." *Athenaeum* (15 February 1896): 207–9.

———. "Reminiscences of Christina Rossetti." *The Nineteenth Century* 37 (1895): 355–66.

Weinstein, Donald, and Rudolph M. Bell. *Saints and Society: The Two Worlds of Western Christendom, 1000–1700*. Chicago: Univ. of Chicago Press, 1982.

Weld, Theodore. "Shakespeare in the Classroom." *Shakespeariana* 3 (1886): 437–50.

Welsh, Alexander. *The City of Dickens*. Oxford: Clarendon Univ. Press, 1971.

Welsh, Alfred H. *Development of English Literature and Language*. 2d ed. London: Truebner, 1883.

Wemple, Suzanne Fonay. *Women in Frankish Society: Marriage and the Cloister 500 to 900*. Philadelphia: Univ. of Pennsylvania Press, 1981.

Wentz, Virginia Leila. "The Browning Love-Letters." *Book Buyer* 18 (1899): 237–38.

Whipple, Edwin P. "Shakspeare's Critics." In *Essays and Reviews*, 2:209–49. Boston: Houghton Mifflin, 1893.

[Wicksteed, Charles.] "Poems by Elizabeth Barrett Barrett." *Prospective Review* 1 (1845): 445–64.

Widdowson, Peter. *Hardy in History: A Study in Literary Sociology*. New York: Routledge, 1989.

———, ed. *Re-reading English*. New York: Methuen, 1982.

Wilde, Oscar. "English Poetesses." In *The Artist as Critic: Critical Writings of Oscar Wilde*, ed. Richard Ellmann, 101–8. Chicago: Univ. of Chicago Press, 1969.

———. "Epigrams." In *The World of the Victorians: An Anthology of Poetry and Prose*, ed. E. D. H. Johnson, 494–97. New York: Charles Scribner's, 1964.

———. *The Picture of Dorian Gray and Other Writings*. Ed. Richard Ellmann. New York: Bantam, 1988.

Williams, Raymond. "A Problem of Perspective." In *The Country and the City*, 9–12. London: Chatto and Windus, 1973.

———. "The Romantic Artist." In *Culture and Society, 1780–1950*, 30–48. New York: Harper, 1958.

Wilson, John ("Christopher North"). "The Young Lady's Book." *Blackwood's* 27 (1830): 267–78.

Wilson, Stephen. *Saints and Their Cults: Studies in Religious Sociology, Folklore, and History*. Cambridge: Cambridge Univ. Press, 1983.

Wingate, Charles E. L. *Shakespeare's Heroines on the Stage*. New York: Thomas Y. Crowell, 1895.

Winkler, Karen J. "A Scholar's Provocative Query: Was Huckleberry Finn Black?" *Chronicle of Higher Education* (8 July 1992): A6–A8.

"With the Elect." *National Observer* 8 (1892): 539–40.

Wittig, Monique. *The Straight Mind and Other Essays*. Boston: Beacon Press, 1992.

Wolfson, Susan J. "Explaining to Her Sisters: Mary Lamb's *Tales from Shakespear*." In Novy, ed., 16–40.

Woolf, Virginia. "Aurora Leigh." *Yale Review* n. s. 20 (June 1931): 677–90.

———. *Between the Acts.* New York: Harcourt Brace Jovanovich, 1969.

———. "I Am Christina Rossetti." *Nation and Athenaeum* 48 (6 December 1930): 322–24.

———. "Professions for Women." In *Virginia Woolf: Women and Writing,* ed. Michele Barrett, 57–63. New York: Harcourt Brace Jovanovich, 1979.

———. *A Room of One's Own.* New York: Harcourt and Brace, 1957.

Wright, T. R. *The Religion of Humanity: The Impact of Comtean Positivism on Victorian Britain.* Cambridge: Cambridge Univ. Press, 1986.

[Wright, Thomas.] "Saints' Lives and Miracles." *Edinburgh Review* (American edition) 85 (1847): 154–68.

Wright, William Aldis. "Edward Fitzgerald: Trinity College, Cambridge, July 16, 1889." *Athenaeum* (1889): 94.

Young-Bruehl, Elisabeth. "The Writing of Biography." *Partisan Review* 50 (1983): 413–27.

Zangwill, Israel. "The Two Empires." In *A Book of Homage to Shakespeare,* ed. Israel Gollancz, 248. Oxford: Oxford Univ. Press, 1916.

Ziegler, Georgianna. "The Actress as Shakespearian Critic: Three Nineteenth-Century Portias." *Theatre Survey* 30 (May 1989): 93–109.

Index

Browning, Elizabeth Barrett (*cont.*)
  as Angel in the House, 2–3, 180
  on familial grounds (as Words-
    worth's niece or Swinburne's
    aunt), 139
  as formerly overrated poet, 11–12,
    151–57, 168, 201 n. 40
  as hysterical heroine, 151–54, 176
  for immodesty, 174–75, 178, 180–
    82, 203 n. 18; *see also* Rossetti,
    Christina, canonization of
  for inadequate mothering, 142
  for stylistic excesses (as source of
    the "Pythian shriek"), 130–
    31, 137, 146, 150, 156–57,
    199 n. 15
  for Victorianism, negatively con-
    ceived, 154–56
  see also Works, *Sonnets from the Por-*
    tuguese
  self-canonization of
  as dutiful daughter, 121–22, 124
    198 n. 6
  as genius, 122
  as secular saint 11, 120–28, 183,
    199 n. 13
  Works
  Aurora Leigh, 2–3, 12–14, 117, 127,
    129–32, 136, 139, 141–42,
    144, 146, 154–57, 187 nn.
    1–2; 199 nn. 13, 15–16, 18;
    200 n. 28
  Casa Guidi Windows, 117, 127–28,
    139
  Complete, ed. Porter and Clarke, 1,
    143, 198 nn. 1, 5
  "A Curse for a Nation," 127–28, 133
  "Fragment of an 'Essay on
    Woman,'" 121
  Letters, ed. R. H. Horne, 201 n. 36
  Letters, ed. Frederic G. Kenyon,
    125, 128, 199 n. 14
  Mrs. E. B. Browning's Letters, 129,
    147–49, 153, 199 n. 14, 201
    n. 38
  Poems (1844), 121
  Poems before Congress, 2, 11, 117,
    127–28, 156, 199 nn. 15–16
  Poetical Works, Cambridge edition
    of, 116–17, 157
  "The Runaway Slave at Pilgrim's
    Point," 199 n. 13

  The Seraphim, 129, 199 n. 16
  Sonnets from the Portuguese, 198 nn.
    2, 4, 8, 9, 200 n. 29, 201 n.
    39; compared to Christina
    Rossetti's "Monna Innomi-
    nata," 175, 179, 181, 204 n.
    24; decanonization of, 150–
    54, 175, 198 n. 8; as expres-
    sions of chaste heterosexual
    love, 138, 200 n. 31, 201 n.
    32; reading of, 118–20, 198 n.
    5; "Reading Edition" of,
    144–45; as relics of poet's "ap-
    otheosis," 12, 140, 144–46;
    Christina Rossetti on, 120,
    163–65; and sexual anarchy,
    138–39, 142–44; as supreme
    works of women's poetry,
    138–40, 162
  "A Vision of Poets," 122–24, 127
  see also Canon, architectural; Wom-
    en's poetry; Woolf, Virginia
Browning, Elizabeth and Robert, *Letters*
  of Robert and Elizabeth Browning,
  148–51, 153–54, 201 nn.
  38–39
Browning, Fannie, 144–45
Browning, Robert, 24, 118, 124, 129,
  136, 140–42, 144, 146–49, 151,
  153, 156, 160, 176, 198 n. 6, 200
  nn. 26–27, 201 nn. 33–36
  Works
  "Andrea del Sarto," 179, 204 n. 23
  "The Bishop Orders His Tomb,"
    28–29
  "Childe Roland," 123
  Letters, 201 n. 34
  The Ring and the Book, 145
  "To Edward FitzGerald," 146–47,
    201 n. 35
  "Transcendentalism," 68
Browning, R. W. ("Pen"), 141, 148–49,
  200 n. 28
Browning Society, 141–44
Burns, Robert, 161
Butler, Judith, 56, 62–63, 92, 113
Butler, William, 66
Bynum, Caroline Walker, 9, 23, 47–49,
  58–60, 191 nn. 4–5, 7–8, 192 n.
  24, 193 nn. 25, 27
Byron, George Gordon, Lord, 149,
  160

Canton, William, 149
Carlyle, Thomas, 18–19, 29, 148, 189 n. 16
  on Shakespeare, 9, 19, 22–24, 28, 31
Carroll, John, 145
Carter, John, 144, 190–91 n. 30
Cary, Elisabeth Luther, 203 nn. 12–13, 19
Catherine, Saint, 114
Catherine of Siena, Saint, 48
Catholicism, *see* Roman Catholicism
Cavazza, E., 197 n. 37
Cecilia, Saint, 84, 195 n. 10
Chamberlain, Alexander F., 203 n. 16
Chambers, Edmund K., 202 n. 8, 203 n. 12
Chandler, James, 6
Character, authors' legendary
  and "characteristic" works, 20, 40–41, 191 n. 32
  and "essentialist biography," 33–34, 190 n. 20
  and literary loss, 10–11, 14, 20, 22, 25–27, 33, 40–44
Charlemont, countess of, 197 nn. 29, 37
Charles, Edna Kotin, 203 n. 18, 204 n. 22
Chaucer, Geoffrey, 92
Chesterton, G. K., 152
Chinweizu, 7
Chorley, Henry F., 128, 199 nn. 10, 17
Cixous, Hélène, 181
Clare of Assisi, Saint, 57–58, 193 n. 25
Clark, J. Scott, 25, 189 n. 10
Clarke, Helen A., 1, 143, 198 nn. 1, 5
Clarke, Isabel, 162
Clarke, Mary Cowden, 101, 104–6, 109, 112, 197 nn. 28, 35, 38
Clausen, Christopher, 187 n. 7
Clément, Catherine, 181
Cockshut, A. O. J., 33–34
Coleridge, H. N., 65–66
Coleridge, Mary Elizabeth, 68
Coleridge, Samuel Taylor, 160
  on Shakespeare, 78, 96–98, 196 n. 15
  on Shakespeare's female characters, 10, 78, 80, 96; and characterlessness, 80–83, 90, 103, 195 nn. 7, 9
Colley, Betty A., 144, 201 n. 33
Collier, John Payne, 190–91 n. 30
Collins, John, 190–91 n. 30

Collins, Mortimer, 130–31
Comte, Auguste, 15, 47, 51–52, 54–55, 112, 121, 134, 192 n. 12
  see also New Calendar of Great Men; Positivism
Conant, C. B., 130
Conduct manuals, 10, 59, 79
  see also Ellis, Sarah Stickney
Congreve, Richard, 188 n. 2
Connelly, Cornelia, 191 n. 2
Connolly, Terence L., 203 n. 17
Conrad, Joseph, 32
Cook, Eliza, 157
Cooper, Helen, 198 nn. 4, 8, 199 n. 15
Couthouy, Marion, 138, 200 n. 29, 201 n. 37
Crashaw, Richard, 172
Crawford, Robert, 13
Crosby, Christina, 51
Cross, Alan Eastman, 147
Crosse, Cordelia, 151
Crowell, Thomas Y., 198 n. 6
Crump, R. W., 201–2 n. 2, 203 n. 12
Cunningham, Allan, 84
Curran, Stuart, 179
Curtius, Ernst, 5, 37–38, 188 n. 11

Dante, 13, 19, 160, 164, 174, 179, 182, 202 n. 8
  Beatrice, 162–64
Davenport, Fanny, 106
David, Deirdre, 121
Davis, Tony, 35–36
Decanonization, literary, 1–2, 121, 152, 156–57, 177, 194 nn. 38, 44; *see also individual writers*
DeJean, Joan, 3, 38, 50, 169, 191–92 n. 10, 194 n. 39
Dennis, John, 150, 200 n. 28
De Quincey, Thomas, 10, 23, 25, 29, 33, 82–83, 99, 195–96 n. 11
Desmet, Christy, 85, 99, 102, 196 nn. 15, 23, 197 n. 31
d'Héricault, Charles, 42
Dickens, Charles, 10, 54, 62, 65, 75, 82, 84
  Characters
    Honoria Dedlock, 75–76
    Sir Leicester Dedlock, 75
    Miss Jogg, 75–76, 84
    Esther Summerson, 62–63, 65

Lesbianism
  and fin-de-siècle critical anxieties,
    169
  and the Muse, *see* "Poetry in Petti-
    coats"
  see also Sappho
Levine, Lawrence, 6–7
Levy, Amy, 170
Lindenberger, Herbert, 160
Linley, Margaret, 192 n. 11, 199 n. 19
Lipking, Lawrence, 192 n. 11
Loeffelholz, Mary, 195 n. 5
Longhurst, Derek, 30
Loomba, Ania, 189 n. 15, 195 n. 5
Lootens, Tricia, 128
Lorde, Audre, 6
Lowell, James Russell, 131, 188 n. 9
Luther, Martin, 39

Macaulay, Thomas B., 32
Maclise, Daniel, 11
Marriage
  celibacy and suspicion of marriage re-
    sistance, 176–77, 203 n. 19
  canonical coverture and the hetero-
    sexual contract, 68–69
  debt, 47, 191 n. 2
  Ellis on, 193 n. 29
  see also Browning, Elizabeth Barrett;
    Rossetti, Christina
Martin, Helena Saville Faucit, 107,
    109–11, 197 n. 38
Martin, Theodora Penny, 195 n. 3, 197
    n. 34
Martin, Wendy, 202 n. 4
Mary, Virgin, 10, 50–57, 67, 192 nn.
    13–22
  Barrett Browning compared to, 137,
    141
  emergence as middle-class figure, 52,
    192 nn. 13–14
  as a mid-century religious figure, 53
  as a miracle in herself, 67, 194 n. 36
  noncorporeal relics of, 67
  as a secular model 50–56, 61, 63, 66–
    67, 75–76, 137, 141, 192 nn.
    19–22; *see also* Angel in the
    House; Postivism
  Shakespeare's female characters
    compared to, 85, 92, 97, 99,
    100–101
  see also Legends

Massey, Gerald, 32, 201 n. 37
Masson, David, 22
Maynooth controversy, 52
McCrea, Brian, 23, 189 n. 9
McGann, Jerome, 175, 182, 192 n. 11,
    201 n. 1, 202 n. 7, 203 n. 12
McNamara, Jo Ann, 60
Mecklin, John, 55, 192 n. 22
Melchiori, Barbara Arnett, 84, 96, 109,
    198 n. 40
Mellor, Anne K., 160
Meredith, George: *Diana of the Cross-
    ways,* 114
Mermin, Dorothy, 120, 193 n. 34, 198
    nn. 2, 9
Meynell, Alice
  on Barrett Browning, 141, 147, 156,
    180
  canonization, as "Woman" over
    works, 67–68
  decanonization, as insufficient em-
    bodiment of "Woman," 67, 193
    n. 35
  on Christina Rossetti, 174, 178, 180
  in triad of great Victorian women po-
    ets, 161
Michie, Helena, 52, 58, 193 n. 26, 194
    n. 38
Mill, John Stuart, 68
Miller, Nancy K., 3
Milton, John, 139, 198 n. 7, 201
    n. 33
Mitford, Mary Russell, 126, 144, 154
Moers, Ellen, 126
Molloy, J. Fitzgerald, 200 n. 29
Montgomery, Robert, 157
More, Paul Elmer, 70, 181, 194 n. 40,
    204 n. 24
Morgan, Susan, 194 n. 41
Morgan, Thaïs, 18
Morley, Henry, 32
Morrison, Toni, 187 n. 4
Moulton-Barrett, Edward Barrett, 122,
    139, 150–51, 201 n. 38
Mulock, Dinah, 124–25
Musset, Alfred de, 149
Myers, F. W. H., 37–38, 56

Neely, Carol, 110
Nemoianu, Virgil, 18, 187 n. 7, 187–88
    n. 8, 191 n. 31

Sacred biography, 33–34, 36–39, 48,
190 nn. 19, 22, 27, 29
Sacred Congregation for the Causes of
Saints, 191 n. 2
Said, Edward, 182
Saint, as watchword, 190 n. 26
Sainthood, female religious, 46–60, 63,
191 n. 2, 4–8
and asceticism, 57–61, 192 nn. 23–24,
193 n. 25, 27
attempts to domesticate, 57, 192 n.
23
conflicts with femininity, 46–50, 56,
178, 191 nn. 2, 4–8
and constructions of feminine literary
canonicity, 46–47, 49–50, 71
exceptional or masculine gendering
of, 47–48, 191 nn. 4, 7
as model
for first-wave feminism, 48, 58,
183
for nineteenth-century femininity,
46–64, 193 nn. 26, 30–31, 33
for nineteenth-century women
writers, 48, 63, 183
physical and spiritual risks of, 48–50,
193 n. 26
and witchcraft, 48–49, 61, 63, 191 n.
8
see also Asceticism, religious; Canonization, religious
Sainthood, religious, general, 3, 5, 8–
11, 18–19, 23, 28, 35–36, 39, 85,
122, 168, 175, 177, 187 n. 6, 188
n. 1, 9, 190–91 n. 30; *see also* Asceticism, religious; Canonization,
religious; Legends, saints'; Mary,
Virgin; Sacred biography; Sainthood, female
Saints' calendars
religious, 34
secular
Pre-Raphaelite Calendar of Immortals, 15–16
Shakespeare's heroines, 77
syllabi as, 34
see also New Calendar of Great
Men
Saintsbury, George, 201–2 n. 2
Sand, George, 149, 169, 174
Sanders, H. M., 149, 153
Sappho, 161, 194 n. 39

critically allied to saints and the
Pythia, 50, 191–92 n. 10
lesbianism and fin-de-siècle critical
anxieties, 169
as inspiration for women poets, 122–
23, 192 n. 11
Sargent, John Singer, 107–8, 198 n. 40
Say, Elizabeth, 55
Schlegel, August Wilhelm, 95, 101
Schoenbaum, S., 189 n. 13, 190–91 n.
30
Schulenburg, Jane Tibbetts, 57
Schuyler, Eugene, 150, 154, 199 n. 15
Scott, Walter, 21, 26, 188–89 n. 7, 190
n. 20
Shahar, Shulamith, 192 n. 22
Shakespeare, William, 15–33, 38–39,
188 nn. 3, 6, 188–89 n. 7, 189 nn.
8, 11–16, 189–90 n. 17, 190 n. 18,
191 n. 32, 41
body of the text, 9, 20–27, 188 n. 6,
188–89 n. 7
"domestication" of, 77, 195 n. 2
expurgation of, 20, 25–26, 41, 77–78,
81–82, 84, 106, 112, 184, 189
nn. 11–12
female characters of, 10–11, 76–115,
195 nn. 4, 6–10, 195–96 n. 11,
196 nn. 12–21, 22–24, 197 nn.
26–38, 197–98 n. 39, 198 nn.
40–43
as anatomical models, 99–100, 197
n. 30
as bodies of the text, 82, 84, 105,
107–9
canonization of: for characterlessness, 80–85, 98, 109, 195 n.
7; as heroines of biographical
narratives, 106, 197 n. 38; and
iconicity, 82; interchangeabil-
ity or lack thereof, 79, 83–85,
96, 101–2, 107–9; historicized
"characteristics" of, 95–115,
196 nn. 19–25, 197 nn.
25–43; as national models,
78–80, 91–93; and secular
sanctity, 77–79, 84–85, 94,
101, 103
decanonization of, 113, 198 n. 43
female readers of: possession of
and by, 96, 110–13, 196 n. 22,
198 nn. 41–42; preference for

Victorian Literature and Culture Series

Karen Chase, Jerome J. McGann, *and* Herbert Tucker, *General Editors*

———••◦∞◦••———